Psalm 1[illegible]

in behalf of [illegible]

Lawanna McIver Fields

For Pat Beckam

with many rich

shared memories!

LMc

Riding the Wind of God

Smyth & Helwys Publishing, Inc.
6316 Peake Road
Macon, Georgia 31210-3960
1-800-747-3016

Printed in the United States of America.

The paper used in this publication meets the minimum requirements of American National Standard for Information Sciences—Permanence of Paper for Printed Library Materials.
ANSI Z39.48–1984. (alk. paper)

Library of Congress Catalogin-in-Publication Data

McIver, Bruce
Riding the wind of God: A personal history of the Youth Revival Movement / Bruce McIver
p. cm.
ISBN 1-57312-373-0
1. Revivals—Texas—History—20th century.
2. College students—Religious life—Texas—History—20th century
3. Baylor University—Religion.
I. Title.

BV3774.T4 M35 2002
269'.24'09764—dc21

2001055008
CIP

Riding the Wind of God

A Personal History of the Youth Revival Movement

Bruce McIver

In gratitude to the late W. F. Howard — educator, encourager,

and organizational genius. He was the "Gentle Giant"

of the Youth Revival Movement

CONTENTS

ACKNOWLEDGMENTS

About 15 years ago several of the early workers in the Youth Revival Movement out of Baylor University in the 1940s felt the stories of the revivals should be written down. "Bruce," they said collectively, "you're the person to do it!" I reluctantly agreed after extracting from them a promise that it would be a shared experience. I owe much to all who assisted in the gathering of these stories. The Oral History Department at Baylor University made available all written and filmed interviews of those involved. This material was invaluable. In addition, faculty members were available to share their memories and insights. Ray Burchette, then the Director of the Baylor Ex-Students Association, sent out hundreds of questionnaires to students who were on the campus during the years of 1945–1955. The response was overwhelming. My frustration is that I could not use all of these in the book and yet stay within the guidelines set by the publisher.

Judy Prather, Katy Stokes, and Charles Wellborn wrote separate articles about the revivals and gave me permission to use them in research. I am also grateful for people like the late Dr. W. F. Howard who made much of his library available to me. And a special thanks to Jack Greever who helped facilitate this project.

Tom Corts, President of Samford University, invited the original Youth Revival team for a symposium on Samford's campus in

June 1999. We were "miked and wired" for the homecoming and spent three days reliving those earlier experiences in the 1940s. The videotapes from these formal presentations and informal conversations were immensely helpful as I began to pull these stories together.

Special thanks must be given to Howard Butt, Jr., Patsy Ayres, Phil Strickland, Roger Hall, and David Clanton as they encouraged me from the start of this project. Also, I'm grateful to Candy and Max Post who researched papers in archives, kept my computer working, and read some of the first drafts of this material.

My wife, Lawanna, is one of the best "hands on" editors I've ever known. She patiently read every line dozens of times, making both corrections and suggestions. My oldest daughter, Kate, an English teacher, was also very helpful.

More than everything else, I'm grateful to a patient God who allowed me to be a part of the Youth Revival Movement and gave me strength to write about it nearly 60 years later.

The winds of God still blow.

PREFACE

In the 1930s America was plunged into the Depression, which brought most families to the brink of financial despair. There was little incentive to dream and plan for the future. The problem was "survival — now." In the early 1940s we found ourselves engaged in World War II. Again, the word was "survival." By the mid-1940s the Depression was behind us and there was evidence that the war would soon end. For the first time the current generation of young people could hope, dream, and plan.

College enrollments doubled, dormitories were renovated, and new classes were added to curriculums. Weary war veterans received loans and grants as an encouragement to pursue their education. They brought to campuses their own experiences of pain and hardship, discoveries and insights, and hopes and dreams for the future. General MacArthur asked for a thousand new missionaries to go to Japan, and hundreds of students across the nation, with little thought of the practical, indicated their willingness to respond. It was an exciting new day of hope.

In this milieu a small group of students at Baylor University began to pray for spiritual revival. We prayed for a new day and new commitments, but we had no agenda. We were not evangelists with a program; we were ordinary students with concerns. The more we prayed, the more we saw evidence that God was ready to answer our prayers. After months of praying we scheduled a revival near the campus. in April, 1945. Students with almost no preaching experience brought the messages. Four thousand people attended the services nightly and 500 public commitments to Christ were made. No one was more surprised than we were. God seemed to take 18- and 19-year-old students, not yet dry behind the ears, and work miracles through them.

To our surprise, invitations began coming in asking us to lead revival services in other cities — Houston, Fort Worth, Dallas, Memphis, Birmingham, Atlanta, Honolulu, and scores of other places. Students from other campuses, in Texas and beyond, caught the vision and soon hundreds of youth revivals were taking place throughout the nation. A movement had begun.

This is not intended to be a thorough history of the Youth Revival Movement. While it is true to history, it is a record of the beautiful, and sometimes ridiculous, ways God used a group of kids to accomplish His purpose. These stories, written for the first time, reflect our immaturity, our mistakes, our laughter, and our tears. But most of all, they reflect God's power at work in surprising places.

These experiences live on in our hearts. Indeed, in some ways they seem as real today as when we first experienced them more than 50 years ago.

As one of the participants in the early days of the Youth Revival Movement said, "We were riding the wind of God." Enjoy the stories. Listen to the wind . . . and ride with us.

PROLOGUE

IN SEARCH OF A FUTURE

The Lord said . . . leave your relatives . . . and your father's family, and go to a land I will show you.
(Gen 12:1)

Dad and I sat painfully silent on the parking lot of the Elder Service Station and Bus Depot in my small North Carolina hometown — waiting. Waiting for the old, often-repaired Continental Trailways bus to belch black smoke, round the corner, and grind to a stop; waiting for the dreaded good-byes soon to be expressed in a handshake or a hug; waiting for the longest journey of my life — 1400 miles to Waco, Texas, and a school little-known to me at the time named Baylor University. Waiting with uncertainty for my future to begin to unfold. I knew the waiting was painful for Dad, who had extended his lunch hour at the furniture factory just to sit with me. Mother also shared the pain and chose to hug me good-bye, and then busy herself with chores around the house. Besides, the so-called waiting room at the bus station consisted of empty soft drink boxes and a few broken chairs. It wasn't the place for lingering, tearful farewells.

Dad glanced at his watch and asked with a halting voice, "Do you have all your luggage?"

"Yes, sir," I replied, pointing to an old tin suitcase and a cardboard box tightly bound by heavy string. All my worldly goods were in those pieces.

"And do you have your money?"

"Yes, sir," I answered proudly, "all $90 right here in my pocket."

Ninety dollars. Enough to get me settled into a rooming house for a few days and enough to convince the registrar's office that I really wanted to get an education at Baylor University. And maybe enough left over to buy a Big Orange drink and a peanut patty! Life was good.

Ten minutes later, I boarded the bus, waved one last time to Dad and settled down in a backseat for the three day and two night trip. The old bus, wearied by the demands of World War II, groaned its way west across the Blue Ridge Mountains, crawled through the Smokies, and leveled off with a sigh of relief through the state of Tennessee. I watched and listened in fascination, like a 10-year-old child on his first trip to the State Fair in Raleigh. As we crossed the Mississippi, I remembered Rocky River, a muddy stream that flowed two miles from my house and was one of the best swimming holes in all of Chatham County, North Carolina. I had played there often as a boy, diving carefully into the muddy waters so I would miss the rocks. I also remembered Tick Creek, a nearly dried up stream that wound through Grandpa Moody's farm. Shubal Stearns, the pioneer Baptist preacher, had preached there 60 years earlier. Rives Chapel Baptist Church was organized out of his revivals. Several years later, both Grandpa and my mother were baptized in Tick Creek. My mother often played the piano in that little church, and the congregation was the first to listen to my stammering remarks when I announced that "God had called me to preach."

Memories. Good memories. Memories that shaped a life.

As the old Continental bus hummed through Arkansas I felt the turning of a page and the opening of a whole new chapter in my life. I also felt the onslaught of questions, and more questions. Why this trip? Why 1400 miles to continue higher education? Why pull up roots and leave a heritage that had been both happy and healthy? Why move away from a father whose only words to me when I got into trouble in high school were, "Son, I want to be your pal"? And, why leave a mother whose eyes filled with tears of gratitude when I told her, "God has called me to preach?"

Why gather my few belongings and leave a white bungalow that Dad and Mother built with their own hands and the only house I had called home for my 18 years? Why leave a well that supplied the best drink of water in the whole area, and a garden that produced the best tomatoes and beans and corn found anywhere? Why give good-bye hugs to friends and neighbors who were as steady as proverbial rocks and as honest as the days were long? And, as my brother asked in total perplexity, why "go off to school when you can make $17 a week driving a truck and delivering gasoline and fuel oil for my oil company?" He just couldn't understand it. Neither could I, but the "oughtness" wouldn't leave me alone.

I had just finished two years of education at Mars Hill, a junior college located in the mountains north of Asheville, North Carolina. My plan was to enroll in Wake Forest University or some other four year college near my home. This was an agreement that I had made with my parents, and it seemed sensible. There were at least five outstanding universities located within an hour's drive of my home. But in a matter of a few short weeks, I realized as the old bus rolled through the hills of Arkansas, all those plans had been laid aside.

Humanly speaking, Ralph Langley was responsible for some of the change in my plans. At the invitation of the Baptist Department of Student Work for North Carolina, Ralph and I had preached youth revivals throughout that summer of 1944 in seven churches in the state. Ralph, a red-headed persuasive debater from Opelika, Alabama, was one year ahead of me in his academic program. After graduating from Mars Hill he had transferred immediately to Baylor University. To no one's surprise, he was quickly recognized as a leader on the campus and was elected president of the Baptist Student Union. Without portfolio, he also became an energetic recruiter for the university. "I need a few minutes of your time . . . without fail," Ralph said to me one afternoon during the last week of our revivals together.

"Need some help on your sermon for tonight?" I asked with a smile. That was the last thing Ralph ever needed. His oratorical skills had already put him in a class by himself as far as student preachers were concerned.

"No," he said, "I want to talk to you about going to Baylor."

"But, Ralph, we've already been over that again and again. You know my answers: money, parents, distance from home, my girlfriend, and a dozen other things make it impractical. Besides," I continued, "what's Baylor got to offer that I can't find here in North Carolina?"

"Just trust me," Ralph replied persuasively, "and then find out for yourself. Besides, I believe some wonderful things are about to happen at Baylor, and I'd like you to be a part of them."

"Well, it just won't work," I protested. "The timing is all wrong."

For nearly an hour, we sparred verbally and finally gave up in exhaustion.

There, I thought, *it's settled. Finished. Over.*

When the final week of revivals concluded I shook hands with him, told him good-bye and wished him well. In all honesty I welcomed facing the next day without another confrontation about Baylor.

"I'll see you in Texas," he grinned. Ralph didn't give up easily.

"And try to get there early in September," he added. "We're having a pre-school Baptist Student Union Retreat, and it looks like we'll have the largest crowd ever. You don't want to miss it."

When the last revival service ended that week, I left quickly for my hometown of Siler City, had dinner with my parents, swapped stories around the table, called my girlfriend, and didn't give Baylor or Texas a second thought . . . until the next day.

Then it began to gnaw on me. What if Ralph is right? Have I really been open about this matter? Does my friend have an "inside track" on God's purpose for my life? Could the Lord be speaking through him to me? And then, I had a downright irreverent thought. I remembered the Old Testament story of God speaking through Balaam's ass. Maybe, I concluded with a chuckle, maybe if God could speak through Balaam's ass, He could also speak through Ralph! But the decision refused to be dismissed with a chuckle. I prayed, counseled with a few friends, talked with my pastor, shared my concern with my parents, added up "pro's and con's," appealed to logic, counted my money, and then, finally, I packed my old tin suitcase — all in less than a month. I wasn't sure what lay ahead, but I didn't want to miss one minute of it.

The bus to Texas was crowded, with standing room only. Soldiers were on the way to and from their posts of service. Their relatives, including an endless number of crying babies, were following them around the country. The days were long; the nights longer, broken only by an occasional rest stop at a dimly lit combination diner and gasoline station. On the second night my body cried out for mercy. Looking around, I noticed that the overhead racks for luggage were not completely filled. By rearranging some of the smaller cases and boxes, I created enough space for one medium-sized body. To the jealousy of those around me, I climbed over the top of seats and laid down in the overhead rack, using my overcoat as a pillow. It was my first sleep in two days.

At daybreak we crossed the Red River that divides Arkansas and Oklahoma from Texas. My heart skipped with anticipation. We were four hours from Dallas and six hours from Waco! There was no turning back.

Dallas was the largest city I had ever seen — bigger than Raleigh, Greensboro, Charlotte, and Siler City combined! The skyline, visible for miles across the flat Texas country, made it appear even larger. And the Magnolia building, with its flying red horse on the top, had become a familiar and classic landmark. I looked out the bus window, surveyed all this and whispered, "Gol . . . lee!" It was an entirely appropriate response for an 18-year old from "Small Town, USA."

There was a two-hour wait before I was to catch the "Interurban," a one-car trolley that made the ninety mile trip between Dallas and Waco. It was a good opportunity for me to take a walk around the heart of "Big D." I carefully placed my battered tin suitcase and cardboard box in a locker, put a quarter in the slot and put the key in my pocket. I felt again to make sure my $90 was still safe and secure. Then, I stepped out the door, asked for directions and walked four blocks to the First Baptist Church of Dallas. Dr. George W. Truett, a native of North Carolina, had served as pastor there for 47 years. No pastor anywhere was more respected than this man. In 1918, at the request of President Woodrow Wilson, he preached to the troops in Europe. In 1927, he was elected president of the Southern Baptist Convention, and in 1934 he became president of the Baptist World Alliance. To the folks back home in North Carolina, he was a legend.

I found the church without difficulty and happily discovered the doors were not locked. I stood at the back of the sanctuary, marveled at the size, and was overwhelmed with a sense of Presence. (Was it God . . . or Truett . . . or both?). Then, in a hesitant sense of wonder, I moved slowly down the aisle of the empty sanctuary to the rostrum, climbed the steps and stood for a moment behind the pulpit. The words carved into the pulpit spoke clearly: "Sirs, we would see Jesus."

Later, I purchased a penny post card and wrote my mother, "Today I stood where Dr. Truett stood." There was not a hint of ego in the statement — just humility and gratitude and respect for this giant of a man who had died only two months earlier. I never met him, but through the years I've cherished that special moment on a hot August afternoon when I stood briefly "where he stood."

It was not until years later that I learned about Dr. Truett's special ties with Baylor. In 1889, Truett and his family moved from North Carolina to Texas where they settled near Whitewright and were active in the church there. He planned to study law, but the little congregation saw in him unique gifts of preaching and pastoral leadership. Against his wishes, the church called him to preach and ordained him to the gospel ministry. The actions of the church were most unusual, and Truett could not deny their deep impressions about his gifts for ministry. More than half a century later, no one could question the wisdom of this little congregation.

Around 1890, Baylor University was in dire financial circumstances, facing a debt of $92,000 and standing at the brink of bankruptcy. Truett, then only 24, was hired as financial secretary of the school and given the responsibility of raising the money to keep the doors open. With a persuasive voice, sincerity of purpose, and the integrity to back it up he traveled the state, urging Baptists to "save Baylor." The people listened and responded to the pleadings of this young man, and the doors of the university did stay open. When the financial campaign was over, Truett himself enrolled in Baylor as a freshman.[1]

Back at the bus station, I gathered my luggage and climbed aboard the Interurban headed from Dallas to Waco. I was only two hours away from walking through those university doors that a young man named George W. Truett helped keep open.

The one-car trolley rocked and swayed through the black land of central Texas. The conductor called out strange names as we hummed along, almost silently, through the countryside — Waxahachie, Ennis, Italy, Hillsboro, Abbott, Elm Mott, and finally, Waco. Weary from three full days and two nights of travel, I breathed a sigh of relief that the long trip was finally over. I gathered my suitcase and cardboard box, checked one last time to make sure my money was in my pocket, asked directions, and began limping down Fifth Street toward the campus of Baylor University.

I found the two-story white boarding house Ralph had mentioned to me, paid a $10 deposit and flopped down on a cot for a few minutes' rest. Later, unable to sleep because of sheer excitement, I walked across the campus, entered the magnificent Pat Neff Hall (appropriately named for the man then president of Baylor and formerly the Governor of Texas), checked with the registrar's office and happily found that all my hours had transferred from Mars Hill, plus one thrown in extra. I never understood how this happened and I never bothered to pursue it! Some things are best left alone. I paid my tuition — with the help of small grants

— purchased some second-hand books and supplies, and still had money left over. Who said you can't get a college education with only $90 in your pocket! But reality said I needed some kind of job.

The 20 minute walk from the campus to the "Square" in the heart of Waco found my emotions bouncing between hope and concern. What if no jobs were available? Suppose the $90 ran out before any money came in? Could this journey halfway across the country be a mistake, or was God really in my decision? It was a lonely feeling, made lonelier because Dad wasn't around to hand me $5 when I was broke. And Mother wasn't around to tell me she was praying for me. With renewed determination I began circling the square (if you can circle a square!), moving from store to store, looking for work.

The stern, no-nonsense owner of the grocery store looked me over, frowned, licked the end of his pencil, and made a few notes on a scrap of paper. I had a funny feeling that he had dealt with other college students looking for jobs. He scribbled some more, scratched his balding head, narrowed his eyes, and looked me over from head to foot while I held my breath. "All right," he finally said, "you look like you'll do okay. But it's hard work. You'll be in the warehouse most of the time, unloading trucks, lifting hundred-pound bags of potatoes and cases of canned foods. Your pay will be 50 cents an hour. Okay?"

"Yes, sir," I said gratefully, knowing full well that orthopedic problems from childhood would make this a miserable experience. But 50 cents an hour sounded good — too good to pass up. In those days a half-dollar would buy five loaves of bread, four gallons of gasoline, and three-fourths of a gallon of milk. A pair of Levi's sold for $2.45 and a new car for $975. The average annual income was $2,378.

"Yes, sir," I responded with a hint of concealed excitement. "Fifty cents will be fine."

"Then I'll see you tomorrow," he said curtly, as he turned to walk away.

"But, sir," I stammered, "I can't begin tomorrow. In fact, I can't start until Monday."

"What do you mean, Monday? Fridays and Saturdays are our busiest days. That's when I need you the most."

"Well, sir, I'm planning to attend a pre-school retreat tomorrow and Saturday. It's very important that I be there."

"What's a retreat?" he asked brusquely.

"I'm not sure, sir, but my friends have told me I really need to be there. That's why I arrived early on the campus."

"You mean you're going to a retreat and you don't know what it's about? Craziest thing I ever heard of. Especially with your need for a job."

"I know it doesn't make sense to you, sir," I pleaded, "but I'll be back in two days and I'll be on the job after classes on Monday."

"Oh, go ahead to your retreat, or whatever. Just don't be late on Monday."

My old limp gave way to a skip as I left the store and danced onto the sidewalk outside. Things were working out faster than I could keep score. I didn't need five loaves of bread or a gallon of milk or a new pair of Levi's, but 50 cents an hour seemed like a lot of money. I could attend the retreat with a sense of financial freedom!

I was richer than I could ever dream. And the future had just begun!

NOTE

[1] Clyde E. Fant, Jr. and William M. Pinson, Jr., eds., *Twenty Centuries of Great Preaching* (Waco: Word, 1971), 129-43.

ONE

THE SOUND OF SILENCE

A time to be silent and a time to speak. (Eccl 3:7)

Pre-school retreats were scheduled regularly on university calendars. They provided an opportunity for campus leaders and selected administrative officials to meet in an informal setting and finalize activities involving students for the year ahead. This was all the more important for a school like Baylor which encouraged students to become involved in a variety of religious activities on the campus and in the community. The average attendance at most of the retreats through the years had been 25–30.

But the fall of 1944 was different. Our nation had been at war nearly four years, both in Europe and in the South Pacific. College enrollment had decreased by at least 50 percent as young men and women were either drafted or voluntarily enlisted in the war. There wasn't a student left on the campus who didn't have a brother, father, husband, or sweetheart in military services. Some had been away for as long as three years with no hope of an early return to normal life. Many of the finest were killed. Baylor lost 122 students in the battles and hundreds of others were wounded. Obviously, news of military actions was meager and highly classified, and students often attended movies, not to see the actual movie, but in hopes of catching some bit of information through the highly popular Newsreels. Sometimes people would stumble upon bits of information in unlikely places.

Katy Stokes, in her *Baylor Line* article "Those Halcyon Days," relates a story about Velma Ray Kay, Baylor's Baptist Student Union President from 1943 to 1944. Velma Ray was engaged to be married to John Hugghins, also a Baylor student, who was serving in the South Pacific. "It seems we went from crisis to crisis," Velma Kay observed. "Just after James Leo Garrett and I, working together on the *Round-Up* (the university annual or yearbook), had been talking about the destruction at Iwo Jima, I picked up *Time* magazine and there was a picture of John's ship landing at — yes — Iwo Jima. I remembered screaming. We were not too frivolous about much; in fact, I remember we felt dead serious and that we had to make things count."[1]

In spite of this passion "to make things count," personal plans were put on hold, marriages postponed, careers delayed, and we learned painfully the meaning of the word "wait." Waiting stimulated a lot of soul-searching, and faith became a day-by-day way of life. So did hope.

This generation of students didn't have a lot of things, but few complained. How could one complain when those closest to him were in the thick of battle? Automobile production lines were now turning out jeeps, trucks, and tanks. Gasoline rationing was the rule of the day, and extra coupons were hard to get. The highway speed limit was reduced to 35 miles per hour. There was no television, and radios were often plagued with interference. National weather reports were canceled in the interest of security. There was no plastic and the "throw-away" lifestyle had not yet begun. Indeed, it was considered a patriotic duty to gather scrap iron or any kind of metallic junk and donate it to be recycled for military purposes. There was little penicillin for public use, few synthetics, and nylons were things that girls only dreamed about. There were no cell phones, no commercial jet airplanes, and no rock and roll.

Area codes and zip codes were beyond the wildest imaginations (my telephone number back home in North Carolina was 8-F, or two shorts and a long, and my address was simply Siler City, or the "white bungalow just past the Dark place"). Airline travel was not a way of life, and there were no interstate highways.

Overcrowded buses and trains were the means of distant travel, and this was often unpredictable because of priority rightfully given to military personnel. Hitchhiking was safe and a common way of travel. It provided a tangible way for those fortunate enough to have automobiles to help those without. (I made several trips with strangers from Texas to North Carolina and back and never had a moment's worry.) Dining out was a luxury that few could afford, and fast food was unknown. There were no parking lots on the campus, and you could count on hands and toes the number of students with their own cars.

But, looking back, I don't think we felt deprived. It's hard to miss what you've not had. The closest thing to sacrifice was walking to pick up your girlfriend for a date because your father's gasoline stamps were about to run out, and he was struggling to figure out how to get back and forth to work for the rest of the month.

Ironically, in the midst of a war fought in two distant areas of the world, life seemed strangely simple. Owning a lot of things didn't matter at all. But some things mattered very, very much: family, friendships, safety for those in battle, learning to wait in the midst of uncertainty and patriotism that touched every area of life. When Dad died in 1976, we opened his safety deposit box at the bank. In the metal box were dozens of war bonds that were purchased while he earned less than $200 a month at the furniture factory where he worked. He never mentioned it to the family, and certainly would have never called it "sacrifice." These things mattered. So did God. Would He, could He, take all the debris and wreckage around us and hammer out His purpose? Would we, could we, be a part of that? Was there some way we could help build a better world? Surely something better — much better — was before us. Or was it?

Those questions, and the vacuum in which they were asked, are why 400 students (not the usual 25-30) showed up for this Baylor pre-school retreat. Many, like me, were new to the campus and had no place of leadership. We were just looking for something that would bind us together in a cause larger than ourselves.

We weren't wise enough to know what that cause would be, but we sensed that it was just around the corner, waiting to be discovered.

Years later, the real story of "the 400" who attended the fall retreat became known. Bob Denny, a Bob Hope look-alike, was the Baptist Student Union (BSU) Director, sometimes referred to as Director of Religious Activities. He was a natural for this administrative responsibility on the campus. Armed with a law degree, a "bushel-full" of wisdom, an easy-going, laid-back leadership style, and a winsome sense of humor, he was a favorite with students. Denny was not an authority figure; he saw himself as a coach who encouraged and taught, and then cheered from the sidelines."Like the Old Testament analogy, he allowed students of all ages to "dream dreams and see visions" (Joel 2:28), rejoicing with them in exciting possibilities and adventures.

So when key student leaders met at the beginning of the summer term in 1944 to prepare for the fall retreat, they began to think big. Then someone exclaimed in excitement, "Let's invite everybody to attend — freshmen, transfers, everybody! Let's have a real gathering!" Denny, never one to squelch student enthusiasm, joined in their excitement and exclaimed, "Why not? Dust off the old mimeograph machine and let's go to work!" They typed the invitation, inserted it in the dilapidated, ink-smudged, hand-me-down duplicator, and began to crank. Denny later added with a wry smile, "We would have had more to attend, but we ran out of paper!"

Leta Beene Woodfin received one of those letters and a lot of encouragement from a Youth Revival team sent earlier to her church. Foy Valentine, Ralph Langley, Asa Couch, and Dot Gilbert were on that particular team. Reflecting on the experience, Leta writes:

> In the summer of 1945, banners and posters around Breckenridge, Texas, proclaimed the approach of a "Youth Revival" at the First Baptist Church. The weekly newspaper and the posters bore pictures of four beautiful young people who were to bring this phenomenon.

> Few young people attended First Baptist in those days. Most of the "boys" seventeen and over were still away in the military. The few girls and younger boys who attended did so mostly at the behest of their parents. Skeptically, I went the first Sunday (My Dad was on the church staff so I had no choice!). By the end of the day I was thunderstruck. Here were four dynamic, intelligent, attractive young students singing "I'd Rather Have Jesus," and showing that following Jesus Christ was exciting, not the big yawn of checking off your "six point" record system envelopes and claiming to have read the Bible daily.
>
> During that week the Christ I had known casually since early childhood became my Lord and Master and intimate Friend. I was bound for Baylor University in a few weeks and this "team," as we affectionately called them, began to talk to me about the Baptist Student Union and Latham Springs, a retreat before the Fall term . . . Latham Springs was crawling with young people just like our youth revival team: enthusiastic, intelligent, dedicated Christians. I had never known there were so many Christian young people in the world, nor that they could have such fun.[2]

The nearly 20 miles over a dusty, "washboard" dirt road to Latham Springs Baptist Encampment grounds jarred every bone in our bodies. But our hearts remained steady. Something good was going to happen. Even the rustic appearance of the camp didn't deter us (and "rustic" is a charitable word). The simple menu was adequate even if the poor cooks had been avalanched by hungry students. We all soon learned that bread and peanut butter are good fillers. The cabins were dilapidated and the beds were "make-do's," but sleep wasn't that important. The nights were spent sharing stories, harmonizing on hit songs like "Sentimental Journey" and "Swinging on a Star," belting out "Accentuate the Positive" and "Don't Fence Me In," and chasing crickets and funny-looking crawly things that also lived in our cabins.

The retreat was certainly nothing to write home about. We were not strong or courageous. We weren't sacrificing anything and, heavens, we weren't heroic. The simple truth is that we were beginning to discover that some things are important, and some things are not important at all. And we were slowly learning, without even being aware of it, that the more profound things in life are found in simplicities.

Looking back, everything about the retreat reflected a wonderful kind of simplicity: the sleeping quarters where sleep was low on the priority list; the showers that supplied only cold water; the roughly-built, open-air tabernacle; the uneven slats in the benches that required a lot of shifting in order to find a comfort zone; the public address system that squawked when someone tried to speak; the naked light bulbs that attracted strange-looking flying insects; and the informal program that majored on building friendships, accepting responsibility, and rebuilding a world that had sacrificed many of its finest young people in a war.

Interestingly, the students themselves did most of the talking at the retreat — not the administration, nor the faculty, nor guest speakers. There was a sense in which it was *our* world, *our* responsibility . . . and *our* special moment in history. This was not a matter of ego; it was a matter of divine urgency.

When the first general worship service of the retreat was over, Ralph Langley called me aside and whispered, "Don't leave yet. We're going to have a brief campfire service, and then a few of us are going to linger and talk about something special that we hope will happen on our campus and in our city." In spite of the late hour and the long week I had experienced, I felt a tinge of excitement. Life was too full for fatigue.

Ralph, BO Baker, Angel Martinez, M. D. Oates, Reiji Hoshizaki, and I were among the small group who lingered. M. D. was Baylor's top tennis player, and he acted as the spokesman. He shared that he and Reiji had recently attended a "Youth for Christ" service in San Diego. Reiji had also attended one in Los Angeles. Their dream was that we have a rally for all the city of Waco, sponsored by Baylor students. M. D. continued to state their case while Reiji listened, adding a brief comment now and then to punctuate his own burden. We were to learn in the ensuing months that this was Reiji's pattern. He dreamed dreams, carried the burden, and allowed others to be the spokesmen. This was not a cultural thing; it was simply a matter of Christian humility.

We listened to M. D. for about 30 minutes, pressed Reiji for more details, and then knelt around the dying embers of the campfire and prayed for miracles. Little did we realize that out of those embers a new flame would soon burn.

Reiji Hoshizaki was the first Japanese I had ever met. Unfortunately, like most Americans, I had my own opinion about the "Japs." As a high school student in North Carolina I sat with my father on a Sunday afternoon in 1941 and listened in disbelief to the news of the bombing of Pearl Harbor. In one surprise attack, the Japanese had knocked out eight battleships (five of them sank in the harbor), nine cruisers, and three destroyers — a total of 19 in all. One hundred and eighty-eight aircraft were destroyed, most of them on the ground. Far more painful was the fact that 2,335 servicemen and 68 civilians were killed, and 1,178 were wounded. A 1,760 pound bomb penetrated the forward magazine of the USS *Arizona*, killing 1,104 men. Our oval-shaped Philco radio continued to blare out the grim messages until long after our bedtime. We listened in disbelief, having no understanding of what the next four years would bring.

The evening following the surprise attack I gathered with my friends at Joe's Drugstore and Soda Fountain, the favorite hangout for most of the kids in Siler City, and heard President Roosevelt address Congress: "Yesterday, Sunday, December 7th, 1941, a day which will live in infamy, the United States of America was suddenly and deliberately attacked by naval and air forces of the Empire of Japan." He then asked Congress for a declaration of war. We cheered when he had finished and immediately began to look for the nearest recruitment office to enlist. I watched with envy as scores of friends boarded buses, hitchhiked, or rode trains to basic training camps. We were all caught up in the *noblesse oblige* — privilege entails responsibility — syndrome. I begged the draft board to consider my case, but they turned me down because of long-standing, chronic orthopedic problems. I was never comfortable with their classification, but there was nothing I could do about it.

Part of this rush to enlistment was youthful excitement, part of it was simple, down-to-earth patriotism, and part of it was the example set by some of our heroes — people like Hank Greenberg, Clark Gable, Jimmy Stewart, Frank Capra, Jackie Coogan, Red Skelton, Henry Fonda, Tyrone Power, David Niven, Joe DiMaggio, and scores of others. These were not only in the military services, but many were in the thick of battle.

For most of us, Japan was somewhere "way out there in the Pacific," and the "Japs," as General Douglas MacArthur first called them, were the enemy. They were fanatical in their dedication to their country, defending it by sometimes living underground on islands like Iwo Jima, Okinawa, Guam, and Guadalcanal. Hara-Kiri, an ancient Japanese act of ceremonial suicide, though officially abolished in 1868, was still the crowning glory of life and the way to an honorable death. This philosophy enhanced the risks of warfare and caused Americans to trust them even less. Every Japanese immigrant, especially those living on the West Coast, was viewed with suspicion.

Strangely, I never thought of this as I knelt next to Reiji and the others around the smoldering campfire. Deeply moved, I glanced to my right as we prayed, and I do believe that I saw reflected in his face the face of Christ. A revival had already begun as God spoke through silence. A small-town boy from the deep South and a "Jap" had become brothers. Though he would humbly deny it today, his story is pivotal to the larger story of the Youth Revival Movement. It needs to be told.

Reiji's parents, Buddhists by tradition, had migrated from Japan and worked as tenant vegetable farmers in the northern part of California. There were eight children in the family. Reiji, one of the older children and a natural born American citizen, was the first to graduate from high school. Upon graduation he moved to the Los Angeles area and worked on a chicken farm. His job was "chick-sexing," a task of dividing day-old male and female baby chicks. Obviously, the job requires special training and keen eyesight. The females, or pullets, were given special food to enhance the laying of eggs. The poor roosters ended up on someone's platter for Sunday dinner.

In 1939, Reiji found a similar job in Dallas that paid better wages, so he moved to Texas. By nature he was a loner and spent most of his time off in his apartment in the Oak Cliff section of the city. One afternoon he met a man named Ellred Thomas in a small grocery store. Thomas, a Baylor graduate and a minister, invited him to attend a revival at a church nearby. Reiji accepted the invitation and attended the service. As he puts it, he was deeply moved and felt a tug to go forward. Later, John Havalick, also a Baylor student, was preaching in a revival in a church in the same area. Reiji attended one of the services and listened as Havalick preached on the crucifixion of Christ. In his message he emphasized Jesus' prayer from the cross, "Father, forgive them, they know not what they do." Reiji was deeply moved and thought, "If that Man can pray for their forgiveness after all they're doing to him, then I need to follow him." This led to his becoming a Christian.

Still later, Reiji attended a service where Angel Martinez was preaching. When the service was over, he said to a friend, "I wish we could get that man to go to California and talk to my friends about what it means to be a Christian." The friend responded, "Why don't you go yourself?" This led to Reiji's commitment to the ministry and to studies at Baylor University.

Meanwhile, his parents and six of his brothers and sisters were caught up in the hysteria that gripped the United States after the attack on Pearl Harbor. Sentiment was especially strong along the Pacific coast where residents feared more Japanese attacks on their cities, homes, and businesses. As a result of this pressure, President Roosevelt ordered the internment of 120,000 people of Japanese ancestry — in spite of the fact that many were citizens and there was no record of disloyalty among the group. Reiji's parents and some of their children were moved to a desert camp near Phoenix, Arizona, with the responsibility to "make the desert bloom." They lost all their personal property and lived in barracks under harsh conditions until their release in 1944. Reiji, a Nisei (an American born Japanese), was not interned. Ironically, he had a brother who served in the United States Army during World War II — as an intelligence officer!

"Were your parents bitter?" I asked Reiji as we visited over dinner one evening long after the retreat we attended as students and the sharing around the campfire.

"No. Not at all."

"I don't understand. How could they not be bitter?" I asked in bewilderment.

"Their lives were rooted in a culture where strict law and order prevailed," he said. "Whatever those in authority said, you were supposed to do it. It's a part of their way of life."

I marveled at their patience and their continuing loyalty to our government in spite of their privations and detention. They suffered in silence and taught us a valuable lesson: *God works miracles out of reversals and fulfills his plans in ways we least expect.*

When Reiji's parents were released from the Phoenix camp, they moved to Chicago to start over. Reiji visited them there and heard of a Youth for Christ rally scheduled on a Saturday night. He attended the service, joined in the singing of the hymns and choruses, and listened to an energetic young man preach. His name was Billy Graham.

It was nearly midnight at the student retreat in the fall of 1944 when the little group finished praying around what had once been a campfire. Words were no longer spoken. They were not needed. God knew our thoughts and our dreams. And He spoke to us that night as he had spoken to Elijah: "through a gentle whisper," or "through the sound of silence" (1 Kgs 19: 12).

As we quietly walked away, all that remained was a wisp of spiraling smoke from a spent fire . . . and a dream.

What irony! God had spoken through silence. And through a Japanese student that some had once called our enemy.

NOTES

[1] Katy Jennings Stokes, "Those Halcyon Days," *Baylor Line*, April 1981.

[2] Leta Beene Woodfin, correspondence with the author.

TWO

AFTERGLOW

Fan into flame the gift of God which is in you.
(2 Tim 1:6)

The two-day retreat was over and students reluctantly retraced the 20 miles back to Waco and to Baylor's campus — never to be the same again. Those who had gathered around the campfire made no formal announcement concerning their dreams for a citywide revival in the months to come. That would have been premature. But quietly small groups gathered to ponder the possibilities and to pray for spiritual awakening. We had no blueprint for such an emphasis, but we had an overwhelming sense that we were involved in something beyond our wildest dreams. We didn't understand it, then or now, but we had a feeling that a movement bigger than life was in its formative stages and had begun to capture our minds and hearts. One thing we did know: we were not instigators; we were mere spectators.

The small group that had listened to Hoshizaki and Oates continued to meet and pray about some kind of student-led revival in Waco. The glow of the campfire embers refused to die. Informal prayer meetings began to take place each night — at Brooks Hall, the men's dormitory; at Minglewood Bowl, where campus intramural games were played; and in the campus building where Bible classes were taught. One of the regular participants in the prayer meetings was Johnny Beard, a freshman from Alton, Illinois. Johnny was eager to learn and to be a part of anything that would prepare him for the ministry.

One morning Johnny was praying with some friends and became convinced that he needed to be baptized, or to be more correct, re-baptized. He had been baptized by immersion in Alton in a Northern Baptist Church, later called the American Baptist Church. Now he had troubling questions about his commitment and the meaning of his baptism. Most of his friends, who were *Southern* Baptists, were anxious to help Johnny out of his "heresy." The more they talked and prayed, the more he wanted it settled right then. But two problems faced them. First, they need plenty of water for immersion. They settled on Waco Creek, a small tributary that flowed (if it rained) through the campus and by the bear pit, the home of Baylor's mascot.

Second, they needed a preacher, preferably someone who had been ordained. We found one in tall, gangling, fun-loving Jess Moody, an 18-year-old son of a liquor store owner, who had enrolled in Baylor as a ministerial student, but, as he puts it, "my knowledge of the Bible was woefully inadequate. I knew the names of more kinds of rum," he said, "than I knew verses in the Bible." About all he brought to college with him was his recent conversion experience, a delightful personality, and a strong impression that the Lord wanted him to preach.

This lack of Biblical and theological understanding was verified during Jess' second week as a student. He sat in a class under the esteemed head of the Bible department, Dr. J. B. Tidwell. The great scholar was lecturing on Judaism when he paused in his lecture, looked over his glasses, and asked Jess a question. There was an awkward moment of silence, and then Jess spoke up with his answer. The professor's response to the answer Jess gave was, "No, Mr. Moody, *Hanukkah* is not a duck call." That was Jess — loved by most everybody, including Dr. Tidwell.

In spite of Jess' limited knowledge of Bible verses and church history, some church had joyfully ordained him. Reverend Moody, armed with his ordination certificate, was now ready to marry people, baptize them, and bury them. So, at two o'clock in the morning there was a knock on Jess's dormitory room door.

"Who is it? And what do you want?" Jess hollered in a non-ministerial sounding voice.

"Johnny Beard wants to be baptized, and he wants you to do it."

"When?" Jess asked sleepily.

"Tonight. Right now."

"Where?" Jess inquired.

"Waco Creek. We told him you would do it."

Jess stumbled around, found his pants and a shirt, and with his Bible under his arm he headed toward the creek. Word had already gotten out, and students swarmed from all directions for the event. When they arrived at the creek they discovered that lack of rain had almost dried up the tributary. In fact, there was only about three inches of water at the deepest part. Undaunted, Jess came up with a plan.

He waded into the ankle-deep water and signaled for Johnny to follow him. Placing one hand behind Johnny's neck, and the other on his chest, Jess began to lower his candidate down toward the water. Down . . . down . . . down they went, until Johnny was lying in a trickle of water, and Jess was kneeling beside him. Jess then turned to Dick Baker, a freshman from Farmersville, Texas, and said, "Dick, cup your hands and splash water all over Johnny's face." When this was over, Jess said, "Okay, Johnny, now roll over and get wet on the other side." As Johnny struggled to turn over, and as Dick continued to cup his hands and splash water in his friend's face, Jess uttered words about "baptizing you in the name of the Father, and the Son, and the Holy Spirit."

Frankly, it wasn't clear whether Jess or Dick was baptizing Johnny, or whether Johnny was baptizing himself. Regardless, it was a wonderful victory, and *Southern* Baptists had won the battle over *Northern* Baptist.

Before noon the next day word was all over the campus about the unusual baptismal service. And, by later in the afternoon, Dr. Tidwell had sent word for Jess to meet him in his office. When

Jess finally showed up, Dr. Tidwell, a soft-spoken scholar, was agitated.

"By whose authority? By WHOSE authority? By WHOSE AUTHORITY did you baptize that boy?" Dr. Tidwell asked, raising his voice with each question.

Jess listened in stunned silence, and then replied in absolute honesty, "Sir, I didn't know I needed any authority." And then Jess asked in naivety and concern, "Do you think the baptism 'took'? Was it valid?"

Dr. Tidwell paused for a moment, and then said with growing understanding, "Mr. Moody, I think God knows your heart and He knows what you and the others were doing down there in that creek last night." Then, he added with a wisp of a smile, "The Lord understands, but I can't say about some of the other professors in the Bible department. We'll just have to work on them. And, it wouldn't hurt if we studied some Christian doctrine and church polity." The "we" said it all, and this was the beginning of a beautiful friendship between the 18-year-old "liquor store boy" and the 80-year-old gentle scholar. Apparently the baptism did "take," for Johnny became the energetic, effective pastor of some wonderful churches for more than 40 years.

The informal prayer meetings continued, and the more we prayed, the more we were aware of practical needs facing us. For instance, what about the location for the revival? What time of the year would be best for all involved? Who should be the speakers? The musicians? Who should be in charge of publicity and promotion? And, what about finances? This was where the genius of Bob Denny's leadership as the Baptist Student Union Director came in, even though many of the students did not recognize it at the time. Denny had a remarkable way of encouraging students, but, like a courtroom attorney, he could ask questions punctuated by lengthy pauses. He could free students up to do their own thinking, but he could also quietly bring them back to reality.

In 1982, the Oral History Department of Baylor University began compiling video histories of those who participated in the Youth Revival Movement. Hundreds of hours of interviews were recorded and thousands of pages of these interviews were filed for research purposes. A careful reading of the oral histories by Bob Denny give a vivid picture of the way he prodded the students to think for themselves; yet, he stood in the shadows to encourage them. An excellent example of this style of leadership is reflected in a conversation he had with M. D. Oates:

Oates: "We need a revival here in Waco designed to reach the youth of our city."
Denny: "I couldn't agree more. Let's get on with making plans for it. There are 18 churches in this area and not a one has had a good revival in years. The truth is, evangelism is relatively dead — if anything can be relatively dead."
Oates: "But we'll have to invite those who led in the Youth for Christ rallies in Chicago to come and lead in the services here."
Denny: "Why? Why do we need them?"
Oates: "Well, because they're the best."
Denny: "Did they ask you to come to Chicago and lead in their revivals?"
Oates: "No. I don't understand what you mean."
Denny: "If they didn't need you to help them, why should you need them to help you?"
Oates: "But who will lead?"
Denny: "Let the students here lead. They can preach and sing."
(Silence)
Oates: "We'll need some money from the administration to pay for the expenses."
Denny: "Why?"
Oates: "Well…er…it will cost money for advertising and maybe a tent and I don't know what else."
Denny: "Let's see if I understand what you're saying. You want a revival but you want someone else to pay for it?"
Oates: "But we don't have any money."
Denny: "Neither does the administration. If you want money, raise it yourself."

Now, this encounter, recorded by Denny and confirmed by Oates, sounds harsh and cold when read in black and white. But behind these words was a "coach" who was trying to get a team to see that they could do for themselves whatever needed to be done — with God's help. It was a lesson none would forget. From that moment through the months of preparation for the 1945 revival, and through the last service of the revival, Denny kept urging the students into places of leadership. He never once sat on the platform, never made an announcement and never led in public prayer. It was a classic lesson in encouragement, servanthood, and leadership wisdom.

Within an hour of that meeting with Denny, Oates found me on the campus. "Bruce," he said with a pained look on his face," "there's no money available from the administration for the revival. We've got to raise it ourselves. I've just met with some other students, and they want you to be chairman of the finances."

"What does that mean?" I asked innocently.

"It means you've got to raise the money."

"How much?"

"Well, it looks like we might need as much as $750, maybe more. And we'd like to raise the money and have everything paid for before the first service begins. No offerings during the week."

I was speechless. I couldn't imagine there was that much money in all of Waco! It had only been a few weeks since I'd arrived on the campus from North Carolina with my $90 "fortune." Seven hundred and fifty dollars was nearly eight times more than that.

"M.D., I don't know a thing about raising money," I protested. And I was telling the truth!

"But we'll pray for you," M.D. answered in a matter-of-fact tone. No more discussion. No meetings. No election. Before dinner that evening it was out all over the campus that I was chairman of finances for the revival. The only person who would have been more frightened than I was would have been my father — if I had dared tell him!

Frankly, I have no idea where the money came from. There was no organized plan for raising it — just word of mouth. One of my first visits was to the office of Mr. Morrell, the owner of the Percy Baby Medicine Company. This kind, gentle man had given me my second job, helping bottle his secret formula for children sick with the stomachache, at the unbelievable wage of 65 cents an hour. Whatever was in the bottles seemed to work and there were times when I thought half of Texas was using it. I trembled as I sat in his tiny office, waiting to share the financial needs of the coming youth revival. He walked in and immediately put me at ease. He listened with deep concern, nodding his near-bald head in agreement as I nervously talked. Before I had finished my "speech" he reached for his checkbook and wrote out a check for $50! It was manna from heaven. Fifty whole dollars on my first visit.

Later, as I walked across the campus to classes, someone handed me a dollar. Crumpled dollar bills came from all directions at all hours of the day and night. Occasionally, a student would give me $5, and not ask for change! It was a miracle.

One coed ran up to me one day on the campus and blurted out excitedly, "My parents are going to help support the revival!"

"Wonderful," I exclaimed, knowing they owned or worked on some kind of farm or ranch in South Texas. "Do you have any idea what they plan to give?" This was important, for every nickel and every dime counted.

"They're going to give a haystack," she said with a proud smile.

"A haystack?"

"Yes, they told me to tell you that they would take all the hay from one of the stacks in the field, sell it, and give the money for the Youth Revival."

I didn't know whether to laugh, dance for joy, or weep. How much is a haystack worth? My Grandpa Moody had some on his dirt-poor farm in the hills of North Carolina, but it was for the livestock to eat during the winter months. I'd never thought of those haystacks amounting to much money. But this was Texas. Things could be different out here.

The gift of the haystack, as I recall, was not a staggering one. At least, it wasn't significant enough for me to remember the amount. But the fact that those parents gave what they had and what they could — a haystack — inspired scores of others to respond with what they could and what they had. To me, it's still one of the warm stories and beautiful secrets of the 1945 Waco Youth for Christ Revival.[1]

Amazingly, no records were kept as money was given, and it didn't seem to occur to anyone to ask for an accounting. This was new territory for all of us. A few churches in the area helped and pastors expressed concern, but they and their churches were also going through a money crunch. The depression, followed by the privations of the war, had touched everyone, and everyone's pocketbook.

Ironically, there was one exception. G. P. Comer was pastor of the First Methodist Church in Waco. In every sense of the word he was a "character." His sermon subjects, printed in bold print in the Waco papers, were sensational ("What I Saw While Standing at the Corner of 5th and Austin Streets" or "The Biggest Sinner in Waco"). His style of delivery was unpredictable. He would move from the pulpit, to the choir, to the congregation, and break into song whenever "the Spirit moved him." The "best show in town" was at First Methodist Church, often to the chagrin of long-time members and to the delight of visiting college students.

Comer had a system worked out when the offering was taken. If someone put $5 in the plate, the usher hollered "Amen!" If it was $10, the shout was "Hallelujah!" And on rare occasions when $20 was put in the plate a little old lady in her eighties would put her fingers in her mouth and give forth with a shrill whistle. She was about the biggest drawing card Comer had, and people would sit in eager anticipation while the offering was being taken, hoping to hear her whistle. Looking back, there may not have been much worship taking place in this part of the service, but there was a lot of entertainment!

Comer was gracious enough to ask me to speak briefly in one of the morning worship services about the coming youth revival.

Waco, Wednesday night; LeRay Fowler, McGregor, Thursday night; M. D. Oates, San Diego, California, Friday night; and, Ralph Langley, Opelika, Ala, Saturday night. A chorus of 150 voices will sing each night and an orchestra composed of young people will furnish music. Services will be held at 8 p.m. If it rains, meetings will be held in Columbus Avenue Baptist Church at the Thirteenth and Columbus Ave. rather than in the tent at the Austin site."

Another news release named the committees for the revival. "M.D. Oates and Reiji Hoshizaki will serve as general chairmen. The theme for the revival will be 'Waco Youth for Christ.' Ralph Langley will head the publicity committee. Newspaper publicity will be covered by Joe Emery, Temple, for the Waco paper; Winnie Dudley of Dallas, for the *Baylor Lariat*; and James Leo Garrett, Waco, for the Waco High School paper. Others on the committee are Bill Liner, Houston, sign advertisement on the site of the meeting; J. C. Moody, Wharton, airplane publicity and a canvas sign at Eighth and Austin Streets; Bill Cumbie, San Diego, radio announcements; Avery Richey, Victoria, public address system; Treysa Seely, Dallas; Jeannette Bullard, Birmingham, Ala, and Beverly Kennon, publicity in churches; Bruce McIver, Siler City, North Carolina is finance committee chairman.

"The music is under the direction of BO Baker, assisted by Kay Timberlake, Earlsboro, Okla., orchestra; Evelyn Alexander, Dallas, violin; and James Robbins, Quitman, sopranos and altos, and James Browder, Groesbeck, male voices. Co-chairmen of the arrangements will be Jack Mason, Tulsa, Okla., and Dub Baker, Farmersville. Their duties will include arranging for the the platform, chairs, electricity, pianos, and organs."

Katy Stokes states that testimonies were given by Evelyn Alexander, Hollis Davis, Dan Rainbold, Elaine Morgan, James Browder, Mayrene Jackson, Winton Swain, and Bruce McIver.[3] Katy also has an interesting paragraph on the music:

> The music included the usual array of Baylor talent. Billy Enete played his marimba; Ann Scott, Ivan Larsen, and Evelyn

> Alexander were a violin trio. Frank McTaggert, then preaching at the "Beverly Hills Mission," soloed, as did Dick Baker and Jane Robbins. Other musical presentations were performed by the trio of Sue and Nancy Anderson and Billie Russell; Baylor's Centennial Quartet: Frank Boggs, Bill Wagner, Bill Cumbie, and Kenneth Balthrop; the trio of Jo Frels, Bennie Mae Oliver, and Eva Marie Kennard and the duet of Sue and Nancy Anderson. Students from five Waco schools comprised a 30-piece orchestra and a 200-voice choir.

In addition to these listed, scores were involved in prayer meetings, cleaning the lot, setting up and dusting chairs, organizing a twenty-block march from the campus to the site on opening night and going to the various schools in Waco urging students to attend. Also, members of a fan-out group visited 2,000 homes in the city, personally inviting people to attend and leaving behind a sheet of publicity concerning the details of the revival. It was a massive undertaking, and one wonders now how any student found time to attend classes!

Those chosen to preach represented the finest leaders on the campus. There were no politics in the choices, and certainly no one ran for the role of preacher. Instead, they were chosen by consensus — by a general agreement of those serving on the Baptist Student Union Council. The only restriction placed on the preachers was the "25-minute" rule. No sermon could go longer than that, and it was strongly suggested that the sermons be kept within a twenty-minute time bracket. Sermon subjects were printed in advance in both the campus and Waco papers and on flyers and posters. Angel Martinez opened on Monday with, "Up Jumped the Devil!" Just before he preached someone rented a devil suit and rode on a fire truck in the parade. On Tuesday, BO Baker preached on "No Draftees in the Army of God," and on Wednesday Reiji Hoshizaki used for his sermon title, "Going My Way." "What's in a Kiss?" was the title of LeRay Fowler's sermon on Thursday, and "Blood Plasma" was the sermon M.D. Oates preached on Friday. Ralph Langley concluded the meeting on Saturday night as he preached, "Don't Die on Third."

Waco newspapers carried large advertisements daily about the nightly sermons. On Wednesday there was a picture of Reiji Hoshizaki under bold words which read, "Hear a Japanese American." Then, in smaller print:

> Hoshizaki, who wants to be a missionary to Japan at the end of the war, quietly disregards insults hurled at him from all sides. Active in Baptist Student Union activities on the campus, he is a regular participant in services held each Saturday afternoon on the city hall square. On several occasions, passerbys have halted to yell insults and threats at him while he was preaching.
>
> When a heckler called out a threat to kill him, Hoshizaki continued talking as if nothing had been said, and sentiment of the crowd forced the heckler to withdraw. He is subjected to insults at every turn. En route home after conducting a series of religious meetings in another city, he was upbraided because of his race by a filling station operator at the station where he had stopped for some gasoline.
>
> He receives innumerable discourteous glances as he walks down the street in the downtown section of the city. He never replies to an insult, never complains or mentions them.[4]

The threat of the filling station operator reflects the love and respect fellow students had for Reiji. When the attendant at the station saw that he was a Japanese, he picked up a tire tool and threatened to kill him. One of the students with Reiji stepped between the two, and said, "If you intend to kill him, you'll have to hit me first. He's with me. He's a Christian, and he's my friend." The would-be attacker looked confused, slowly lowered the tire tool, and walked away.

The attendance at the services soared nightly above the 3000 mark — beyond the wildest imaginations of those in charge of planning and promoting the meeting. There were 281 public commitments made to Christ and to Christian ministries. These decisions were made without the pressure of lengthy invitations or dramatic "begging and pleading." The students came, they sang and shared their personal experiences, someone spoke (or "preached") for about 20–25 minutes, we sang a hymn or chorus, and then we stood back and watched God work in the lives of people. At times, it was as though we were spectators, caught up in a movement we could never have planned and did not understand.

Looking back, Ralph Langley, one of the leaders in the 1945 Youth Revival, observes:

> It was an atmosphere of electricity and excitement. It was new. There's always something exciting about something new that people think and feel is God-blessed. There was a kind of charisma in some of those involved, charisma in the healthiest sense of the word, of holy expectancy. We were excited beyond words when we saw people arriving early, 30 minutes early, to get a good seat. And that always spreads its own kind of divine electricity. There was a holy hush — a group of kids leading a group of kids, with adults around . . . quietly affirming them with an amen from the heart. It was a beautiful spirit of community and campus light blending together, a marriage. We were seeing a holy marriage between a Baptist university ministering to a community that probably wanted it but didn't know how to ask for it, and suddenly God had given them a technique and a strategy and a handle.[5]

Winnie Dudley wrote for an article for the *Baptist Standard*, May 17, 1945:

> Success of the Baylor youth revival conducted by undergraduates and held under a tent in downtown Waco is reflected by the fact that other colleges and cities are asking for information on how to promote a similar meeting . . . . During the first four nights of the six-day revival, Baylor students marched over 20 blocks from the campus to the tent. The parade, which reached 600 marchers, were joined downtown by the Teen Age Club. Accompanied by a motorcycle escort students carried large banners advertising the revival and sang as they marched. Rain the last two nights of the week prevented parades and caused the

services to be taken indoors at nearby Columbus Avenue Baptist Church.

But even the rain seemed symbolic, as God seemed to say to some immature students, *"I will pour out my Spirit on all people..."* (Joel 2:28a).

So, keep fanning the flame!

NOTES

[1] The 1945 revival was called the "Waco Youth for Christ" revival. Other revivals that grew out of the Baylor-Waco revival used the same term until 1946 when the name was changed from "Youth for Christ Revival" to "Youth Revival." There was no competition, but this change was made out of respect for the Youth for Christ organization that conducted their own rallies and revivals. In the mid-1950s the "Youth Revival" name was changed to "Youth-led Revivals" to emphasize the involvement of adults along with the youth.

[2] Reiji Hoshizaki, correspondence with the author.

[3] Katy Stokes, "Those Halcyon Days," *Baylor Line*, April 1981.

[4] *Waco News-Tribune*, April 18, 1945.

THREE

OVER THERE

May the Lord watch between you and me when we are absent one from another. (Gen 31: 49)

Meanwhile, as we slept in rustic cabins with scurrying insects, some of our classmates slept in shallow foxholes partially filled with icy water; as we ate peanut butter and beans, they dined on bland K rations; as we sang and prayed around campfires, they inched their way through bombed-out, burning buildings; and as we greeted our friends with hugs and friendly embraces, they buried their comrades in hastily-dug graves. They were "over there"; we were "over here." It wasn't fair, but there is never anything "fair" about war.

WWII had taken a heavy toll on both campus enrollment and student leadership. Hundreds of Baylor students either enlisted voluntarily or were drafted into military service. One hundred and twenty-two did not return, giving their lives in battle. A heavy pall hung over the campus. Those who remained seemed to redouble their efforts in practical ministries. It has been estimated that during those long war years, 96 percent of the students at Baylor were involved in at least one religious activity each week.

There are hundreds of moving stories about Baylorites in the thick of battle. For example, Captain Joe Dawson, Commanding Officer of G Company, 16th Regiment, 1st Division, was the first American to reach the top of the bluff at Omaha Beach on D Day, June 6, 1944. Stephen Ambrose writes about Captain Dawson in his book, *Citizen Soldiers*: "By mid-September he had been in battle for 100 days. He had learned through painful experience how to fight in the hedgerows, how to work with tanks and planes, and how to pursue a defeated enemy in the dash across France. He was 31-years-old, son of a Waco, Texas, Baptist preacher. He had lost 25 pounds off his already thin 6'2" frame"[1]

Captain Dawson's father, Dr. J. M. Dawson, was the distinguished pastor of the First Baptist Church in Waco. He was a tireless worker on behalf of world peace and a leader in the founding of the United Nations. Little did we know at the time that his son, a Baylor student, was to become one of the heroes of the war because of his courage and leadership. He lived through the battles, came home and settled in Texas and died in 1999, still a hero in every sense of the word.

Others come to mind. Joe Canzoneri flew navy rescue missions in the South Pacific. He returned to the campus in time to sing in a quartet in the 1946 revival. He also met and married Jeanette Bullard, a leader in the Friday night mission program and involved in a variety of other religious activities on the campus.

Joe Morman was a paratrooper assigned to the South Pacific. Joe also returned in time for the '46 revival and was placed in charge of the parade of 500 students who marched from the campus, through downtown Waco, and on to the revival site each night. Dressed in army fatigues and paratrooper boots, he marched those students as straight as any military leader ever marched his troops into battle while they sang, "Onward Christian Soldiers."

Mark Moore was a POW who was released in time to preach in the '46 revival. His sermon, "Don't Fence Me In," was deeply moving as he shared his own testimony of deliverance and freedom. It was the first time most of us had seen or heard a prisoner of war.

George Stokes, another veteran and a communications major, was chairman of radio publicity for the revival. Bob Mitchell, a laid-back, easy-going character with an infectious sense of humor, helped set up benches under the tent. One day, with his back aching from the weight of his job, he complained loudly, "I'm tired of this hard work. I want one of those glory jobs on the committee. " Apparently all the glory jobs had been taken, but Bob and others like him, with aching backs and blistered hands, took care of the practical needs involving thousands of people.

Thankfully, the veterans returned to the campus in record numbers. Their return lifted the spirits of students and faculty who had once told them good-bye. Obviously, this also led to a dramatic increase in enrollment which gave new life to the financial needs of the university. In the fall of 1945, Baylor's enrollment reached 1,816, an increase of 400 students. By the spring of 1946, enrollment had leaped to 2633. Of this number 1,160, or 44 percent, were former servicemen. They came, some with scars on their bodies, others with scars on their hearts. And the vast majority returned with a yearning that "swords would be beaten into plowshares and we would train for war no more" (Isa 4:2).

Dwight Baker, a chaplain during the war and a member of the class of 1944, has made some interesting observations about the climate in which the youth revivals took place:

> Remember it was immediate post-war time and the nation's surviving young men had just come back from up to four years in Europe, the Far East, or on the high seas. They had been through hell; their families had been through it, too, praying the entire time for their safe return. Many, aside from experiencing the horrors of war, close brushes with death, and knowing suffering first hand, had walked through that seamy side of life from which they had been sheltered at home. Some had succumbed to temptation and weren't pleased with their lives up to that point. This, despite the fact that many returned as military heroes.
>
> Now they were home and they yearned for a better life, perhaps the life they remembered as being a part of themselves before they went to war. Others, were deeply shattered and were ready to put the pieces of their lives together. Many families, in gratitude to God for their sons' and daughters' safe return, were ready to dedicate themselves to God's service. The reunion at

> home triggered a deep desire for reunion with God on the spiritual level.
>
> The pastors were ready for it as well. For some it was a nostalgic trip back to their own now faded youth, when, in their earlier days, they had set out to save the world on weekends, between classes at college or seminary.[2]

Into this milieu they returned, and their world...and ours...would never be the same.

Two veterans stand out in special ways as we think of "Over There." Their stories deserve to be told.

JIM COLE
D-DAY, JUNE 6, 1944.

> On the beaches of Omaha and Utah, and anywhere else on the coast of Normandy where a boat could land, 175,000 Allies began the push that would eventually lead to some of the fiercest and costliest fighting the world has ever known. Within three weeks, the Americans alone had 452,000 in the thick of the battle. Of this number there were 27,000 casualties, with 11,000 fatalities and another 1,000 missing in action.[3]

Interestingly, the typical American soldier was not a professional. Instead he (or she) was an amateur, or, as Stephen Ambrose calls him in the title of his book, a "Citizen Soldier." He was young and inexperienced at first, but he learned quickly on the job and he deeply believed in the cause for which he fought — from Omaha Beach through the infamous maze of Normandy hedgerows, to and through the Siegfried Line and the Battle of the Bulge, in the Hurtgen Forest (where you could see nothing but trees), across the Rhine and into the heartland of Germany. Then, finally, victory on May 7,1945.

The last lines of Ambrose's *Citizen Soldiers* sum up the remarkable commitment of those who endured these battles:

> At the core, the American citizen soldiers knew the difference between right and wrong, and they didn't want to live in a world in which wrong prevailed. So they fought, and won, and we — all of us — living and yet to be born, must be profoundly grateful.[4]

Jim Cole was one of those "citizen soldiers."

Jim, a 17-year-old from Memphis, Tennessee, enthusiastically enlisted in the army, but he was eighteen when he was actually called up. Like thousands of others he wanted to get into the thick of battle, settle the issues, and get on with the life before him. The "thick of battle" for him began on the beach at Omaha on June 6, 1944, but the issues were not settled quickly. Jim, who was assigned to the First Army, fought in every major battle for the next 11 months. In these experiences, Jim said quietly, "young men became old men overnight." He then added, "Wars are planned by old men, but never fought by them."

"Let me tell you about my first day in combat," Jim said in an interview. "That was the day I saw my first American soldiers killed. I dug a foxhole in the hedgerows of France that was at least 12 feet in depth. I was trying to find China, I guess. But then we moved positions and I went over to a foxhole that had already been dug and started to get in it. Then I spotted one about 50 to 75 feet away, covered with an old door and a mound of dirt. I put my pack and rifle down, pulled out a cigarette and lit it. In that moment a shell came in and killed two guys who had gotten into the foxhole I had started to get in."

"What did you do then?" I asked.

"I flipped my cigarette away and had a deep feeling that God was speaking to me." And then he added with a wry smile, "Of all the times to give up smoking, that was not the time!"

"But," he continued, "I sensed God speaking to me. And I can recount other experiences where I had a near brush with death and I felt God's hand on me."

When the war in Germany was over, Jim returned to the States. As his ship came into New York harbor, he looked at the

Statue of Liberty and said, "Honey, if you see my face again, you're gonna have to turn around."

Jim came home with a deeper conviction that we are "created in the image of God," and with a growing understanding of the "brotherhood of man." He didn't want to talk about the war; he just wanted to get on with his studies and his commitment to the Lord made in a foxhole. One of his first accomplishments was making the Dean's List during his first academic term.

Jim received a degree in business at Union University in Tennessee. He then signed a contract to work for a popular chain of men's varsity shops. But his experiences in the war kept bringing him face to face with reality. "Here we are," he said, "killing one another, and I kept asking the question — why? We're created in the image of God and we're supposed to be brothers, and yet, we're seeking to slaughter one another. I turned my life around at that point and came to Baylor because I had surrendered to preach and wanted a graduate degree in religion."

The dramatic post-war increase in enrollment, enhanced by the return of so many veterans, created some "happy problems" for Baylor. Dormitories were crowded beyond capacity, and dozens of homes around the campus became "boarding houses." Jim lived on a vacated military base near Waco that Baylor was able to lease from the government.

At 5:30 p.m. on Tuesday afternoon, April 2, 1946, tires screeched in front of Jim's make-shift apartment. Jess Moody, one of the preachers in the student-led revival that began the day before, jumped out of the car, dashed to the door, and announced, "Jim, you're to give your testimony at the youth revival service tonight. I was told by the committee to ask you last night, but—"

"Tonight?" Jim interrupted in disbelief.

"Yep," Jess replied, "I'm sorry I didn't get the word to you sooner."

But what Jess didn't know was that Jim had a premonition that he was going to be asked and he was already prepared. Besides, he had participated in many of the pre-revival prayer services held nightly in preparation for the revival. Two hours later, he stood before nearly 4,000 students and shared some of the stories he shared with me in the interview fifty years later. A quiet sense of awe fell over the students as he talked of God's grace and presence — even in the midst of battle. Later, Jack Robinson, who preached after Jim's testimony, said, "There was no need for a sermon tonight. His testimony said it all." In humility, Jack had captured the moment, or had been captured by the moment. So had scores of others as they moved forward at the conclusion of the service in public commitment of their lives to Christ.

Jim Cole, who was in every major battle in the European Theater of Operations, from June 6, 1944 to May 7, 1945 when the Germans surrendered, has spent nearly sixty years living out that commitment made in a foxhole in the hedgerows of France. He married Helen Whitten (class of '47), pastored several churches, served for 20 years as editor of the *Baptist Message*, the Louisiana state Baptist newspaper, and then returned to Baylor University to serve as the executive vice president of the alumni association for 11 years prior to his retirement.

BILL LOGUE

The date was December 8, 1941. Bill Logue and two of his friends, Marion Pierce and Raymond Fisher, sat outside Pat Neff Hall at Baylor University and listened to the radio as President Roosevelt addressed Congress and called for a military response to the bombing of Pearl Harbor. Their emotions were stirred and, like thousands of other young people, they marched straight to the recruiting office and volunteered for duty. Within a few short weeks they were processed and assigned to different branches of the service. They never saw each other again.

For several months Bill moved from camp to camp, training as a foot soldier in the infantry. He missed D-Day and Normandy but found himself in the heat of the Battle of Bulge, in December 1944. The fighting was foxhole-to-foxhole and building-to-building. Then, the word came that the Germans were sending in their "Tiger Tanks," the most powerful tanks used by either side in the battle. "They're gonna blow the thunder out of us," a sergeant said. "We'll have to surrender." Painfully, there seemed to be no other alternative.

Bill Logue's 21st birthday was far from anything he had imagined or dreamed — even in his worst nightmares. On that January day in 1945, he was a prisoner of war in a camp near Nuremberg. His feet were frozen and he had gone without adequate food for weeks.

"Did you see the movie *Schindler's List*?" Bill asked me as we visited one day.

When I told him I had, he replied quietly, "I've been there."

Then he talked, almost reluctantly, about the Battle of the Bulge, the encirclement of his outfit by powerful Tiger Tanks, and, finally, his capture on December 17, 1944. He was then herded onto a train and placed in an overcrowded boxcar. There was no place to sit or lie down. He, like all others, stood body to body throughout the seemingly endless trip across Germany. No water, no food, no privacy. On Christmas Day, 1944, his overcoat and overshoes were taken from him and he stood in the snow all day with his feet frozen — still without food or water. This led to more than one subsequent bout with pneumonia and the loss of 40 pounds of weight.

But several times as he described these experiences, he would pause and say, "I'm ashamed to talk about this and my own hardships, for so many of our friends had it so much worse in the South Pacific." His humility helped redefine the word "greatness."

"How did you keep your sanity?" I asked in all sincerity.

He paused for a long moment, and then said, "I had faith in the Lord, and I loved my Momma and my Daddy and my brothers and my sisters. I hoped the good Lord would spare me, but I knew if He didn't, I was going to have eternal life."

I smiled with gratitude that a distinguished man, now retired and a grandfather, would speak in such simple, yet profound, language about "Momma and Daddy . . . and brothers and sisters . . . and eternal life." V-Day was May 8, 1945. Bill got to Paris on May 9, purchased a box of Hershey Chocolates, and ate the whole box!

Several days later his ship sailed into New York Harbor and passed by the Statue of Liberty. As he reflected on that moment, he said, "At times, grown men cry. It was a very moving, emotional experience."

"Did you go straight home — back to Waco?" I asked.

"No," he replied, "I got to New Orleans and then took a couple of days and visited a mother and father in Pineville, Louisiana. Their son, Bill Hickson, was one of my buddies in the war. He was killed in a foxhole next to me. I promised I would look up his parents before I returned to my own home."

On November 30, 1945, he was finally discharged.

"What were the first things you did?" I asked.

"The first thing I did was to go to my church, Seventh and James Baptist, located next to the campus. Then I enrolled in Baylor . . . about the time plans were being made for the 1946 campus revival."

Bill Logue wasn't a highly visible leader in that 1946 revival. He didn't sit on the platform nor did he sing in the choir. He served on no committees. He didn't participate in the nightly prayer meetings in preparation for the revival because he was working two jobs trying to make ends meet. But, like hundreds of others, he returned from the worst the war could offer with a quiet commitment to help change the world. He's done this in his own way — by teaching Sunday School through the years, by quietly suffering through and winning the battle against cancer. He has been called the "neighborhood paper boy" because, on his early morning walks, he picks up neighbors' newspapers, often thrown on the curb or casually pitched the shrubbery, and quietly walks them to the front door (Few things please a senior citizen on a cold morning more than this. I know).

At the time of his retirement, the local Waco paper observed, "Judge Bill Logue has stood as a cornerstone of compassion, integrity and fairness":

> Bill Logue, known affectionately as "The Judge," has been a tireless advocate for the welfare of children by presiding over

1500 adoptions. Through the years he has presided over 30,000 divorce cases, each bringing pain to a heart committed to family life. "The Judge" retired recently from the 19th District Court, holding the record of 37 continuous years of service on the bench, the longest tenured judge in the state of Texas. The eyes of the world were focused on him as he was given the awesome responsibility of placing 17 children of the Branch Davidians in homes or institutions after their parents and the religious sect's leader, David Koresh, died in a fiery confrontation with federal agents on April 19, 1993. A total of 80 members of the sect died in the flames and four agents who had tried to serve them papers were killed in the longest stand-off in U. S. history — 51 days.[5]

Today, between Pat Neff Hall and Waco Hall on Baylor's campus there are 122 lamp posts, each dedicated to a Baylor student who died in World War II. Two of these have plaques in memory of Marion Pierce and Raymond Fisher, Bill Logue's friends who left school and enlisted with him. Bill was the only one of the three who made it home.

These stories remind us that "over there," tragic and painful as it was, paved the way for spiritual awakening . . . over here.

NOTES

[1] Stephen Ambrose, *Citizen Soldiers*, (New York: Simon and Schuster), 117.

[2] Dwight Baker, correspondence with the author.

[3] Ambrose, 117.

[4] Ibid., 472.

[5] *Waco Tribune-Herald*, January 17, 1999.

FOUR

LESSONS ON THE BANKS OF THE BRAZOS

By the rivers . . . we sat down and cried. On the trees nearby we hung our harps. (Ps 137: 1-2)

It was the end of April in 1945. The first Waco Youth Revival was over, and we were physically exhausted. For weeks our time and energy had been consumed by prayer meetings, planning sessions, raising money and door-to-door visitation. In spite of our fatigue, we had been on a spiritual "high." In a way, we were like the disciples who had spent time with Jesus on the top of the mountain, away from daily assignments and basic responsibilities. When Jesus told the disciples it was time to leave, they protested, "But, Lord, we like it here. Let's build some shelters and just stay up here." The answer of Jesus was crisp and to the point, "Get up!" And they made their way from the top of the mountain to the valley.[1]

The Youth Revival had been a mountaintop experience for us. Many had confessed their faith in Christ, our own hearts had been revived, and the unity we discovered in praying and working together had bonded us for life. But it was time for us to "get up" and move in other directions — toward the library, the classroom, and toward a world where history was being written faster than we could internalize. The war, the death of world leaders, and the challenge of new directions were greater than one generation had ever faced. The urgency of "Get up!" was upon us.

It was a good time to lean back, ponder, and thank God for more miracles than most of us would see in a lifetime. Our lives had been so centered in the revival and the aftermath of it that we had missed much of what was happening around the world. Of course, we had heard the news, but we found it difficult to internalize. There's just so much a person can absorb at one time. "History was moving at a breakneck speed," observed William Manchester.[2] On April 12, 1945, just four days before the first day of the revival, President Roosevelt died at Warm Springs, Georgia. Within four hours Harry S. Truman was sworn in as our new president. On May 1, the death of Hitler was announced. On May 2, the city of Berlin fell to the Allies, and later the same day the Germans in Italy surrendered. Two days later, the German commanders in Holland, Denmark, and northwest Germany signed an unconditional surrender document. On May 8, the birthday of our new president, V-E Day was announced.

The war in Europe was over. By July, 1945, the troops in Europe were coming home in record numbers. "On one day seven transports docked in New York with 31,445 GIs on board. The Queen Elizabeth brought one division; the Queen Mary another. The Army Transport Service flew in 125,370 veterans from the European and Mediterranean theaters. By summer over half a million men were home . . . . "[3] This obviously was a time of unbridled celebration for thousands of families, but the battle in the South Pacific raged on in desperation. For several months the Allied forces had fought from island to island. Names like Guadalcanal, Bataan, Corregidor, Midway, Okinawa, and Iwo Jima were daily reminders of the fierceness of battles. The cost in lives was beyond comprehension.

In his magnificent book, *Goodbye Darkness*, renowned author William Manchester shares his own personal experiences in the battles. He enlisted as a 17-year-old and fought island-by-island until the war was over. One of the most strategic battles of the entire campaign was the capture of Iwo Jima. This tiny island was an eight square mile piece of lava rock with thousands of hidden caves. "Iwo" is Japanese for "sulfur," and "jets of green and yellow sulfuric mist penetrated the entire surface of the isle, giving it a permanent stench of rotten eggs."[4] The caves were inhabited by the Japanese and the only way to take the island was through hand-to-hand fighting. The price of this property for the Americans was 25,851 Marines, including 19 battalion commanders. James Forrestal, Secretary of the Navy, said of Iwo Jima: "I can never again see a United States Marine without a feeling of reverence."[5]

Why *this* price? Why *this* island? B-29 Superfortresses had begun regular bombing raids on Tokyo. If planes were damaged in the attacks, they could never make it back to some of the more distant airfields. Iwo Jima became a welcome emergency landing strip for planes in trouble. In fact, the first B-29 bomber to crash-land on the island while returning from the bombing of Tokyo was piloted by a man that I met years later in a small church in Texas. "Iwo Jima saved my life," he said with deep emotion, "and it saved the lives of my crew."

In spite of Manchester's statement that history was moving at breakneck speed in 1945, I was dragging my feet throughout the summer. Painfully, I learned at the close of the spring term that I needed to take Chemistry 101 in order to graduate the following year. My high school back in North Carolina offered very few science classes when I was a student there. We had no facilities for a lab, which meant that some courses simply were not a part of the curriculum. I do remember taking a class in biology and studying a frog in a jar. At least, they told me it was a frog! We're often afraid of the unknown, and chemistry was about as big an "unknown" to me as anything I could imagine. So, I put it off . . . and off . . . and off. Ironically, I was a decent student in almost every other subject.

So, in the heat of the summer in Waco, Texas, after a "high" of a youth revival and wishing every day I could be out preaching revivals with my friends, I had to continue my education "on the banks of the Brazos." Early every morning I struggled sleepily just to stay awake in Chemistry 101. Dr. William R. Stephens, a short, stocky, soft-spoken scholar was the professor. But I wasn't ready for an early morning class in chemistry in the basement of a building that was already sweltering hot by sunrise! And what an amalgamation of odors! As kind and gracious as Dr. Stephens was, I wasn't ready to greet him at that hour, and I couldn't understand why he seemed so pleasant day after day. No, I didn't want to be in that lab, and I didn't want to be at "Baylor on the Brazos," a term often used since the Brazos river flowed nearby. I wanted to be out preaching like my friends.

Needless to say, it was a long summer — until August 7, 1945. On that particular morning the disciplined professor walked slowly to the podium, stood in silence without a smile for about a minute, swallowed hard, wiped a tear from his eyes, and quietly said, "Yesterday, August 6, we dropped an atom bomb on Hiroshima." Another pause, and another tear as he slowly pulled his handkerchief from his pocket. Then he added, "I doubt that any student in this classroom understands the implication of what I've just said." I didn't. I'd spent two months merely trying to learn the valance chart!

We sat in stunned silence, not comprehending the depth of his words, but moved and puzzled by his tears. Then, just above a whisper, he said, "Class dismissed." We slowly filed out, still unable to grasp the magnitude of what had just been said. We had never heard of "The Manhattan Project," (neither had President Truman until the day he was sworn in as the leader of the nation). And terms like "Tube Alloy," "X," "S-1," "S-Y," "The Gadget" — all code names for the atom bomb — were foreign to us. Nor did we know at the time that nearly 8,000 human beings died in Hiroshima and thousands of others were burned and scarred for life. Three days later a second bomb was unleashed on Nagasaki. When I heard the news, I walked in stunned disbelief across the campus toward my dorm room, hoping to pick up pieces of news through my inexpensive radio. As I reached the dorm, I bumped into a new student who had just enrolled in Baylor. We went to my room and tried to listen, in spite of static, to the radio newscaster, "As many as 75,000 are feared dead."

My new friend, the second Nisei, or Japanese-American, I had ever met, looked at me in stoic silence, and then said, "My family lives in that city."

Silence. Words would have been empty and hypocritical. We both knelt. And prayed. And history that moved at breakneck speed paused for a moment that day.

I had signed up for Chemistry 101. What I got was a course that jolted me into a new understanding of life . . . and relationships . . . and world vision. The Great Commission of Jesus, "Therefore go and make disciples of all nations," (Mt 28:19) no longer meant a small town in North Carolina, Baylor University, Waco, or even the state of Texas. "Into all the world" became a shocking reality.

On a steamy hot August morning in 1945, a chemistry classroom had made the world look much smaller, a compassionate professor became a prophet, and the lesson I learned on the banks of the Brazos River would never, never allow me to be the same again.

NOTES

[1] See Matt 18:1-7.

[2] William Manchester, *The Glory and the Dream: A Narrative History of America, 1932–1972* (Boston: Little, Brown, 1974), 270.

[3] Ibid., 388.

[4] William Manchester, *Goodbye Darkness: A Memoir of the Pacific War* (Boston: Little, Brown, 1980), 337.

[5] Ibid., 343.

FIVE

"THY KINGDOM COME"

Thy kingdom come, Thy will be done. (Matt 6:10)

"How do you explain the Youth Revival Movement?" That question has been asked for almost 60 years. How do you explain 4,000 people meeting nightly in Waco in 1946 with 500 public commitments? Is there any human explanation for students digging deep into empty pockets and paying for all expenses before the revival services began? And how do you account for 19-year-old kids, who didn't know what the word "homiletics" meant, preaching before thousands of people in the months that followed in cities across the nation — Houston, Fort Worth, Dallas, Birmingham, Atlanta, Memphis, Honolulu? And what about the hundreds of documented miracles when God seemed to supply the needs at the last minute? More than this, how can one explain thousands who moved into vocational Christian ministry as a result of this movement? Missionaries, pastors, musicians, professors, college and seminary administrators, denominational leaders, and a host of laypersons point to the Youth Revivals as the "turning point" in their lives.

Frankly, after thinking about this every day, I've come to the only conclusion that satisfies: there is no explanation apart from prayer. And, just as amazing, we discovered the meaning of prayer by being forced to pray. Without exception, those of us involved in planning the revivals were in situations over our heads. As one said, "We didn't know, and we knew we didn't know." All we did know was we'd make fools out of ourselves if God didn't rescue us. There were no guidelines on how to plan a citywide, or a campuswide, revival. Most of the students had never been involved in this kind of emphasis. Remember, this was before we'd heard of words like "crusades" or "campaigns" used in describing religious gatherings. Billy Graham had just begun his own ministry, and Youth for Christ rallies were limited to larger cities like Los Angeles and Chicago. That's a long way from Waco, located on the Brazos River in Central Texas!

When Reiji Hoshiziki gathered with a few of us around a campfire at the retreat in 1944 and shared his concern for revival, we prayed. That's all we knew to do, and, without knowing it, that's all we needed to do at the time. As dreams took form, others joined us and we continued to pray. When the revival services concluded in the spring of 1945, we began immediately to pray for another revival in 1946. There was hardly a break in our schedule as we moved from one year to the next. University enrollment had more than doubled as men and women were released from military responsibilities. There was an urgency about "reaching the world" and an optimism that it could be done. The world had few borders, and the sky was the limit!

So we prayed. We prayed not out of piety, but out of need. We prayed about completing our education, receiving degrees, and finding the right jobs We prayed about bills that had accumulated while we pursued an education. (Most of our parents, still trying to shake the privations of both the Depression and WWII, couldn't carry the entire load.) And we prayed about dating and developing meaningful relationships. In all honesty, most of us prayed about the possibilities of marriage. In the new world of opportunities facing us, family was very important. Looking back, many of us have thanked the Lord for relationships that led to the altar and "I do"; others are just as thankful for relationships that ended in "I don't!"

Once, several of us got together and prayed for a car. To us, talking to God about this need was as natural as talking with one another about it. On Friday nights, scores of Baylor students were involved in mission activities working with boys and girls, mostly black by race, who lived in low-income houses near the campus. These mission points were located on street corners under street lights, in tiny yards and on porches of houses, and anywhere else you could gather 30 or 40 little children in relative safety. Each mission point had a student leader who enlisted several other students to work with him. Games were played, choruses were sung, Bible stories were told, and scripture verses were memorized. When the various mission activities were over the students would gather back on the campus for a time of sharing and "singspiration." While it's not possible to gauge the lasting results of these Friday night mission services, many students became sensitive for the first time to world mission needs. "Red and yellow, black and white, they are precious in His sight" became more — much more — than a chorus to be sung. For the first time ever, well-dressed university students held unkempt little children in their arms. Some never got over it, and spent the rest of their lives doing the same thing around the world.

As the Friday night mission program grew, so did the need for some kind of transportation. Trying to move musical instruments and other pieces of equipment from one place to another became difficult and time-consuming. Most students could not afford automobiles, and the university had no vehicles available for this ministry. So we prayed. The *Baylor Lariat*, the campus newspaper, tells the story:

> The Baptist Student Union needed a car and needed it desperately.... A few students began to talk about it, and finally, Bruce McIver, BSU president, started out to raise $500 to buy an old car — something of about the speed and vintage of a Model A Ford. Several BSUers held a prayer meeting Friday morning and decided that Bruce should visit a Waco businessman who had been very generous in his gifts to the Baylor BSU, hoping he would contribute again. That afternoon, with another campus prayer meeting in progress to back him up, Bruce went to see the businessman.

"What would you do if I were to give you a car?" the man asked when Bruce had explained his mission. Speechless, the astonished Baylorite just sat and listened while the man explained that he had an unused car at home. He had purchased it for his wife but she never drove it. "It's ten years old," he said apologetically, but then added, "It's in good shape and has only a few thousand miles on it." To Bruce, with thoughts of a Model A rapidly fading away, it looked like a new limousine.

As Bruce tells the story: "He kept apologizing about the looks of the car, and even got out a dust cloth and dusted it himself. He insisted on taking me for a ride in it so I could see whether I wanted to accept the car. I didn't need to see it, and I didn't need to ride in it. I knew! All that time I was changing the subject to keep from shouting. Our friend said he had a feeling that something like this would come up, and he had already filled up the gas tank, just in case, and equipped the car with a stack of 'Gospels of John' for its first mission. He said if it was what we wanted, I could take it back to the campus that afternoon and get the title the next morning. Then he added he had promised BO Baker, a graduate student from Farmersville, Texas, $175 for use in the Ninth Street Mission, a little church in a pocket of poverty near the campus, that BO served as pastor. He said if we thought the car was worth $175, we could give that amount of money to the mission church. One hundred and seventy-five dollars for a car worth $600 at that time! Then he said he'd like to have the car washed before he gave it to us. 'Would it be okay for you to pick it up about 4 o'clock this afternoon?' he asked. At the Singspiration that night, following the usual mission activities, the wonderful news was announced and the 225 students in attendance gave one dollar each to fulfill the $175 commitment to BO's church. The Gap was ours!"

The "Gap?" Strange name?

Not to the students who prayed for the car — God Answers Prayer.[1]

The prayer services, or "gatherings," were informal and usually unannounced — until a need arose. Then the grapevine, or network, would begin humming. "We've hit a snag in securing the tent. We'll meet to pray at 10 tonight." "There's been a misunderstanding. We need to pray about it." "We're low on funds; we need a miracle to pay for some of these bills." Within an hour students would begin gathering for prayer. No problem was allowed to lie on the table and not be dealt with. Every situation, every need, and every crisis was discussed and prayed about, regardless how painful the issue was. This openness and honesty brought the Youth Revival leaders together in remarkable ways.

One student finished his own verbal prayers one night, rose from his knees, and said to the group, "Fellows, I've been jealous of some of you. I haven't been asked to do some things in preparation for the revival that I wanted to do. This is hurting me, and it's hurting my relationship with you, even though you may not be aware of it. I'm asking you now to forgive me, and I'm asking God to help me get my attitude corrected."

Another student shared the tension he had experienced with his pastor. "I've said some things about him that I shouldn't have said," he confessed with deep emotion. "Pray for me." He then moved toward the door, and someone asked where he was going. "I've got to call my pastor and apologize," he said tearfully.

"But it's 11:00 at night," he was reminded.

"That doesn't matter," he exclaimed as he walked out the door. "I've got to get this settled." And he was gone, and we continued to pray for him. The next morning I saw him on his way to his first class — all smiles. The matter had been settled and he and his pastor were now reconciled.

One night, Jim Wimpee, a junior student, asked the group to pray about his getting into medical school. Jim felt his destined call was to be a doctor, and he felt it as strongly as some others felt called to the mission fields. But he faced a problem: his calling came after two or three not-so-good grades had been recorded. Now, Jim took full responsibility for the grades, but, in spite of that, he felt a spiritual tug in the direction of medicine. He wasn't asking God to grant him special favors, but he did ask us to pray about the situation, that God would give him a sense of peace regardless the answer. Both his humility and his commitment spoke quietly to his friends who gathered to pray. A few months later, Jim was accepted into medical school and eventually completed his training as an orthopedic surgeon. We knew then, and we know now, that prayer is not a magic wand that makes bad grades look good. That wasn't our prayer, and it wasn't Jim's prayer. But until he died recently, Dr. Jim Wimpee looked back on that prayer service as a turning point in his life.

No one was elected or appointed to preside over the informal prayer meetings. No outlines for worship were followed, and no schedules were kept. People were free to come and go as they chose. They could voice their prayers, or they could simply pray silently. There were often prayers of adoration, petition, confession, praise, and thanksgiving. There were times when students wept; there were other times when some expressed genuine rejoicing.

One student prayed out loud one night, "Lord, they tell me the Baptist Student Union is a clique. Well, Lord," he continued, "if that be true, it sure is 'clicking' around here today!" I listened to a room full of students strangling back chuckles. The thought occurred to me, irreverent as it might seem, that God also chuckled.

Howard Butt was the chairman of the Youth Revival committee in 1946. Howard was thorough, gifted in organizational abilities, persuasive, and passionate in his conviction that the same God who parted the Red Sea could solve any problem we faced. His faith was contagious. One night, long after midnight, we were praying about some seemingly overwhelming need. Howard prayed, "Lord, You can do it." Pause. In a louder and more enthusiastic voice, "Lord, You can do it!" Another pause. Howard then got his breath, raised his hand over his head from his kneeling position, made a fist and burst forth, "LORD, YOU CAN DO IT!" With those words echoing throughout the small room in which we were praying, he banged the wooden seat of the chair he knelt beside. The seat shattered into pieces as a hush settled over the room. No question about it, God could do it. And He did! At least no more chairs were broken.

Fifty years later I learned that some sleepy neighbors, wanting to be encouraging to the revival effort, ran out of patience when as many as 200 students would leave the building joyfully singing and celebrating two hours after midnight! And, 50 years later, I'm wondering should someone pay Seventh and James Church for that broken chair!

In all honesty, our girlfriends and dates also had difficulty understanding the urgency we felt to gather for prayer almost every night. Strict curfews, rigidly enforced, already limited the time a couple had together. You can imagine the reaction when some messenger interrupted a dinner date or a stroll on the campus or a trip to the movies to say, "we're meeting in 30 minutes for prayer." Not the most romantic thing a girl wanted to hear! It definitely put a strain on relationships and ended a few. It's not hard to imagine. "Are those guys becoming fanatical?" "Can't you pray during the day as well as during date time in the evening?" "Does it take that much praying to get anything going?" "Is this what it means to be married to someone thinking about Christian ministry?" Fortunately, however, most of our girlfriends tolerated this — even though they didn't like it — and several formed their own prayer groups in their dorms. When the dates of the revival, April 1-6, 1946, arrived, none were more supportive that the women on the campus.

Some other students also had difficulty understanding the prayer meetings. The lack of structure, the freedom of expression, and the boldness about praying for specific things bothered them. Wayne Smith, a freshman, was one of these people. In a lengthy letter, written July 1, 1998, he shared his dilemma. He had come to Baylor eager to be involved in as many activities as possible. When he was invited to attend a prayer meeting he readily accepted. "But," he wrote, "I didn't understand some of the things that were going on and I really felt that it was a bit beyond where I was and perhaps wanted to be at that particular time. So I made my way over the bodies of these young men . . . and went outside and sat down on the curb."

A few minutes later an older student approached him and sat down beside him. Wayne looked up and said, "I'm not sure I understand everything that is going on and I'm not sure I like everything that is going on. This is something I haven't experienced before. And I don't know if it is good, or something I should be striving for, or if it's something that I'm lacking; it's just not a part of my repertoire. I don't understand. And I don't know what I should do. I don't know if I should just quit the ministry at this point, because if I am not like they are, then I must not be what God wants me to be."

The older student listened, and then said quietly, "Wayne, you don't have to be like everybody else in that room. You don't have to feel the way they feel. You don't have to act the way they're acting. What you need to do is to feel the way you feel and act the way you act in accordance with what God is asking you to do."

A little later Wayne was walking near Brooks Hall. Dick Baker, just back on the campus from the Navy and destined to be one of the great music leaders of the Youth Revival Movement, showed up and they started talking. After a few minutes of conversation, Dick said, "Wayne, why don't we just kneel right here and pray." Wayne adds, "I don't know of a better time in all my life that I had in prayer than I did with that great young man, Dick Baker."

Still later, Wayne attended another prayer meeting. He writes ("tongue-in-cheek"), "You know how it is when you get a bunch of preachers together — everybody tries to out-preach everybody else when he's praying. I guess God's ears really get pounded by preachers whenever they get together and start having a prayer meeting. Everybody in the room prayed, and they prayed with their heart. I appreciated that." The prayers went on and on and on. When it came time for the last person to pray, Wayne braced himself, fearing that the meeting was far from over. There was a pause, and Jess Moody, one of the preachers in the 1946 revival, simply prayed, "Lord, teach us to pray. Amen." Wayne adds, "It was the most profound prayer I have ever heard."

Reflecting on that lonely moment when he walked out of the prayer meeting at midnight, confused and uncertain about what was expected of him — how he was to act, and sound, and pray — and wondering about his own call to the ministry, Wayne concludes: "I am now in my 53rd year of preaching, and I can't tell you all the great blessings that God has given me during these years, but I can tell you, 'Yes, He has used me as Wayne Smith.'"

Wayne's commitment was not recorded on a card at the close of a revival service, but it's about as significant as any you'll see. And it's the story of a campus that was saturated in prayer.

Charles W. Bryan was a Baylor student who met nightly with others to pray for revival. One night the informal prayer meeting was held in a classroom where Charles sat daily for a Bible course. The prayer meeting had lasted until 2:00 a.m. Unfortunately, he had a class in that very room at 8 a.m. As his class began Charles, sleepy-eyed and confused, stumbled through the door and found the chair where he sat daily. He paused for a moment, and then immediately knelt beside it! It would be nice to think Charles was so renewed in his spiritual life that he knelt and prayed in every classroom. That wasn't the case; instead, he was so drained, physically and emotionally, that he wasn't sure where he was . . . or why!

But the prayer meetings left a deeper and more positive impression on his life. "In one of those prayer meetings," he stated, "I faced the question, 'Would you be willing to serve as a missionary in the Soviet Union if God called you?' This was my first missionary impression." And then Charles added, "When I preached in the First Baptist Church of Moscow, I told them that story. It was a moving experience for me . . . and for them." Charles served as the Senior Vice-President for the Foreign Mission Board of Southern Baptists until his recent retirement.

Bob Harris, a veteran of the war, returned to the campus in time to participate in planning the details of the revival meeting. He was also a part of the prayer meetings. Here is his observation:

The prayer meetings continued every few nights. There didn't seem to be any special schedule for them, nor did I ever hear any announcement of them or promotion of them.

Nevertheless, they grew. I counted over sixty men one evening. No one seemed to be in charge, but occasionally some of the leaders gave some guidance. There was great freedom in prayer, but there was no shouting. There was weeping, and there was assurance of victory and blessing. I believe this was the dominant strain which my heart picked up on. In fact, there were continual answers to prayer before the services began. Finances were prayed for and secured. Unsaved students came under conviction and were led to Christ as prayers spread to the dorms and across the campus. A prime downtown lot was secured right beside the First Baptist Church. Across the front of the lot was a large commercial billboard. We wanted that billboard to carry the key announcement for our "Waco Youth for Christ." I was supposed to arrange that, as a member of the publicity committee. I went to the sign company in downtown Waco and laid out our need and request before the owner. He seemed unmoved by our plight and said that sign had been rented for weeks. I took the disappointing news back to the prayer meeting that night. There were already other answers to prayers that made us rejoice. Our hearts ran the gamut of emotions as we opened that to the Lord. In my own heart there began to form an incredible assurance that we would get that billboard. I had never felt anything like that before.

The next morning I could hardly wait for a class break so I could call the sign company. The owner answered. When I told him who I was he immediately responded, "Yeah, we've been thinking about that sign you asked about yesterday. Look, we're going to let you fellows have that sign. In fact, we're going to put it up for you for free. Just a minute (and I could hear him yell to his partners somewhere there in his shop), you guys want to give your work to paint the sign for this Youth For Christ thing?" The answers came back, "Yeah — sure thing!" The owner said to me, "Okay, you got it. We're proud of what you're doing. Get the copy to me sometime today."[2]

The prayer meetings continued nightly throughout the 1946 revival. On Monday night, after our first service, I was kneeling next to one of the most gifted students on the campus, Jack Robinson. He was scheduled to preach on Tuesday night, less than twenty-four hours away. He was overwhelmed with the responsibility facing him and moved from a kneeling position to lying prostrate on the floor. I still remember verbatim his prayer: "O, Lord, use me. Use me as I try to preach." And then there was a sob as he struggled to continue, "But, Lord, if you can't use me, let me die, for I'd rather be dead than to be unusable." When we rose to leave, I lingered for a moment, and saw a puddle of tears where he had prayed with his face on the concrete floor. There's no need for me to tell you that God did use him then, and for more than half a century that followed.

These prayer experiences are not shared in piety or self-righteousness. On the contrary, they are glimpses into the lives of college students, many still in their teens, who are meeting for the first time the fundamental issues of life — God, forgiveness, relationship, commitment . . . and grace. In the words of Howard Butt, "We talk about the prayer meetings because they were wonderful. They were times of very earnestly seeking God's face and celebrating His love and grace and power . . . and in confidence believing He was going to give us a revival at Baylor, that He was really going to do something in those meetings."[3]

Jess Moody was right, "Teach us to pray."

NOTES

[1] *The Baylor Lariat,* Sept. 25, 1945.

[2] Bob Harris, correspondence with the author.

[3] Thomas Charlton, Oral History, 13 May 1982.

SIX

"THINE IS THE POWER"

Thine is the power. (Matt 6:13)

In 1853, nearly 100 years before the 1946 Waco Youth Revival, Yorkshireman Hudson Taylor went from England to China as a missionary. He encountered a variety of problems, some involving his own health, and he came home to England to recuperate. During this interim period he graduated from medical school, founded the China Inland Mission, and returned to China in 1865. Taylor later said that through this experience he discovered three echelons, or levels, of praying:

First: "O, God, let me do your work."
Second: "O God, let me help you do your work."
Third: "O, God, do your work through me."

A century later, hundreds of students at Baylor moved through these same echelons. There was no feeling that the Kingdom of God would collapse if we did not "do God's work" or "help God do God's work." Nor was there any urgency to outdo the revival in 1945. In a deep sense that can only come through prayer, there was a quiet cry, "use me" or make us "usable." We were still 19 or 20 years of age, and, happily, we had not yet grown accustomed to the fact that God could do some rather remarkable things. But along with this child-like excitement about prayer, there was a corresponding voluntary commitment to work that would make most organizations envious.

Howard Butt was the general chairman of the 1946 revival. I was the chairman of finances, commissioned to raise at least $2100. Students gave $2400! Jess Moody was in charge of general publicity; George Stokes was responsible for radio announcements and programs; and Bob Harris worked with the newspapers. Arrangements (and this meant almost everything!) fell on the shoulders of Bill Cody and Hollis Davis. Dan Rainbolt worked with churches and schools, Dale Fisher was responsible for the choir, and Tom Cole had charge of the orchestra.

All of these students were elected to their positions by the Baylor Baptist Student Union. Working with these various committee leaders were scores of less-recognized students. It is conservatively estimated that at least 250 people were involved in the behind-the-scenes organizational framework for the revival. The campus daily newspaper, *The Lariat*; Waco's two newspapers; oral histories; Charles Wellborn's classic little book, *He Lives*; Katy Stokes' article "Those Halcyon Days"; and other documents indicate the range of their responsibilities. These included:

- Correspondence with each pastor in the area requesting both his support and the names of outstanding young people in his church who could be contacted.
- Interviews with these young people and assigning them to committees.
- Visits to civic clubs and community organizations asking for their support.
- News releases to the university newspaper and to the local newspapers.
- Announcements in university chapel services and other student meetings.
- Distribution of 500 large posters throughout the city.
- Contacting every home in Waco on Saturday before the revival services began on Monday (led by Ronald Hill who enlisted 150 students to help).

• Placing placards on the backs of all city buses and 250 banners on the backs of cars.
• Showering Waco with 10,000 handbills dropped from an airplane.
• Stretching a huge banner in five-foot letters across the main street in Waco and stenciling the sidewalks below.
• Numerous radio programs and spot announcements, especially the week prior to the revival services.
• Full-page advertisements and news stories in high school newspapers throughout the city.
• A special announcement in every church in the Waco area by a young person on Sunday, March 31, in behalf of the revival.

And, freshman Milton DuPriest found an old cow somewhere, painted a huge sign and hung it around her neck, and led her through downtown Waco. The sign read: "This is no bull; Come to the Youth Revival Tonight!" In spite of the cow, Dr. W. W. Melton, pastor of Columbus Baptist Church, Waco, and former executive director of the Baptist General Convention of Texas, said, "This thing is better organized than any revival I've ever seen."

All of this, with a few exceptions, was before the modern day of mass evangelism, crusades, and rallies. We had no models, no patterns, and no guidelines. We just climbed out on a limb, whimpered, and prayed for wisdom beyond our years. We also asked God to bless our efforts and to forgive our mistakes.

On Monday evening, April 1, several of us gathered under the tent long before the services were to begin at eight o'clock in the evening. It was our last chance to go over the checklist one more time. Nothing could be left to chance, or "hope so." Is the electricity working? Are the chairs in order? Is the public address system balanced? Obviously, we had worked tirelessly for weeks and months on these and other questions, but we sought perfection in the "little things." God's work deserved the best we could offer, not a mere concern that things "fall together" at the last minute.

On the first evening, the Devil began to work me over with the "What if?" game. *What if* no one showed up? *What if* the public address system crackled? *What if* these were our dreams and not God's plans? *What if* our own egos had gotten in the way of God's purposes? I think I must have wrestled with half the imps in Hell in those moments. Then I heard it. Music in the distance. Music from the downtown area of Waco. Singing. Louder. More distinct. Listen. "Onward Christian Soldiers."

Then I saw them! Baylor's cheerleaders, several police cars, a fire truck, and 600 students marching down the main street of Waco. They were in a straight line because veteran paratrooper Joe Morman in battle dress marched with them shouting orders: "All together! Keep those lines straight! Heads high, shoulders back! Now let's hear it!" And hundreds burst out singing the revival theme song, "He lives! He lives! Christ Jesus lives today!" Like the disciples who "disbelieved for joy" (Luke 24:41), I made a panoramic turn and saw hundreds of students and townspeople coming from every direction. Within 10 minutes the tent that seated 2,000 was filled and overflowing. A total of 2,500 attended on the first night! The crowds grew nightly from 2,500 to 3,600 to 4,000. These were the largest crowds ever for a religious service in Waco.

It would be impossible to name everyone involved in the music for the week. But, again, largely with the help of Katy Stokes and Charles Wellborn and newspaper clippings, here are the names of several persons who contributed: The Lengfeld sisters (all four of them) — Jeanne, Rose, Shirley, and Doryce; the trio of Bennie Mae Oliver, Eva Marie Kennard, and Violet Rogers (Orr); the quartet of Joe Gilmore, Asa Couch, Bob Mitchell, and Joe Canzoneri; and the trio of Nancy Biles (Miller), Shirley Polk (Corrie), and Mary Ila Ullom (Colvin). Tom Cole directed the 30-piece orchestra, and Dale Fisher and BO Baker led a 200-voice choir and the congregational singing. Lil Brown and Virginia Clower played the pianos, and Bill Enete played his marimba.

The preachers for each night were also chosen by the Baptist Student Union. The "line-up" was as follows: Monday, Jess

Moody — "Aren't You Glad You're You?"; Tuesday, Jack Robinson — "No, Devil"; Wednesday, BO Baker — "Wake Up and Live"; Thursday, Mark Moore — "Don't Fence Me In"; Friday, Howard Butt — "What's the Hurry?"; and Saturday, Bruce McIver — "One Thing Lacking."

Now, some brief footnotes to the sermons:

•The first public decision made in the entire revival was made when Jess preached. The first person down the aisle was a girl by the name of Doris Cummings. She did not know Jess. But she came to know him "real good," as they say in North Carolina. She and Jess have just celebrated their 50th wedding anniversary!

•The printer made a terrible mistake. He left out the comma when he printed Jack's sermon title, "No, Devil." I got word in my room at Brooks Hall one afternoon that a very angry, elderly man was down on the quadrangle looking for Jack, or "any one of those preacher boys I can get my hands on!" I was asked (begged is a better word) to go and try to calm him down. He had a handbill in his hand, listing the preachers and sermon titles. The comma was not there. I must have spent 30 minutes with him trying to explain the obvious error in printing. He never did understand. He left mumbling something about "liberal colleges" and "preachers who didn't preach the Bible." I don't think he ever understood what a comma was!

•Mark Moore had been a prisoner of war in the hands of the Germans. He shared his own experiences as a POW and his sermon was appropriately titled "Don't Fence Me In."

•The sermons were relatively brief — not more than 20-22 minutes. The invitations were not "dragged out" or unduly prolonged. About 295 decisions had been made by Wednesday night. At the close of the service on Saturday exactly 500 decisions had been recorded. At the conclusion of the Saturday night service, I asked those who had made a public commitment to form a circle around the tent. The circle grew...and grew...and grew. It encompassed the entire block with some standing in ditches because there was no more room on the lot. We then sang, "Blest Be the Tie That Binds." Fifty years later that circle has encircled the globe!

Dr. W. F. Howard, director of Baptist Student Work in Texas, had driven down from Dallas for the Saturday evening service. This is his account as it appeared in *The Baptist Standard* two weeks later:

> *I was there* at the closing service when the last person walked the aisle to register publicly a life-changing decision. That last response of the revival — the forty-sixth — was the five hundredth of the six-day meeting!
>
> *I was there* when Bruce McIver, BSU President and closing night preacher, asked the audience of nearly 4,000 to remain seated while all who had come forward during the week moved to positions just outside the vast crowd . . . I saw this audience deeply moved as this group of approximately 500 joined hands and were led by BO Baker in singing "Blest Be the Tie That Binds."
>
> *I was there* until nearly midnight, listening to students as they broke up into little groups to talk it over — then out to (the BSU office) to listen in on a large group of boys who had gathered in the BSU Center to talk it over some more — mostly all at one time!
>
> *I was there* to see these visible results — but *I was not there* to catch the real secret of the mighty week. I had seen evidence of extensive and detailed planning. I had heard the wonderful singing. I had been lifted by student testimonies. I had sat praying earnestly for Bruce as he brought a strong message — but, I repeat, I was not there in time to catch the story-behind-the-scenes which explained it all.
>
> But they told it to me. The composite testimony of all was that the victory had occurred before the revival services began. In the words of one leader, "The preaching and everything else was incidental; prayer had already brought Pentecostal power."

> Until two and three o'clock in the morning for days preceding, groups had prayed: confessing their sins to God and to one another and praying for souls by name. As nearly as I can tell, that's how it happened at Pentecost!
>
> So — the answer is not found in the "new" or the "unique." Indeed the methods appear entirely incidental. The secret of such a revolutionary revival experience is revolutionary praying!
>
> Youthful emotionalism, dramatic tactics, superficial mob psychology, a frenzied passion that will soon vanish — perhaps some will explain it on this basis, but not me because, thank God, *I WAS THERE!*

Like Dr. Howard, *I was there* also. But, as is so often the case, the highlight of the week was not in the obvious, open meetings. It was in a dimly-lit Sunday school classroom at Seventh and James about two o'clock on Tuesday morning of the week. The first service was over, and, tired as we were, some felt the need to slip away and pray — just to thank God for the service, the crowds, and the commitments. All of this was beyond our comprehension.

On the way to our place of prayer, Jack Robinson, the all-American basketball player who was to preach Tuesday night, ran into Charles Wellborn on the campus. Charles had just served three years in Italy as a member of the army ski patrol and had witnessed war at its worst. Some of his best friends had been killed in battle, leaving Charles bitter and cynical. He had a brilliant mind and had been National Debate Champion twice before entering the military service. But there was little place in his life for God. Ironically, he had been asked to write some radio scripts to be used in promotion of the revival. To everyone's surprise, he agreed to do this. He also was deeply impressed by Jack, a star athlete with a keen mind and a solid Christian commitment. So many miracles had already taken place that it should not have surprised anyone when Charles walked into the prayer meeting long after midnight. But it did. We struggled to continue praying without appearing to be overly excited by his presence. When eight or ten who had gathered that night had finished, there was a long pause. Then Charles, now on his knees, groaned, "Fellows, I gotta pray." You could have cut the silence with a knife.

"Lord," he said, "when I think of all I've done, how can you love me?"

More silence.

Then, "Lord, I don't know what it is you want me to do, but I'll do it!"

The line of an old gospel song became real in that moment, "Heaven came down, and glory filled our souls!"

But Charles tells it in his own words:

> After three years in the military, I was discharged in October, 1946, just in time to return to Baylor to complete my undergraduate work. I lacked only one quarter's credit, which I completed in the winter quarter, 1946–47.
>
> I was a nominal church member, but not, as I came to realize later, a "born-again" Christian. I was indifferent to the claims of religion and, in a mild way, hostile to the church, which I regarded as hypocritical and simplistic.
>
> I became involved in the Youth Revival movement at Baylor in two ways. First, I was asked by some of the organizers to assist in the publicity plans for the revival. Second, in a chapel service, I heard Jack Robinson give his testimony, which deeply impressed me. I was invited to join the core group of organizers of the revival in a nightly prayer meeting at Seventh and James Baptist Church. In one of these prayer meetings, I had a deeply emotional conversion experience. Fifty years later, I have never doubted the reality of that experience. It dramatically changed my life.
>
> I had made careful plans to go to law school and had been accepted for entrance into Harvard Law School in September, 1947. My religious experience changed all my plans, and although at that time I had not seriously considered entering the Christian ministry, I became heavily involved in the Baylor Youth Revival, where I gave my testimony at one of the services. Later, I was asked to be one of the speakers in the citywide youth revivals that took place in the summer of 1947–48, and in the overall youth movement.

During that period I committed myself to the ministry. After seminary training at Southwestern Baptist Theological Seminary in Fort Worth, I returned to Baylor to teach in the religion department, but, after only one quarter of teaching, I was called as pastor of Seventh and James (1951), the church where I had been converted and later baptized. I served in that position for ten years, 1951–61.

In thinking back over the youth revival phenomenon, several major reflections intrigue me.

First, the way in which the atmosphere of the entire Baylor campus — faculty, administration, students — was markedly affected and changed by the revival and its aftermath. Anyone on the campus — in classes, chapel, or otherwise — could not have helped but see and feel the difference.

Second, the way in which the appeal and influence of the revival extended not just to young people, but to all types and ages. Recently, in going through some old papers, I came across a letter written to me after the Waco revival by an elderly retired Waco banker, who, out of curiosity, had attended the services. He was an Episcopalian and did not make any kind of public decision, but he wrote to tell me that the revival experience had renewed his Christian faith in "the most remarkable religious experience I, and I believe many others, have ever had."

Third, the lasting influence of the revival. Through the years I have frequently encountered people, both ministers and lay people, whose lives were changed in meaningful ways by the revivals. But I especially have reflected on the fact that, to my knowledge, all the young revival preachers — most of them almost totally inexperienced in planning, preaching, etc. — have continued, each in his own way, in fruitful Christian ministry.

Looking back, I can find no viable human explanation for what happened in Waco and in Houston, Dallas, Fort Worth, Birmingham, etc. in those months of 1947–48. Looked at from a hard-nosed secular viewpoint, the revivals should have never happened. The organizers and preachers were naïve and inexperienced; many mistakes were made in plans and operations, but the revivals still happened. I have no explanation except to attribute what happened to the power of God.[1]

On June 18, 1999, Wellborn spoke on the campus of Samford University in Birmingham, Alabama. He referred to that Sunday School classroom and his conversion there, and then added, "During those years as a pastor of the Seventh and James Church, when I felt overwhelmed with the burdens, I'd slip again into that room which, for me, had become 'holy ground.'"

There is a sense in which Charles speaks for many of us. The entire 1946 Youth Revival was holy ground for us. It was a never-to-be-forgotten experience, and it has shaped our lives for half a century. It's good to hear team members and leaders who participated in the revival recount their own experiences; it's refreshing to hear and read how pastors and religious leaders across the nation evaluate it; but, in many ways, the best commentary on what happened comes from our peers — those who sat with us in classrooms, roomed with us in the dorms, and participated with us in sports. Bill Hailey was one of those "peers."

Bill enrolled in Baylor in 1940 and entered the Air Force in 1943. Three years later he returned to continue his studies and to play basketball. He and Jack Robinson were teammates. Today, Bill is an attorney who lives in San Antonio. Here are his reflections:

> I lived on the fifth floor of Brooks Hall, and late one night in 1946, Jackie Robinson called from the Seventh and James Baptist Church. He had someone in my suite on the 5th floor call me to the phone in the office of the dorm. Jackie was very excited and told me that during the prayer meeting at Seventh and James he had just heard the most impressive testimony he had ever heard. It had been given by Charles Wellborn . . . .
>
> The revival was the first to my knowledge that was completely conducted by youth. In my opinion, the many revivals and participation by youth in religious activities for a number of years thereafter was the greatest happening in religion in the history of the United States. I know that my dedication to Christ was greatly increased by that one revival . . . . [2]

NOTES

[1] Charles Wellborn, correspondence with the author.

[2] Bill Hailey, correspondence with the author.

SEVEN

THE ENCOURAGERS

Encourage one another daily. (Heb 3:13)

The final service of the 1946 Baylor revival was over. The tent was taken down and shipped back to Dallas, the chairs were returned to the rental company, and the pianos were carefully hauled back to the music stores that had graciously loaned them to us for the week. Even the sign came down. The lot was vacant, but our hearts were full — never to be the same again.

We were excited beyond words because of the thousands who had attended the services and the 500 who had made significant commitments throughout the week. We were grateful for pastors and church leaders who followed up on those making decisions, encouraging them to become active in local church worship and ministries. It was a never-to-be-forgotten week, one that had changed our lives forever.

What next? The answer was simple. Next were classes the following day, the writing of overdue papers, and the rediscovery of the route to the library. Thankfully, most professors had been patient and understanding, but the college catalogue listed no credits given for city-wide revivals, regardless how many people attended the services. The spring term would conclude in two short months. For me, also, it would mark the date of my graduation — maybe. Painfully, I realized that I hadn't made that three day trek from North Carolina to Texas, bringing all my worldly goods, to miss my own graduation. So, "next" became "now" as I resolved to meet and make those deadlines.

Things went smoothly for three or four days, until W. J. Wimpee, the Director of Religious Activities, called some of us into his office.

"Fellows," he began, "I've just been contacted by the Houston Baptist Pastor's Conference. They'd like to invite you to come to Houston and lead a week's city-wide youth revival."

We sat stunned for a moment, and then someone asked, "When?"

"The date hasn't been set," he replied, "but they're talking about the first week in July."

"July? This year?"

"That's right," Wimpee responded. "That's three months from now."

Everyone started talking at once. "There's no way!" "Do they have any organization?" "What about basic preparations?" "Where will we have the services?" "What about money for publicity and a hundred other things?" "Do they realize it took us a year here at Baylor with nearly 300 volunteers?" "What about our personal schedules?"

W. J. Wimpee, one of the best friends students ever had, simply looked at us, grinned, and said, "I'm just the messenger. You fellows will have to make those decisions. Quickly."

We were overwhelmed and caught completely off-guard. We had no organization, and saw no need for one. We were not professionals. We were just a bunch of college kids — 18, 19, or 20 years of age — who had rallied to a specific challenge before us at a specific time. We had no plans beyond Waco, except those that God revealed to us person by person. The idea that we were a team had never entered our minds. Now, if we accepted the Houston invitation, all of this was about to change, and it frightened us. We sat in Wimpee's office with no sense of direction, and an hour later we walked out no wiser than when we entered.

"Look," someone suggested. "This is heavy. We've got to get away and do some serious thinking and praying. This could be God trying to show us something."

Howard Butt's family had a ranch home 18 miles southeast of Kerrville in the Texas Hill Country. Howard also had a car, one of the few on the campus. After class on Friday, six of us climbed into his new Ford and made the 200 mile trip. We drove south toward Austin, turned west at Georgetown, and passed through "exotic" Texas towns and communities like Liberty Hill, Llano, and the quaint, historic German town of Fredericksburg. Late in the evening, we pulled up at the ranch house located on Palmer Creek, a tributary that flows into the Guadalupe River. The house, surrounded by majestic live oaks, cedar elms, and magnolia trees also had a pool, which was just what we needed. And we had the whole place to ourselves! We swam and talked and prayed through most of the night. When we had exhausted a subject, or were physically exhausted ourselves, we would drop off to sleep. Inevitably, within an hour or two, someone would wake the whole group up with some thought, or insight, or "what if." This went on through the night and into the next day.

Money became a genuine concern as we pondered the invitation to Houston. The concern was not about our personal needs since it had not occurred to us that we would be paid anything. But we were concerned about the financial needs involved in communicating with more than a million people in the largest city in Texas. From experience we knew that things like newspaper ads, radio commercials, billboards, and posters would take money. It also took money to rent sound systems, print special worship guides, and rent adequate facilities. Most pastors had not been involved in emphases of this magnitude, and most churches were struggling to meet their own budget needs.

After several hours of talking and praying, Howard volunteered to call his father to ask if Mr. Butt would underwrite some of these practical needs. He picked up the phone and talked with his father in Corpus Christi while we prayed . . . and eavesdropped!

"Good news," he exclaimed when the conversation was over. "Dad says he'll underwrite the needs up to $5,000!" Now, in 1946, $5,000 looked like $100,000, especially to a bunch of college kids who stayed broke most of the time. It was a signal to move forward. Mr. Butt's help should not have surprised any of us. It was a reflection of who he was and a tribute to his roots.

In 1905, Florence Butt, Howard's grandmother, affectionately called "Grand" by the family, moved her family from Tennessee to the Texas Hill Country. Her husband, Charles, suffered from tuberculosis, and she faced the responsibility of taking care of him and supporting their three sons. She said a prayer, borrowed $60, leased a small two-story building in Kerrville for $9 a month, and opened a cash-and-delivery grocery store. While sweeping out the downstairs of the dilapidated old frame building, she found a New Testament under one of the shelves of her new store. She dusted it off and said, "This is a good omen." Grand then knelt on the dirty floor, waving the New Testament in her hand, and prayed, "Lord, I take you as my partner."

As Florence Butt stocked and ran this first family grocery store, her son Howard, then about 10 years old, could be seen after school with his little hand-drawn red wagon delivering groceries to customers' homes. Because of his mother's increasing reliance on him early in life, Howard developed the attributes of a much older person. By age 16 he was managing the store and later converted it to cash and carry, a change that was viewed at the time as an uncertain gamble since credit was still the order of the day. With his innovative ideas and hard work, he began the ground work for one of the largest private chain of grocery stores in the nation — the H-E-B stores.[1]

Forty-one years after Grandmother Florence Butt found a New Testament and said, "Lord, I take you as my partner," her son, Howard Butt, Sr., said to his own son, Howard Jr., and to a bunch of wet-behind-the-ears college students, "I'll partner with you." It was a turning point in the Youth Revival Movement. We said "yes" to the Houston pastors.

Within days other invitations were extended to us. One was from the Pastors Conference in Fort Worth asking that we conduct a citywide youth revival there, and another was from Dallas with the same request. In spite of the generosity and encouragement of Mr. Butt, we still had some reservations. We felt we needed guidance, a sense of direction, and accountability. Admittedly, it was nice to be wanted, and it was a thrill to see the Youth Revival Movement begin to spread; however, our experience was limited, and we knew that we would soon be in situations over our heads. It was not a comfortable feeling.

W. J. Wimpee, who served as the director of Religious Activities at Baylor, was a steady encourager of students. But he was concerned by the number of calls that began coming to his office, asking for help in organizing youth revivals, both in local churches and in city-wide efforts. Wimpee, 29 years of age, had been a star football player at Baylor in the late 1930s, and also excelled in the academics. When he and his wife, Lillian, arrived on the campus in the fall of 1945, plans were already in motion for the 1946 revival. In every sense of the word, Wimpee was a friend of students and a strong supporter of the revival efforts. Time and time again his wisdom got us through difficult situations.

But one man can do only so much. In addition to serving as the Director of Religious Activities, he taught at least one course in the religion department each term, and had also begun his graduate studies toward a doctorate in theology. All of this, plus raising a young family, was more than one person should do. Wimpee also knew that youth revivals were taking place on other campuses in Texas. In his wisdom he sensed that, although the more dramatic experiences had happened at Baylor and the crowds were by far the largest at Baylor, something was taking place much larger than one campus and one group of students. Baylor should not, and could not, hold on to this new movement.

One afternoon, shortly after the brief retreat in Kerrville, six of us got in Howard's car and drove hurriedly toward Dallas for a brief conference with Dr. J. Howard Williams, the executive director of the Baptist General Convention of Texas. We hurried because Wimpee was preaching a revival service that week in a Waco church and needed to get back in time for the evening service. Happily, we found a parking place near the Baptist Building in downtown Dallas, paid 50 cents to park the car, caught an elevator, and quickly found Dr. Williams's office.

"Come in, young men. Please come in," he called in a warm greeting. "How can I help you?"

We told him our story. He listened as if he had all the time in the world, slightly nodding his head at times in affirmation. The way he received us, the patience with which he listened, and the occasional smile of genuine concern were gifts of grace to college students who were floundering for answers. When we had finished, he sat silently for a moment. Then he said with deep feeling, "I know the very man who can help you. He's the director of the Department of Student Work for Baptists in Texas, and his office is just down the hall." Then he added, "His name is W. F. Howard." Our hearts leaped. Every one of us knew W. F. Howard. He had been on Baylor's campus many times, and, more importantly, he had contacts with every student group in Texas, and many beyond the state. He was the logical choice.

Looking back, that moment was one of the most historic in the entire youth revival movement. Other campuses were also experiencing revival. This could unite us — from the Big Bend Mountains in west Texas to the piney woods of east Texas; from the Red River in the north to the Rio Grande along the Mexican border. We sensed immediately that this man was to become God's special gift to us — and to youth revivals. We left Dr. Williams' office at six o'clock in the evening, too late for an in-depth conference with Dr. Howard about the future. We arranged for another meeting with him within two weeks. Meanwhile, we had nearly 100 miles to travel back to Waco if Wimpee was to make his revival meeting on time.

The three-lane highway between Dallas and Waco was filled with chug holes. Bill Cody, Howard Butt, Jack Robinson, Charles Wellborn, and I cheered Wimpee on as he dodged those holes and broke all speed records racing through Waxahachie, Italy, Hillsboro, West, and Elm Mott.

"Faster, Wimpee! Faster!" we urged. "You'll make it to the church in time!"

Talk about immaturity and needing a sense of direction, guidance, and accountability! W. F. Howard had no idea of the job cut out for him!

Finally, we topped a slight hill, saw the lights of Waco, and cheered like little kids that Wimpee would make it back in time for the service. We breezed through the suburb of Bellmead like a blur and headed toward downtown Waco. After a right-hand turn near the town square, we burned rubber as we sped in the direction of Cameron Park and the church. By now Wimpee was deep in thought about the sermon he would preach in twenty minutes. It had been a good day. Things had worked out well. Then red lights behind us flashed and the siren sounded repeatedly.

Wimpee meekly pulled over, rolled his window down, and said to the burley policeman, "Sir, I'm on the administrative staff at Baylor University and preaching a revival at a church not far from here. Unfortunately, I'm a little late. Could you give me an escort to the church?"

"Escort? Escort?" the policeman shouted (sounding like he had just graduated from Texas A & M!), "I'll escort you to jail. I've been chasing you since you came through Bellmead!"

Somehow, perverted as our sense of humor was, we got tickled — everyone except Wimpee. He wasn't taken to jail; he did make it to the church — late; and none of us dared asked him the following day about the service the night before. In fact, that was over 50 years ago and we still haven't asked him. I'm not sure how much "love offering" they gave him at the close of the week, but it would have had to be a big one to cover the traffic ticket! But, even more important, through the years he has cheered thousands of students as they dodged the chug-holes of life, and he's cheered them as enthusiastically as we cheered him on that memorable drive from Dallas to Waco. And, sometimes, I think it's a miracle that any of us made it!

Bob Denny, W. J. Wimpee, J. Howard Williams, Howard Butt, Sr., W. F. Howard, and scores of others encouraged us beyond our imaginations. Denny, in his wisdom, challenged us to think things through and not to depend on others to think and act for us. Wimpee, new in his work with students, listened patiently and never once placed restrictions on what we could or could not do. On second thought, that's not entirely correct. In the early stages of planning for the 1946 revival, we met for prayer at night in the Baptist Student Union office building adjacent to the campus. Wimpee and his family lived upstairs. As the prayer services lasted longer and became more spontaneous, he gently, but firmly, suggested we meet elsewhere so his family could get some sleep! To his credit, no one has ever criticized him for protecting his family from an excited group of students who found it difficult to tone down their enthusiasm, even when praying about a revival.

Dr. Williams was a gracious, caring pastor–educator–administrator. With one negative word, or with an impatient sigh, he could have dismissed us and sent us on the 100 mile trip back to Waco — depleted, confused, and discouraged. On the contrary, he took time, affirmed us, and prayed with us.

The Houston revival, and the hundreds that followed, might never have taken place without the generosity and the grace of Mr. Howard Butt, Sr. He was not offering to help financially because his son was involved. Not at all. He was underwriting the basic needs because he believed in a group of 18- to 20-year-old students who wanted to do something for God. Interestingly, his $5,000 pledge to underwrite the Houston revival was not used. As the people of that city became more and more involved, their own gifts poured in, and all needs were met before the first service of the revival. But the generosity of Mr. Butt was a constant source of encouragement.

Words of encouragement were happy surprises throughout the Youth Revival movement. Charles Wellborn, in his little booklet *He Lives*, lists several quotes from professors, pastors, and businessmen concerning the 1946 Baylor Youth Revival:

• This is the greatest undertaking that a group of Baylor students has ever accomplished. (Dr. Monroe Carroll, professor, Baylor University)

• It is my belief that the Waco Youth Revival was one of the greatest advertisements for our Lord which our city has seen. (Dr. Woodson Armes, Waco pastor)

• I feel utterly ashamed of what everyone else is trying to do in comparison to what these youngsters have done. (Dr. A. J. Armstrong, professor, Baylor University)

• This is the greatest thing I've seen since my mother took me to hear Dwight L. Moody. (E. L. Morrell, Waco businessman)

• I thank God for our young people who follow our risen, reigning Lord...God grant that this revival may spread. (Dr. George C. Humphrey, head of Baylor's Bible Department)

• I have been in Waco for a good while, and have seen some good revivals, but this is the greatest thing I have ever seen. (Dr. W. W. Melton, Waco pastor)

The support of the pastors in churches across the land was overwhelming. This was new territory for them. Their confidence in opening their churches and their pulpits to "acne-faced 19-year-old kids" (as Jess Moody describes us) was amazing. They greeted us when we arrived, prayed with us before each service, shared with us their own needs, sat on the front rows and nodded their heads in approval, and cheered us on to the next revival! What encouragement! What respect.

Bill Tanner and Doug Dillard were invited to preach a revival at the First Baptist Church in Nederland, Texas. Ray McCollum was the pastor. He had been the pastor there for a number of years, and, as Bill puts it, "he had paid his dues." In his first meeting with Bill and Doug he said, "Fellows, I'm not putting any fences around you, whether it concerns the fellowships, the after-service seminars, the music, or the preaching. I am trusting you not to embarrass yourselves, our young people, our church, or the Lord."

Years later, Bill Tanner observed, "Maybe it was this unlimited trust that pastors placed in us — this no-strings-attached attitude — that supplied the grit and the willingness we had to be honest in our efforts and to make every attempt to do our best . . . . There was absolutely no way I would have offended, embarrassed, or knowingly disappointed Ray McCollum. He trusted us, and I think that is a good bench-mark for all of us in the ministry — to be trusted, and to be worthy of the trust. You have to keep the trust."[2]

In the summer of 1948, a citywide revival was held in Birmingham, Alabama. Dr. James G. Harris was pastor of the Calvary Baptist Church in that city at the time. In the July 4th edition of his church paper he wrote an article under the title, "As I saw it."

> It wasn't in Jerusalem on the Day of Pentecost in the early '20s, but in the modern, industrial steel city of Birmingham in 1948. It wasn't the delightful fall months, when church programs and individual enthusiasm pick up in tempo, but in the sweltering days of mid-June, when it is a foregone conclusion that church work will slump. I saw nearly 5,000 people come to the city auditorium one hot June Sunday afternoon to hear a sermon by Charles Wellborn . . . . I even saw more people come through a rain storm the following Sunday afternoon to hear Jackie Robinson preach . . . . I saw almost 6,000 people jam into the auditorium on a June Wednesday to hear a young layman, Howard Butt, dramatically picture a crucified and risen and reigning Savior. I heard BO Baker lead the thousands in singing, "I'd Rather Have Jesus" and "He Lives!" until the melodies and messages from those marvelous songs re-echoed in my heart all day long. I saw Bill Cody lead hundreds of Birmingham young people into agonizing prayer, intensive

> visitation, and careful organization for a great revival in our city. I saw about 500 young people walk the aisles for Christ. I'll never forget the scene of young people, standing joined by handclasp that encircled the vast auditorium, who had walked the aisles, and I saw other scores rise from their seats to break the circle and join with them. I saw Birmingham, our beloved city, impressed with Christ, and the implications of separated living as never before. God gave our city a revival....
>
> I was told the revival would not be church-centered, but eighteen walked the aisles at Calvary last Sunday, and two others have given their hearts to Jesus who plan to come next Sunday. Eight volunteered for special service, and they are among our choicest and most gifted young people. I was told the revival would be excessively emotional, but the team did not capitalize unfairly on any possible religious hysteria, but gave sane, dignified, fair invitations, after stirring sermons, and left the results with God.
>
> What is the secret of this team? It is not talents — although they are all ten-talent men — for there are many ten-talented men. It is not eloquence — although they are eloquent — for I have heard equal eloquence without being so moved. The secret is that these young men love the Lord with all their souls, and each has decided, "I'd rather have Jesus than anything this world affords today!" That is the secret, and it will be the secret of our power as Christians, and as a church. The world would bid high for them, but they belong to God.

Now, every member of that 1948 Birmingham team would be embarrassed by the words of this highly respected pastor. But, knowing James Harris, as I came to know him after he moved to Texas a few years later, he meant every word he wrote. And the generous, gracious words of pastors like him made the team humble, grateful . . . and usable.

NOTES

[1] Notes taken from the files of H-E-B. Used by permission.

[2] Bill Tanner, correspondence with the author.

EIGHT

ENLARGING THE TENT

Enlarge the place of your tent . . . for you will spread out to the right and to the left. (Isa 54:2a, 3a)

The challenge of leading that 1946 citywide revival in Houston, the largest city in Texas, with little more than two months preparation was overwhelming. Indeed, it was downright ridiculous! We had just concluded a revival in Waco that had the support of 300 volunteers working daily for nearly a year. Houston had no organization, no funds, no committees, no visible goals, and no place to meet. And, to make matters worse, they wanted the revival to be held the first week in July, which, of course, included July 4th. "No one will attend a revival on July 4th," some suggested. "They will be on the beach down the road at Galveston. We'll all be embarrassed," others said, suggesting plans be postponed for a year. These well-measured responses made sense to everyone — except to an ever-growing number of young people and adults who felt with passion that "*now* is the time." The urgency for spiritual renewal could not be calendared, but it had captured their lives.

Thankfully, W. F. Howard had been officially approved as the coordinator of all youth revivals in Texas. This meant that all correspondence, all advance work, all assignments and travel arrangements and all evaluations were now cleared through his office. Obviously, this was a heavy load off the shoulders of a bunch of 20-year-olds who were already over their heads and in desperate need of both wisdom and guidance. There was no question in our minds that Dr. Howard was the very person to give this, and we welcomed him almost gleefully. Now we could concentrate on refining our *one* sermon and maybe come up with a *second* one!

One of the first things Dr. Howard did was assign Bill Cody and Bob Harris to advance preparation in Houston. They were the best. Bill Cody grew up on a farm near Farmersville, Texas. For the first five years of his public education he was the only child in his class. Later his high school days were spent in a one-room building. The area in which he lived had no all-weather roads, so on Sundays they had "preaching" when it didn't rain. And preaching was about the only thing on the menu! There were no training activities, no choir, no order of worship, and no organized Sunday School. Bill once observed, "Church music was what the women did while the men stayed outside and smoked. When the men finished smoking and came in, the women quit singing and the preacher started preaching."[1]

Obviously, Bill experienced some loneliness in this, for deep inside he knew that another kind of world existed — a world of delightful, creative people, a world waiting for exciting discoveries, and a world celebrating every one of those discoveries with exuberant "A-has." As a super-achiever he needed the challenge of this world, and he found it when he stepped onto the campus of Baylor University. It was as though all his creative abilities, yearning to be expressed, were released in the form of meaningful ministries. In 1946 he was the capable co-chairman of all arrangements for the Waco Youth Revival. After that, he became the indispensable advance team member in scores of citywide revivals throughout the nation. Bill made things happen, and he kept the preaching-singing team in line. With a clipboard always in hand he would say, "Jack, you have a radio interview at 10:00; Bruce, you're to meet some pastors for lunch; BO, the choir will gather one hour before the service; Howard, don't forget to call the local chairman of publicity; Charles, don't forget your radio talk program this afternoon at 2:00..." and on and on. Bill reviewed his notes while leaning against a chair or a table, holding his trusted clipboard in his left hand and a pen in his right, resting the bottom of the clipboard against his protruding stomach about two inches above the belt. Jess Moody observed, "I became so accustomed to Bill and that clipboard that I thought the clipboard was a growth on his body." But Bill and his clipboard kept us out of trouble and helped us stay on schedule. It was a learning tool for Bill . . . and for us.

Bill died in 1995 — all too young. He was still learning, seeking, exploring and watching things work. I have a feeling his last word was, "A-ha."

Bob Harris was the other advance man sent to Houston. Bob, a native of the university town of Chapel Hill, North Carolina, had graduated from Mars Hill Junior College in that state. After a tour of duty as a navy pilot during the war, he transferred to Baylor University — just in time to become involved in the 1946 revival. The early deaths of each of his parents made Bob more sensitive to responsibility, having promised his parents that he would take good care of his siblings. He was thoughtful and kind, warm and compassionate, and thorough without being tedious. He could charm a room full of people with his smile without ever being aware of what he had done. That was Bob, and along with Bill Cody, his ministry was desperately needed as we looked toward Houston.

During the last weeks of the spring semester they made four trips from Waco to Houston, laying the foundation for what was needed as we faced the first week of July. After considering all alternatives, the decision was made to have the revival services in the auditorium of the First Baptist Church in downtown Houston. Attendance would necessarily be limited to 3,000 persons with overflow rooms accommodating another 500–600. This was not ideal, but it was the best under the circumstances.

When classes were concluded in the spring of 1946, Bill and Bob moved to Houston and lived there until all arrangements were completed. In a whirlwind of activities they not only met with pastors and youth leaders, but they also arranged small luncheons with influential laypersons, asking for their support through prayers, creative suggestions, and personal involvement.

In Bob Harris's own words:

> First of all we organized a prayer meeting. We sent out notices to all the churches that we needed to have prayer support and that we needed a prayer chairman and a prayer group in each church in the city. We met first with the prayer chairmen, and then he, or she, followed through with the prayer group in his church. Then we worked on advertising. We had advertising chairmen in each of the churches. All of the chairmen then met together and shared ideas. Out of this, new ideas kept flowing. For instance, we wrapped flyers around all the milk bottles announcing the revival services. The kids painted footsteps around the theaters in downtown Houston pointing to the First Baptist Church saying, 'This way to Houston Youth for Christ.' Fortunately, the police gave them no trouble. And, amazingly, we were able to stretch a banner across the busiest street advertising the revival. It stayed up throughout the entire meeting.[2]

But Houston is a massive city, and communicating to churches alone was a major task, to say nothing of trying to get the word out to hundreds of thousands who never entered a church building. Two dramatic things happened to make the people more aware of the scheduled youth revival.

Mr. H. E. Butt, Sr., Howard's father, had a friend and business competitor in Houston named Weingarten, who also owned a chain of grocery stores. One day Mr. Butt said to Mr. Weingarten, "Some boys from Baylor are coming to Houston for a city-wide youth revival. They're interested in reaching the youth of this generation, and they need our help. Now, I've put up some money to underwrite their needs, and I'd like for you do something also to help them."

Mr. Weingarten, a Jew, thought it sounded like a good idea. He pondered it for a moment and said, "Howard, I own several billboards on major streets and highways in this area. What do you think about my donating 14 billboards to help them in their advertising program?"

The answer was obvious, and throughout the city huge billboards announced:

"Follow the Living Christ"
HOUSTON YOUTH REVIVAL
First Baptist Church Auditorium
Lamar at Fanning
July 1st through July 6th

And very few people ever realized these signs were donated to a Baptist youth revival by a wonderful Jewish man!

But young people do not automatically respond to signs, regardless who contributes them. There was still a need to make more of the city aware of what was happening. Frankly, the press had not been very helpful. They loved the ads we purchased but the writers had shown little interest in the revival. A noonday prayer service, involving youth throughout the city, had been meeting for weeks at First Baptist Church. Bob Harris spoke with genuine concern to several newspaper reporters: "Just come and see for yourselves how concerned these young people are," he pleaded. One of the writers for the *Houston Post* showed up the next day, and the following day her column was given a prominent place in the paper under the title, "The Devil Takes No Holiday." She wrote:

> The Fourth of July was not a holiday, but a holy day to thousands of Houston young people who cheerfully abandoned plans of former years for recreation and gaiety, and dedicated the Fourth to prayer and church-going. Undaunted that the holiday came right in the middle of their one-week youth revival, they redoubled their efforts, with the retort, "The devil takes no holidays — why should we?"
>
> For nearly two hours, approximately 200 young men and women knelt in a noon-day prayer meeting...and petitioned God to save their friends — to save Houston . . . and, strangely

> enough, some pleaded with God to save their parents. Scores wept. One beautiful blue-eyed, golden-haired girl, who forgot to bring her hanky, picked up the corner of her fresh blue chambray dress and wiped her tear-stained face.
>
> "God, you've gotta help us," several of the suppliants begged. "We know the newspapers can't do it. Ads won't do it. Publicity won't do it. Nobody can do it, Lord, but you."
>
> Among this group of earnest young men and women are former bomber pilots, well-known high school and college athletes, and girls and boys with lovely voices, many of whom until recently had plans for worldly honors. They have placed "on the altar" their talents to be used for God in helping point America to the way of peace.
>
> Interspersed with the fervent prayers were songs softly sung. The revival theme song, "I'd Rather Have Jesus," was sung with such sweet simplicity and impressive earnestness that it made one feel: "These young people really have something," as we pictured in our minds the tragic contrasting anti-God indoctrination of Hitler youth a few years ago, the results of which plunged a world into war.
>
> Undoubtedly, the effects of the youth revival movement will aid in the long up-hill climb toward peace and happiness for a war-weary world.[3]

Other papers began to give serious coverage to the revival and overflow crowds numbering 3,500 gathered nightly for the services. The youth preachers were Jess Moody, Jack Robinson, BO Baker, Charles Wellborn, Howard Butt, and Bruce McIver. BO and Howard shared in leading the congregational music.

Jess Moody preached on Monday, July 1, 1946, the opening night of the revival. His sermon topic was "Aren't You Glad You're You?" Twenty-two young people drove from Wharton to hear their hometown hero speak. The *Houston Post* quoted from Jess's message the following day:

> "God is just as big as you let Him be, or just as little as you want Him. The youth of Houston are going to get revived. We are young, but we love God. We don't know much about

> organization, but we love God. We don't know much about denominations, but we love God. I'm glad I've got Jesus. I've got something I wouldn't trade for anything, not even popularity. If you only knew how weak I am but how mighty my Christ is!" Over 150 young people responded to the public invitation to commit their lives to Christ.

Movie star Dennis Quaid wrote the foreword to Jess's book, *Club Sandwich Goes Great With Chicken Soup*:

> Randy Quaid is my brother, and we have a wonderful mother, Nita Quaid. When she was about 16 years old, she was a close friend of a young preacher named Jess Moody. In those days there was a great movement of spiritual power amoung the young people. In the North, there was Youth for Christ, spearheaded by Billy Graham and others. Jess Moody was one of the others, and was present at the founding of Youth for Christ in Winona Lake, Indiana. Billy Graham and Jess traveled separately, but unitedly, for that organization.
>
> In the South, there was the Baptist Student awakening, and thousands attended in the major cities. My mother was one of those in Houston. The young preachers, like Jess, were almost like modern rock stars. Young people, by the thousands, thronged to hear them.
>
> Years later, when Randy and I came to Hollywood to try to break into the movies, Mother said, "When you boys get there, be sure and attend Jess's church, the Shepherd of the Hills." We did just what Mother told us to do, and Randy served on Jess's board for seven years.[4]

Jack Robinson preached on Tuesday evening. Jack was a statewide and nationally recognized basketball star. We expected an overflow crowd because of Jack's popularity as a basketball star, but our hopes were dashed when a deluge of rain flooded the city. But the rain seemed to make the occasion more exciting and exhilarating as people crowded into every "nook and cranny" of the church house. Finally, when all space was gone, they stood in the streets outside in the rain, hoping for a glimpse of their athletic star.

Records are incomplete, but we do know that from Monday through Thursday night there were 27 professions of faith, 50 who dedicated their lives to Christian ministry, and 250 rededications. Eighty-five of these came forward on Thursday night as Charles Wellborn brought a dynamic message, "Face to Face." Scores of others responded publicly on Friday and Saturday nights, but those actual figures are not available.

The newspapers mention several Houstonians who were involved in places of leadership. R. F. Boston was the general chairman; Gale Burton, a medical student, and Frances Redman, a student nurse, spoke of their commitments to medical missions; Betty Kesterson, from Sam Houston High School, and Francis Ball, director of the Christian Servicemen's bureau, shared their personal testimonies; senior Bill Dyal and Bill Corrigan led some of the noonday prayer meetings; Bert Kadell presided over many of the services; Adele Muirhead sang a solo; and Mary Albertson, Winnie May Acord, and Ruth Hutcherson — all three students from Jefferson Davis High School — sang in a trio.

By the way, one of the rewards in doing research is the delightful serendipity that comes while studying old photographs, reading news clippings and probing the minds of people. The trio of attractive girls from Jefferson Davis High sang the night BO Baker preached. In the files I came across a picture of BO standing behind the pulpit with the trio seated immediately behind him on the first row of the choir. BO seemed to have the attention of the overflow crowd, but, in a special way, he held the attention of the three girls. There are no records that any of the girls came forward to register public commitments at the close of the service, but several years later, Ruth Hutcherson became Mrs. BO Baker! Now, who says life isn't filled with happy surprises!

It was in that same Houston revival that a high school boy named Bailey Stone made his commitment to Christ. I listened in fascination as he shared his story with me:

> My mother and dad were not Christians, nor did they go to church. My mother was an alcoholic. I had a friend, Henry SoRelle, who played football with me in high school. Henry took me to the first citywide revival in Houston. The only reason I went was to see and hear Jack Robinson, the basketball star. Henry didn't just say, "Come to the meeting," because I would have never gone. He took me, and we went back to hear Charles Wellborn, BO Baker, Howard Butt, and the other fellows who were preaching. On Saturday morning Henry took me to his father. "Dad," he said, "Bailey is under conviction and I know that you know how to tell him how to be saved."
>
> Mr. SoRelle told me a simple Bible story that illustrated how much God loved me and wanted to forgive me. Then he said, "Son, that's what Jesus Christ did for you on the cross." It was there that I received the Lord Jesus as Savior. That night I returned to the revival. You, Bruce, were preaching when I publicly accepted Christ. I then joined the Second Baptist Church, where the SoRelle's were members and where Dr. Kyle Yates was pastor. He baptized me.[5]

Bailey had athletic scholarships to Texas A and M, Rice, and the University of Houston. He chose Baylor because he felt God was leading him into the ministry. "I needed scripture," he said. "Real growth began to happen in my freshmen year when I started a Bible study in the freshman dorm that grew to about 75–100 attending each week. I began to grow and to sense what God was doing in my life." Some became Christians through those Bible studies and others surrendered to the ministry.

Later, Dr. Yates invited Bailey to return to Second Baptist Church and preach a youth revival. In the months following his own conversion Bailey had prayed for his parents, but they showed little interest in becoming Christians. On Sunday during the revival, Bailey had tried to witness to his father, but felt like he had failed. "I went down to the prayer room of the church, and opened the door of that little room. Rupert Wright (a Baylor friend and member of the football team) was not on his knees —

he was on his face, down on the floor crying out to God to save Bailey's mother and daddy tonight."

Bailey continued, "I went to that service and I preached the worst sermon I have ever preached, but my mother and daddy were saved that night . . . . From that day on you couldn't root them out of the church. In fact, one time I called them and couldn't get them until later. I asked where they were. Mom said, 'We were at a Baccalaureate service out at Jeff Davis High School.'

'Who do you know out there?' I asked.

'No one. Your dad just thought we should go because our preacher (Kyle Yates) was preaching the Baccalaureate, he felt we needed to support him by our presence.'"

Later, Bailey himself preached in numerous youth revivals throughout Texas, served as pastor of First Baptist Church, Odessa, First Baptist Church, Bryan, and First Baptist Church, McKinney. For eight years he has served as Director of Evangelism for the Baptist General Convention of Texas.

Bailey ended our conversation with a quiet verbal postscript. "When I came home that Saturday night of the city-wide youth revival and told my parents that I had become a Christian, Mom never touched another drop of alcohol for the rest of her life." Her commitment, like so many others, was not recorded on a card during the revival meeting — just in the heart . . . and in the home.

The crowds in Houston overflowed the facilities each night — in spite of heat and storms. One of the great pastors in that city, Dr. Kyle Yates, sat on the steps leading to the balcony and prayed throughout the services. Local churches swamped the temporary Youth Revival office with invitations for the team to speak in their churches, schools, or special rallies they had arranged. The press gave front page stories on the revival with pictures of the throngs attending, and radio stations called for personal interviews. Hundreds of commitments were made to Christ and scores of young people volunteered for Christian ministry.

Meanwhile, Dr. W. F. Howard's office in Dallas was overwhelmed with invitations for teams to lead citywide revivals in places like Ft. Worth, Dallas, Birmingham, and Atlanta. And, it seemed that half the churches wanted a Youth Revival in their local church. When they were questioned about possible dates, the answer usually was, "Right now!"

We looked at the crowds, listened to the invitations, opened our Bibles and checked the notes on the two or three sermons we had outlined, and wondered, "What on earth is God doing?" How in the world did we get involved in this!"

And, "What's next?"

NOTES

[1] Bill Cody, Oral History, 24 May, 1982.

[2] Bob Harris, correspondence with the author.

[3] Gladys Carroll, *Houston Post,* 5 July 1946.

[4] Jess Moody, *Club Sandwich Goes Great with Chicken Soup* (Nashville: Broadman: Holman, 1999), 3.

[5] Baily Stone, correspondence with the author.

NINE

BEYOND EXPECTATIONS

No one has ever imagined what God has done for those who love him. (1 Cor 2:9b)

When do movements begin? Is it possible to track them adequately? Why is so much of our information discovered through what Frederick Buechner calls, "listening back"? I'm not sure of the answer to those questions, but I do know if we had the answers at the time, we would be so overwhelmed that we might be paralyzed in the process. It was years before any of the team members referred to the Youth Revivals openly as a "movement." To us, they were remarkable events on the calendar, wonderful relationships with youth and adult leaders and thrilling experiences of watching God do miracles beyond our wildest dreams. But not a "movement." Not yet.

Of course, the seeds for a movement were sown during the two campus revivals at Baylor in 1945 and 1946. More seeds were sown on other campuses across the state and the fruit of those seeds was becoming obvious.

Fleta Lindley was a student at Howard Payne College during the 1946 revival at Baylor University. She heard from friends about the revival at Baylor University. Fleta and a friend got on a bus, rode from Brownwood to Waco, attended the Saturday night services, and returned to report to their fellow students at Howard Payne. This led to an outdoor revival on the campus in Brownwood conducted by the students. S. L. Harris, who later married Fleta, was one of the preachers. So was Jimmy Allen, who years later was to become the president of the Southern Baptist Convention. Students on other campuses, in Texas and beyond, inquired about the revivals and rallies and asked for help in planning for them and promoting. This amazed us. Something was happening. We weren't sure what it was, but we were sure that it was beyond our doing. We felt like spectators, standing on tiptoes, watching and waiting. Many times we read and quoted the verse of scripture, "No one has ever seen this, and no one has ever heard about it, no one has ever imagined what God has prepared for those who love him" (1 Cor 2:9).

About the time we received the invitation to lead the Houston Crusade, some of us also were invited to speak at the Ridgecrest Baptist Assembly, the largest gathering of Baptist students in the nation. Each year at the close of the spring semester, between 2,500 and 3,000 students from campuses across the country gathered at the Assembly in the heart of the Blue Ridge Mountains in North Carolina. The gathering afforded those attending a remarkable opportunity for congregational worship, hearing messages from some of the outstanding leaders in the world, participating in stimulating small-group discussions on how to apply these messages to daily living, and meeting new friends destined to become world leaders. All this, plus some of the richest fellowship to be found anywhere. Students would sacrifice throughout the year, organize carpools, and share food and housing expenses just to be able to attend this one exciting week of spiritual renewal.

You can imagine our surprise when W. J. Wimpee called four or five of us into his office and said, "Fellows, they want you to speak at Ridgecrest."

"Ridgecrest? What in the world do they want us to say?"

"They want you to tell them what happened here at Baylor in the citywide revival. There's a genuine interest among students across the nation that this same thing happen on their campuses and in their cities."

A myriad of feelings flooded through our minds. We were overwhelmed, amazed, bewildered, awed, just plain scared. These students represented the sharpest minds in our colleges and universities. How would they receive us? How could we tell the story without sounding "Texanic?" We didn't understand ourselves what was happening, so we certainly couldn't boast about it.

"Just be yourselves," Wimpee encouraged. "They just want to hear what's on your hearts."

We quickly shifted our limited schedules, made travel plans, and headed 1,300 miles for the mountains of North Carolina, my home state. In the *Baptist Standard*, June 20, 1946, Winnie Dudley wrote an article titled, "Texas Youth Revival Catches Fire at Ridgecrest":

> As quickly and contagiously as its theme song, "I'd Rather Have Jesus," has been caught up and sung by college students, the idea and the power of the Texas youth revivals have spread at the . . . retreat of Baptist students at Ridgecrest, N. C., during the past week.
>
> "This is what I have waited a generation to see — a real revival in America — and now I can return to China satisfied," said Miss Martha Franks, veteran missionary to China, after hearing the testimony of those who had been in the meetings. She believes the Texas movement is the beginning of a revival such as the noted Shantung revival which swept China in the early thirties. When 400 Texas students, the majority from campuses where the first youth revivals were held, hit the Ridgecrest encampment grounds on June 6, they had a story to tell and they lost no time in telling it. They had been present at the beginnings of the Texas youth movement and had seen the power of God — they were there. Knowing that God had given them something too big for them to hold, they had prayed definitely for weeks that he would help them share it. They told it in the assembly where 2,600 student leaders heard it; they told it to their prayermates and cabin-mates; they told it in conferences and forums; they told it in prayer meetings into the night.
>
> Ralph Langley, Bruce McIver, and Jack Robinson, Baylor students who helped promote the Waco revival meetings; John Earl Seelig, cheerleader and yearbook editor at Hardin-Simmons; Charles Wellborn, faculty member and national

> debate champion at Baylor, who was converted in the youth revival on his campus; and S. L. Harris, BSU president of Howard Payne, told what youth revivals meant to them and to their colleges.
>
> And, as it has been from the beginning of the movement, when two Baylor students who knelt in prayer conceived the idea, prayer was the keynote and basis for the movement. In state groups, students from university after university rose to pray and to ask for prayers for a youth revival on their campus. Students pledged themselves to do all within their power to have a revival on their campus, and to prepare themselves by removing everything from their lives that would hinder a revival.

Dudley concluded her article: "When Dr. Marshall Craig, pastor of Gaston Avenue Baptist Church in Dallas, gave an invitation for personal surrender at the close of his message Sunday morning, some 400 students came to the platform of the Ridgecrest auditorium to publicly register their decision."

Miss Franks' prayers were being answered . . . indeed.

Within days, we came from the "high" of the mountains to the rugged inner-city of Houston to find the same outpouring of concern and commitment. Whatever was happening (and we had no name for it), we felt like amateurs. Our primary concern was that we not hinder whatever God was doing! This involved everything from attitudes to public and private actions, from dispositions to diplomacy, from a grand overview of changing the world to a genuine respect for immature high school students whom God would use in the changing process. All of this involved prayer . . . and a whole lot of patience!

About a week after the Houston revival had concluded, Dr. Howard called me from his Dallas office. "Bruce," he said, "I have your schedule before me and see that next week is open as far as your preaching responsibilities are concerned."

"Yes, sir," I replied, trying to hide my relief that I had a few days off. I had hoped to see my fiancee and also welcomed the time to work on another sermon. Most of us were painfully stuck with the one or two messages that we had when we began preaching in youth revivals. Not a one of us had ever had a class in homiletics or sermon preparation, but God seemed to honor the simple messages and the freshness of new experiences every day, and accentuated them with vitality and new meaning whenever we spoke. And, it didn't hurt to have your best friends praying for you, even though they may have heard that very sermon 20 times.

Dr. Howard listened sympathetically, and then said in a pleading voice, "Please, Bruce, I need you in Dallas Monday morning. Bill Cody and Bob Harris are both working on the arrangements of this revival, but they are overwhelmed and time is running out. We still need help."

"What kind of help?" I asked innocently. Bill and Bob were the best when it came to details, and it never occurred to me that they would ever need help from anyone, especially from me.

"To begin with," Dr. Howard responded with obvious fatigue, "we have a young man who is the chairman of one of the local committees for the revival."

"I know him," I answered. "He's got lots of energy."

"He means well," Dr. Howard groaned, "but his energy is about to drive us nuts! Only yesterday we learned he has chartered an airplane and has planned to drop 50,000 handbills about the youth revival over downtown Dallas. He may have us all in jail for littering the city if he follows through."

"What do you want me to do?" I asked with a muffled chuckle.

"Just get up here immediately, cancel the plane he has chartered, shadow that young man, and don't let him out of your sight!"

I don't know how we were able to pull it off, but it was a master coup. It demanded all the diplomacy we could muster, but the plane was grounded, the handbills distributed through other means, and his wild-eyed enthusiasm channeled through half a dozen creative public relations programs. Dr. Howard was relieved, Bill and Bob were ecstatic, and I was exhausted!

Now, whether one preached, led the music, or made arrangements for the revivals, the honorarium was the same — $50 per week, plus a meager allowance for expenses. I guess I am the only person in the history of youth revivals who made $50 for "shadowing" a local committee member. But it was a small price to pay since we stayed out of jail!

The revival services were scheduled to be held in Cole Park, a lovely open area just north of downtown Dallas at McKinney and Cole streets. Six thousand seats were ordered for Monday night and a choir platform was built for 500 singers, four pianists, and an orchestra. For weeks several hundred young people had worked with Bill Cody and Bob Harris on arrangements. And, during that same time they had also prayed together. Four weekly prayer meetings grew in numbers from 400 to 1,300. Obviously, their prayers were answered. Before the first service on July 29, 1946, there was a ground swell of excitement — more than we had seen in any other city.

Unfortunately (for me), I was the first speaker. On Monday night as we gathered, every one of the seats had been taken, and BO Baker was "warming up" the 500-voice choir. From all directions people were slowly trying to get near Cole Park. Policemen were directing traffic all the way to downtown Dallas. The atmosphere was electric with anticipation. Everyone was excited — except me. I took one look at the "multitudes," more than lived in my entire county back in the hills of North Carolina, and collapsed. I dropped to my knees, not in humble prayer, but in stark terror! Never had anyone felt more out of his element than I was in that moment. Dr. Howard knelt with me; so did Jack Robinson and Howard Butt. Then they took me by an arm and lifted me to my feet, half-dragging and half-carrying me toward the podium. I paused, took a deep breath, and began slowly mounting the steps as though I were heading toward my gallows. As the service began I was aware of what sounded like several people talking at once. This bothered me since I was trying to concentrate on my message and pray for those participating. At least 20 minutes passed before I realized what was happening. Several dozen young people had gathered beneath the choir platform — completely out of sight of the congregation — and were praying in quiet voices, barely above a whisper, for the service. This continued throughout the message, the singing of the invitation, and until the last note had been sung. My heart became strangely calm, and a sense of peace enveloped me as I preached to the largest crowd I'd ever seen gathered in one place — 6,000 people.

Both the *Dallas Morning News* and the *Dallas Times Herald* gave us brief daily stories, listing the local committee chairmen and the preachers for the week. Dr. W. A. Criswell, pastor of the First Baptist Church of Dallas, served as co-chairman of the revival campaign. Joe Boyd, a Texas A & M all-American tackle on the national championship 1939 team and pastor of a new church in Dallas, was the other co-chairman. Rang Morgan was in charge of finances, and Bud Dosher handled the publicity. Ruby Matejka led in the pre-revival visitation emphasis, Louise Steindam was chairperson of spiritual preparation, Eugene Quinn served as music chairman, and Bill Odam and Jim Haley were responsible for arrangements. Bobby Nell Simms organized follow-up contacts, Henry Lyles was responsible for ushers, and Virginia Tapscott arranged hospitality and entertainment. Hundreds of young people from scores of churches worked on these committees, and many more stood ready to do whatever needed to be done at the moment. It was a marvelous display of unity as people from all sizes of churches in Dallas worked hand in hand. The *Dallas Times Herald* reported on July 28, 1946, "that 12,000 personal letters had been mailed to Dallas High School students, and that a concentrated campaign, designed to cover every home in the city, has been conducted in the interest of the revival."

Speakers for rest of the week were Jack Robinson, Tuesday; Ralph Phelps, Wednesday; Charles Wellborn, Thursday; Howard Butt, Friday; and BO Baker, Saturday. On the night that BO preached, Howard Butt led the congregational singing and Dick Baker, BO's brother who had just returned from military service, sang a solo.

Beginning with the attendance of 6,000 on Monday night, the crowds grew by 1,000 to 1,500 more each night. Daily, more chairs were rented and delivered to the park. Bob Harris, one of the advance persons in charge of arrangements, had pleaded with a photographer with the *Dallas Morning News* to take a picture of the crowds for his paper. The photographer had shown little or no interest. Finally on Wednesday, Bob said to him, "There will be 8,000 people in the service tonight. We have that many chairs set up and every one of them will be filled."

The photographer chuckled and said, "Son, if you have half that number, call me and I'll be there."

As the crowds gathered for the evening service, Bob scanned the audience and saw that all seats were filled. He called the photographer and said, "Do you remember your promise? It's time for you to grab a camera and get out here!" During the service later that evening the photographer climbed a step ladder near the podium, doing a tricky, balancing act, hanging onto his camera with one hand and trying to keep from falling with the other. The next morning, what has become a classic panoramic picture of the Dallas revival appeared in the *Dallas Morning News*, covering the entire eight columns across the newspaper. We budgeted a lot of money on publicity, but this was a picture money could not buy.

"Bobby-Sockers Flock to Mammoth Revival" was the title of a story in the *Dallas Times Herald*, July 31, 1946. Sue Stinson wrote:

> If the Dallas Citywide Revival in Cole Park Tuesday night was an example of where the "bobby-sox" will go if given the opportunity, then the delinquency experts might well divert the larger part of their efforts toward the problem of adult delinquency.
>
> Of a crowd of 7,000, 5,000 were of the 'bobby-sox' age. The response was something that hasn't been seen in Dallas in a long time. Before the meeting began, an observer might have believed there was going to be a jitterbug contest! That is, he might have believed it until he noted the serious expression on their faces and the sincerity in their voices as they gathered in small groups before the meeting opened.

> Jack Robinson, all-Southwestern Conference basketball star and a sophomore at Baylor University, was the main speaker for the meeting Tuesday night.
>
> "Youths our age are the ones faced with the future and we must have faith in God because that's the only way of facing the issues of life," Robinson said.

Dr. W. F. Howard reflected on the Dallas revival in the *Baptist Standard*, August 15, 1946:

> It (the revival) lives on in the hearts and lives of 732 persons — most of whom were young people — who registered publicly their various decisions for Jesus Christ. There were 94 who found Christ as Savior, 120 who surrendered for full-time vocational Christian work, and 518 who came forward in sincere rededication of their lives to consecrated Christian living.

Dr. Howard then quotes three Dallas pastors, giving their evaluations of the week:

- "It was the greatest campaign for Christ that I ever saw in Dallas," said Dr. Wallace Bassett, pastor of Cliff Temple Baptist Church.

- "The recent youth revival was one of the greatest meetings I have ever known," observed Dr. Marshall Craig, pastor of Gaston Avenue Baptist Church.

- "The greatest spiritual blessing the city of Dallas has ever experienced!" declared Dr. C. E. Colton, pastor of North Temple Baptist Church.

On August 6, 1946, Dr. Robert S. Jones, then the associate secretary of the Relief and Annuity Board of the Southern Baptist Convention, wrote a letter to Mr. H. E. Butt, Sr.[1] In the letter he expressed his reactions to the Dallas revival:

> I wish you could have been in Dallas last week for the Youth Revival . . . . I was in the Dallas Pastors' Conference meeting yesterday morning, and it was the opinion of all the pastors that Dallas has never experienced a week that meant so much in the lives of Baptists in this city, both young and old, as did last week.
>
> The power of the meeting was reflected in the churches of the city last Sunday, and several of the pastors said that never in all the history of their churches had they ever experienced such a day. How thankful I am for this group of young men who have been able to stir cities as they have stirred Waco, Houston and Dallas.
>
> I had a long visit with Mr. W. F. Howard this morning, and we went over the results of the work of last week, and we both agreed that only eternity would reflect the good that was accomplished. I told Mr. Howard that I believe this was the only program I ever saw that seemed to be absolutely perfect. Looking back over it, I would not suggest any change that would improve it. It was a masterful presentation of the Gospel of Christ, and how your son and his co-workers did exalt our Savior . . . .

Without a doubt, the Dallas revival of 1946 became the "high water mark" of youth revivals. The size of the crowds, the support of churches and pastors, the large number of public commitments, the positive attitude of the secular press, and the willingness of hundreds of young persons to work for weeks in preparation for the services, all contributed to the success of these remarkable six days.

Two "afterglow" experiences linger from that Dallas revival in 1946. Nearly twenty years ago my wife, Lawanna, served as a trustee of what was then known as the Southern Baptist Home Mission Board. Occasionally, mission awareness trips were planned to better acquaint trustees with the diversity of the ministry of field missionaries. On one such awareness tour, spouses of the trustees were invited to be a part of the tour group. We were in Montana and were approaching an Indian reservation by chartered bus. As the bus inched its way through the narrow gate leading to the reservation, a slightly-built man ran out and flagged it down. The driver opened the door and the man climbed up on the first step, briefly looked the group over and then said in an excited voice, "Bruce McIver? Is Bruce McIver on this bus?"

My heart skipped a beat. Lawanna and I immediately feared something had happened to one of our children back in Dallas, or someone in the church where I served as pastor had died. Others on the tour shifted in the aisle and let me pass to the front where the man was standing.

"I'm Bruce McIver," I said to him. "Tell me what's happened."

In that moment he beamed, shook my hand and told me his name. Then, he proudly announced to everyone, "I set up chairs in the 1946 youth revival in Dallas!"

I listened in disbelief, and then asked, "What in the world are you doing up here?"

Again, he smiled proudly, "I've been teaching English on this Indian reservation for 31 years."

It was his mission, his calling, and his life's work. And it began when he was a high school student as he set up chairs for a revival meeting back in Dallas. And it just might be that what he did was the most important work anyone did all that week.

The second experience concerns a young man whose name is known: Buckner Fanning. Let him tell the story in his own words as he wrote them to me.

> I grew up at First Baptist Church, Dallas. My mother and my father were very active there. George Truett was my pastor. I graduated from high school in 1943 at the age of 17 and left immediately for the Marine Corps. I was gone three years, serving as a PFC in a rifle company in the Pacific. I was a long way from home, and a long way from the Lord. I believe only God or my mother believed I was a Christian. I didn't act like one, and wasn't living like one. But my mother had given me a Bible which I had put in my sea bag. I hadn't taken it out or read it in years, and hadn't gone to church . . . .
>
> Shortly after the atomic bomb was dropped on Nagasaki on Aug 9, 1945, we went ashore. I was among the first to land

> there for occupation duty, and I can't describe the devastation of that event. It overwhelmed me. The bomb incinerated a huge area of that city. It killed 40 or 50 thousand people instantly and thousands more died later . . . . It was a horrible event.
>
> Some personal things happened there that began to turn my life around. I began to see that the way I was going was destructive — just as destructive as bombs, except in a less dramatic way. But I saw the power of evil, and I saw the power of what happens when people no longer communicate. I knew very little about ethics . . . but I just felt like that here the innocent were suffering . . . . All the men were gone. They were in the military. Only the elderly and the women and the children were there, so they were the major victims of that bomb. They knew less about World War II than our little daughter knew about Vietnam.
>
> I started going to a little Japanese Methodist church . . . . There were only about thirty or forty people there, and I'd help them set up the chairs and put out the hymnals. I couldn't understand a word they sang or said; the preacher and I would bow to each other. I would sit in the back and read my Bible. I didn't know straight up from sideways about it, but I would open it and start reading it, and when (the service) was over, I would help them clean up. "Sayonara, see you next Sunday," and I would leave . . . . What those people did — and I didn't understand till later the full significance of it, but they served communion every Sunday, and at the end of the service they served me communion. I thought they were being polite Japanese, but then it began to dawn on me that I was the enemy. I was occupying their country. I was a symbol of that bomb, and of all the hatred that had existed in the war. And here they were saying to me in effect, "we consider you one of us." As I look back, I think they were seeing that faith in Christ and a commitment to Christ transcends hatred and war, violence, national origin, and race and culture, language, and everything. So, ever since, a kind of bomb went off in me.[2]

When Buckner had been home four or five days, his mother and dad said, "You know, Buckner, there's a big youth revival going on down in Cole Park right back of North Dallas High School.

"What's a youth revival?" Buckner asked.

"Well," they said, "it's a bunch of young guys — all students at Baylor and terrific kids — and they're down there preaching and singing, and having about 10,000 people every night. Why don't you go?"

"I thought that sounded a little kooky," Buckner later confessed. He had never really known but one preacher — George Truett, his pastor — and he knew him as a stately gentleman in his 70s. "I thought God made preachers and made them 30 years old and put them in a blue suit and behind a pulpit. They had never been 17 years old."

He attended the first night and was impressed that these guys and girls leading in the revival were not just leftovers, people who couldn't make a living or be successful doing anything else, so they were doing this. That was not true. "I didn't want to go back the second night," Buckner adds, but his mother told him she had invited the entire revival team over to their house after the services for refreshments and fellowship.

"I was trapped!" Buckner recalls. But the surprise of the evening was the fun everyone had. "I had never been around people who enjoyed laughter and hilarity like those guys. I didn't think it was possible, especially if you were in the ministry!"

"I had this date and we were going to LuAnn's or the Plantation to meet some friends and dance." But, after he had picked up his date, he said, almost impulsively, "You know, I think we ought to do something different. I want to take you to this thing." And they headed for Cole Park. When the services were over he took his date home, drove around the streets of Dallas until nearly 3:00 a.m., then sat on the back porch of his home and prayed, "Lord, I don't know what you want me to do, but I know that you want something from my life; you want me. As best I know how, I want to give you my life."[3]

The next night Buckner was back at Cole Park. Ralph Phelps preached a sermon titled "The Tragedy of Almost." A beautiful girl, Martha Howell, sang a solo just before the sermon. When the invitation hymn was sung, Buckner went forward and was greeted by Bob Harris, who had worked for weeks on preparations for the revival.

"What decision are you making?" Bob asked Buckner.

"I don't know," Buckner responded hesitantly, "I just need to turn my life around and get right with God."

Without him realizing it, a lifetime of wonderful decisions came out of that one commitment. A life was turned around. Within two months Buckner was headed for Baylor University. Within a few weeks he was sharing his own testimony, and one year later he himself preached in a citywide revival in Dallas. Three years later he and Martha Howell were married. Thirty years later at the invitation of the mayor of Nagasaki he returned to the Japanese city and preached a revival in Peace Park; a television documentary, shown nightly in Japan, was made of his return and the messages he preached that week. For the last 45 years he has served as pastor of the Trinity Baptist Church in San Antonio, and after 50 years he and Martha are still writing their own love story.

Buckner would be the first to say, "God keeps on 'turning things around' . . . and adds a surprise at every bend of the road."

NOTES

[1] An interesting "sidelight" to Dr. Jones' letter to Mr. Butt. In 1944, two years before the Dallas Youth Revival, I was hitch-hiking from Waco to Abilene for a Baptist Student Union Convention. A gracious man stopped and said, "Get in, son." He then introduced himself to me as B. B. McKinney. I was a young Christian but I recognized the name immediately and knew that he had written dozens of hymns and gospel songs that I loved. All the way to Abilene I asked him how he came to write certain songs. He patiently told me the story behind each one. "Tell me," I said, "about my favorite one, 'Wherever He Leads, I'll Go.'"

"I had a friend," he said, "who went as a missionary to South America. I was surprised to see him a few months later at a retreat back in this country. I asked him what had happened, and he told me he and his family had to resign and return to the States because of health problems. I asked him, 'What on earth are you going to do?' He looked at me and said with a steady voice, 'I don't know, B. B., but wherever He leads I'll go.'"

And then Dr. McKinney added, "My friend's name was R. S. Jones. I went immediately to my cabin at the retreat center, and in one sitting I wrote all the verses to 'Wherever He Leads I'll Go.'"

[2] Buckner Fanning, correspondence with the author.

[3] Buckner Fanning and Richard Baker, Oral History, 1982.

TEN

ALOHA

Come over.... and help us. (Acts 16: 9)

In the summer of 1946, Rev. and Mrs. Victor Koon, missionaries to Hawaii, were on the campus of Baylor University. Everywhere they turned they heard exciting reports of the citywide revival that had been led by the students in April, resulting in 500 public commitments. They also had heard that invitations had come to the team to conduct campaigns in other major cities.

In conversations with their friends, Rev. Woodson Armes, Pastor of Seventh and James Baptist Church, Waco, and with W. F. Howard, who had just assumed responsibilities as the coordinator of the youth revival ministries in Texas, Rev. Koon urged that a team be sent to Hawaii during the Christmas holidays of that same year, 1946. Such a possibility seemed like a dream, if not downright ridiculous, to everyone — except to the 22 Baptist missionaries who served on the small chain of inhabited islands. During the 1940s most of these had begun their missionary work in China and were forced to leave because of World War II. Some stayed in the Philippines for a brief period of time before relocating in Hawaii. They had known privation, personal loss, reversals, and overwhelming obstacles. They now ministered among fewer Baptists, numerically speaking, than had made public commitments in either the Waco or Dallas revivals. Yet, with amazing faith and unbelievable commitment, they wanted to plan and promote a city-wide revival in Honolulu scheduled to begin in only four or five months. This was even more of a challenge since Hawaii at this time was still a territory and mission work there was considered "foreign."

In preparing to write this chapter I had long conversations with W. F. Howard. He shared experiences out of the Hawaii mission trip that must be told if we are to understand the far-reaching influence of the Youth Revival movement. Sadly, he died in 2000 at the age of 91 years, but I'm glad he lived to see some of these stories on paper for others to read. In one of our conversations, I said to him, "I can't begin to imagine the problems you faced in trying to put together a team in such a short time for this project. The logistical problems alone must have looked like a nightmare — financial costs, selection of preachers and singers, travel schedules, classroom responsibilities, Christmas holidays, and pre-revival preparation without the help of either Bill Cody or Bob Harris."

"Bruce," he chuckled, "anyone who knows the truth about that revival also knows that God is a God who works miracles. That's what it was — an absolute miracle."

The practical problems were obvious, but there were deeper emotional issues that needed to be faced. To some, these seven or eight inhabited Polynesian Islands were the garden spots of the world; to others, they had become a graveyard five years earlier on December 7, 1941. To some, this was a land of beautiful music where the "Hawaiian Wedding Song" brought tears of joy to people; to others, it was the land of a dirge where the National Memorial Cemetery of the Pacific was located. The area is commonly called "Punch Bowl Crater." The Hawaiian word is actually "Pouwaina," or "Hill of Sacrifice." To some, Hawaii was a land of sunlight, with gorgeous rays shining on exotic flowers; to others, it was a land of darkness, where homage to strange gods was paid. Even more important, to some it was a land of less than ten struggling Baptist churches; to others, it was a South Pacific door to mission opportunities in the Far East.

The response was immediate. Dr. Howard agreed to put a team together and to assist the local committee from Hawaii with suggestions, ideas, and materials that might help them in their preparation. Baptist student directors from campuses across the nation, meeting in Nashville, Tennessee, pledged continuous prayer support. Students from those same campuses united to pray for the revival. The Southwide (National) Department of Student Work for Southern Baptists became vitally interested, and one of their leaders, Dr. William Hall Preston, accompanied the team and assisted in numerous ways. What had begun as a single college endeavor had now caught the imagination of students throughout the nation. Without our realizing it at the time, the youth revival movement was taking on a new shape, a new mission, and a new challenge. And it wasn't anything that we created or controlled. Like hot lava, flowing where it willed, the Spirit of God was moving, and every eruption, every breaking out, created a little more of paradise.

Records indicate that the first Youth Crusade Executive Committee for the revival in Honolulu met on October 25, 1946. Rev. Koon spent much of the time sharing his burden about the need for a citywide youth revival and recounting his conversations with Dr. Armes and Dr. Howard. He explained that the team from Texas would take care of all their own travel expenses, with the churches in Hawaii handling hospitality, publicity, and other related costs. It was also reported that several denominations had agreed to cooperate with Baptists in supporting the revival. Specifically mentioned were the Church of Christ, Lutherans, Nazarenes and Congregationalists. The date for the revival was announced — December 19-22, 1946 — and the services were to be held in Honolulu's McKinley High School auditorium.

The second meeting of the Committee was held on Nov. 8, 1946. Interestingly, the one asked to serve as treasurer had declined. (After my own experience of serving in this capacity twice at Baylor, I smiled and understood!). Another pastor indicated that it was "too far ahead of time to know whether his church would be available for a youth rally prior to the revival." (The revival was scheduled to begin in five weeks!).

On the other hand, Rev. Lindell Harris, chairman of publicity, and his committee pulled off some "miracles" in a matter of days. For instance: spot radio announcements were arranged to be broadcast over most of the local stations; articles and ads were written for the newspapers; 5,000 tickets were printed for rallies held in churches prior to the revival meetings, and 10,000 tickets were ordered to be distributed for the services at McKinley High School. Apparently, there was also a curfew in effect in Honolulu. Hundreds of small cards were printed that read: "Bearer on Police approved travel after Curfew from Youth Crusade Meeting to home. This permit good only on date hereon stamped." These were to be given to the young people attending the services. Harris also wrote in a letter to Dr. Howard:

> We are making a large number of bumper posters and banners for the rear end of cars. In addition, we are putting posters in half of the city buses for the month preceding the meeting. We are to distribute 25,000 handbills in various gatherings, i.e. house to house . . . .
>
> Another feature is a parade on Monday morning of the first day. Assemblies are being planned for as many high schools as we can get into, with posters being placed in all schools. These posters will also go in all businesses that will permit them. Another plan is to divide up the telephone directory among 150 young people and ask them to call every person listed in their section.

Harris concluded: "Baptist are very much a minority in Honolulu; yet, we are looking forward to a great meeting." That last line by Lindell Harris reflected the spirit of the twenty-one other missionaries who served with him.

Students on the mainland slowly but surely began to catch that same spirit. We began to look forward to something beyond ourselves, our campuses, our goals and careers. The lava was flowing, and something great was about to happen.

The team for the crusade was carefully and wisely chosen. Dr. Howard, who left Dallas for the Islands on December 3rd, introduced them by sharing brief biographical sketches on a radio program, "The Baptist Hour of Hawaii." Here are his introductions lifted from his manuscript used in that program on December 8, 1946.

> Jackie Robinson is a 6 foot 1 inch All-Southwest Conference basketball star on the 1946 championship Baylor team. Robinson's home is Fort Worth, Texas. His high school won the state championship during his senior year and he was voted the outstanding basketball player in the state. In his first year at Baylor he made the varsity, was the team's high scoring ace, and was the unanimous choice of sports writers for a place on the all-conference five. He is taking a leave from the team in order to make the Honolulu trip and will fly home December 23 to join the Baylor squad for the opening of the regular season. When you hear Jack Robinson, you will thrill to a spine-tingling, Christ-centered message coming from one of the most popular and best known college men of the United States.
>
> Howard Butt, a Baylor senior, is one of the most talented students in the party. Howard is the son of a Texas multimillionaire wholesale grocery merchant and is preparing himself by studying for a degree in business administration to take over the management of his father's vast business empire within the next few years. But, as in the case of young Robinson, this young man's appearance on the youth Crusade for Christ team is because of one thing, and one thing only: his consistent practice of putting Christ first in his interesting and privileged life. Howard can grip an audience with his dynamic speaking style and with his excellent vocal numbers, but more important, he brings to Honolulu youth a story of how Jesus came into his life when he was 15 years of age and gave him the one thing he lacked. He had money, automobiles, clothes — all that many young people consider so very essential to happiness, but not until he surrendered to Christ, he says, did he find full, thrilling, and completely satisfying happiness for which he was seeking.

> Ray Hoshizaki, a young Nisei, born in California and educated in Texas, entered Baylor University during the war years and soon made a place for himself in the hearts of students on the campus as evidenced by the fact that he was elected to Who's Who in American Colleges for 1945. Young Hoshizaki compiled one of the best scholastic records ever made by a Baylor student and has come to be sought after throughout Texas and far beyond as a speaker for youth rallies and crusade campaigns. Hoshizaki has a number of personal friends here in Honolulu and so will be no stranger with many of his own race.

Dr. Howard closed his message with a strong appeal from his own heart to the radio audience:

> If we could speak to every boy and every girl, to every young man and every young woman in the city of Honolulu and throughout the Islands, we would say the same thing to each one: you simply cannot afford to miss this opportunity of a lifetime. You must, in all fairness to yourself, come and see and hear and experience the greatest youth movement of your generation. In complete confidence we promise you that if you will come for the very first service, you will not want to miss a single one during the week. You will find no high pressure applied. You will not be embarrassed in any way. The program is simple, streamlined and planned by youth for youth. The messages are straight from the shoulder and right to the heart.

All of this sounded good in a radio address, but the logistics of getting the team from the mainland to Hawaii was a challenge. Obviously, every member of the team had to juggle his own personal schedule. For instance, Robinson had to work around some basketball games and special practice sessions. Thankfully, the coaches were understanding in giving him permission to make the trip. Woodson Armes, the only pastor on the team, faced the problem of being away from his congregation during one of the busiest times of the year for a church. And, for some, finances seemed insurmountable.

I chuckled as I read recently through files relating to the revival. Ray Hoshizaki had graduated from Baylor and had enrolled in Southern Seminary in Louisville. In one of his telegrams to Dr. Howard he wrote, "Plans ready to leave. Wire $100." I read that and smiled, wondering how far Reiji would get toward Hawaii on $100! But, amazingly, most of the problems were solved and the needs were met day by day.

Except one.

Howard Butt's parents refused to give him permission to fly. There were concerns about the safety of air travel, but there were also corporate concerns since Howard was an officer in the family business and heir apparent to major responsibilities with the company. Finally, after much discussion, passage was secured on a ship that had been used in WWII to transport both supplies and military personnel. That was in 1946 and some of the amenities associated today with luxury liners were missing, but the crossing turned out to be a pleasant one — especially for Howard. Each evening he had dinner with an elegant lady and her beautiful niece. As Howard tells the story, "I was caught up in youth revivals!" Now, for those of us who know Howard, being "caught up" can mean an exciting all-consuming experience. "Man," he exclaimed, "I told them about the Waco revival, the Houston revival, the Dallas revival, and I told them what God was going to do in Hawaii." I'm sure his "telling them" was accentuated by more than a gentle tapping on the table. Howard didn't tap in those days; he banged! This went on from California to Honolulu — every meal.

As they sailed into the harbor in Honolulu they politely said their good-byes and best wishes. Then the elegant lady could no longer hide her feelings. "I must confess I'm disappointed," she said, without a hint of embarrassment. "I had *sooo* hoped my niece would meet some handsome, wealthy young man on this cruise and that something might come of it." She then looked at Howard for the last time, lifted her nose about two inches, took her beautiful niece by the arm, and marched off the ship.

Poor old Howard had never set foot on the islands, but he had already lost two converts! And a haughty, overly-ambitious aunt, without realizing it, had lost the handsome, wealthy young man she hoped her niece would meet. What she didn't know was that Howard's closest friends, in jocularity, had dubbed him "The Rich Young Ruler!"[1]

On December 10, 1945, Dr. Howard wrote some friends back on the mainland, sharing progress that had been made and the burdens on his heart for the revival. He indicated that a city-wide prayer meeting would be held on Friday night prior to the first service in McKinley auditorium. The next day a parade through the streets of Honolulu had been organized and approved by the city. "We expect to have a minimum of 50 cars," he wrote, "and 100 banners (cloth with red stencil lettering) have been made and will be used in the parade." He asked for prayer for those who preached: Woodson Armes, Monday night; BO Baker, Tuesday; then Jackie Robinson, Howard Butt and Reiji Hoshizaki; Jackie again on Saturday with Howard closing the revival services on Sunday evening.

He closes with this word of hope:

> Too many evidences of God's blessings upon this effort have already been clearly manifest to allow a moment's doubt as to the outcome of the revival. It is certain to bring a great impact for Christ to the city. Radio, press, letters, signs, invitations cards, programs in eight public schools, contacts with church meetings through the city, person-to-person work — all these and many more channels are being used to awaken the city to wide interest. The problems are many and the needs alarming, but surely God is using this endeavor in a mighty manner.[2]

In spite of inclement weather, the crowds grew each night, reaching more than 2,000 for the closing service on Sunday. Over 100 professions of faith were made, 144 young people rededicated their lives to Christ, and twelve made commitments to full-time Christian service.[3]

In addition to the obvious success of the citywide revival, two serendipities came out of the emphasis that would have far-reaching results. First, the foundation was laid for what is now called the BSU (Baptist Student Union) Summer Mission Program. Charles Ashby offers helpful insight concerning this program that stirred college students on campuses throughout the nation:

> When the week was over the people were so impressed with the students' efforts that they extended an invitation for a similar group to return the following summer. It was felt by the Texas Student Department leadership that it would be unwise to try to duplicate this effort, whereupon the Hawaiian Baptist leaders requested that a group of students come to the Islands and work in Vacation Bible Schools and in a small Baptist camp. Dr. Preston returned to Nashville and began to correspond with some of the other state student secretaries asking if they would be interested in joining Texas in sending such a group of young people. Other states were interested, and on June 9, 1947, twelve college students, including a Texan from Baylor, Dan Rainbolt, arrived in Honolulu.[4]

Rainbolt had been a key person in the preparations for the two citywide youth revivals in Waco in 1945 and 1946. He was assigned to work on the Island of Molokai, the "Leper Island." There were only twelve Baptists on the island. How ironic! From 4,000 persons attending the revival in Waco to twelve in Molokai. But those of us who knew Dan knew without doubt that those 12 lepers received as much love and compassion as any 4,000 people have ever known.

In an article written for *The Student,* February 1992, Dr. Howard shares his excitement:

> You may have guessed it. This was the birth of BSU summer missions — a world-wide missions program which has involved thousands of students in ministries at home and overseas and has seen students raise tens of thousands of dollars in support of the work.

Dr. Howard's excitement was based on solid facts and figures. For instance, in the decade of the '50s, students in Texas alone raised more than $95,000 to send 152 students to mission fields around the world, working hand in hand with career missionaries for the entire summer. Those fields, carefully chosen, included Mexico, Cuba, San Andres, Nigeria, Hawaii, Jamaica, Italy, Southern Rhodesia, Alaska, Philippines, and Indonesia. In addition, scores of students during that same period of time were assigned to mission fields within the borders of the United States. The steady increase in summer mission ministries continues to this day.

Now, what happens when college students voluntarily give their summers to the challenge of "doing missions" in another land or with another ethnic group? What happens when they discover what the world is really like beyond their hometowns, their campuses, and their local churches? What happens when they realize that missions involves more — much more — than "pith helmets" and "slow boats" to some distant land? What stirs within them when they realize that their talents, their skills, can be used wherever people live? What is their reaction when they begin to understand that foreign missions is not nearly as foreign as they once thought? Preliminary studies indicate that as many as 30 to 40 percent felt their calling to career missions through that introduction of the BSU Summer Mission Program and through firsthand exposure to the needs of people around the world. And it began in a youth revival in Honolulu in December, 1946!

Another serendipity of the Honolulu revival, less publicized than the Summer Mission Program, was the granting of scholarships to students from the Islands who wished to study on campuses in Texas. In Dr. Howard's personal files there are copies of a letter written to the presidents of each Baptist college and institution. The letter requested that each president consider offering at least two scholarships to students from the Islands who met both academic and Christian standards. Indications are that the vast majority of the presidents and deans responded positively. That means, of course, that within a year of the revival in Hawaii between 20 and 30 students from Hawaii began receiving scholarships to study on the mainland.

Amid stories of conversions and rededications, the birth of summer missions, generous scholarships for academic studies, and enough "Alohas" to last a lifetime there's one more story that needs to be told — just to keep the record straight.

W. F. Howard was one of the most disciplined, correct, moral, and ethical persons I've ever known. He wouldn't think of doing anything that bends the rules — even slightly; neither would he tolerate the bending of the rules by any youth revival team member. When the revival was over in Hawaii, most of the team wanted to stay two or three extra days. They were able to change their tickets without difficulty. On the other hand, Dr. Howard was anxious to get home. After all, he had been there since December 3rd, and even the beauty of the "paradise islands" couldn't keep one from being homesick, especially during the Christmas season. For two or three days Dr. Howard explored every avenue possible, but there was no space on earlier flights. It looked as though he was destined to spend Christmas Day apart from his family, until Jack Robinson came up with a brilliant idea.

"Look," Jack said, "It's simple. You want to go home, and I want to stay. We'll just trade tickets. You'll be Jack Robinson and I'll be W. F. Howard. No problem. It's done all the time."

"But it doesn't sound right," Dr. Howard protested. "Besides, you're an all-American basketball player, and your face has been on leading sports magazines across the nation. Suppose somebody wants an interview? What do I do then?"

"Don't worry about it," the 19-year-old "moral authority" assured him. So, with a great deal of hesitation, Dr. Howard became Jack Robinson, the All-American basketball star, and Jack became the distinguished professor of English who was the Director of Baptist Student Work for Texas.

At the first counter: "Your name, sir?"

"W. F . . . er . . . Jack Robinson."

Upon entering the gate: "Your name, sir?"

More "er's."

As he looked for his seat on the plane: "Your name, sir?"

Finally, with his conscience in turmoil, he found his seat, slumped down with a newspaper in front of his face, and hoped no one would ask him about the upcoming Olympic Games in which Jack had been chosen to play. Thirty-six years later, in an oral history interview at the university where he had been an English professor, he confessed, and said he felt much better.

Did we say that there were 100 conversions in the citywide revival in Honolulu? Make that 101. After 36 years the distinguished Director of Baptist Student Work for Texas confessed the error of his ways! Thankfully, no one confused Dr. W. F. Howard with the *other* Jackie Robinson who within weeks would break the racial barriers and play baseball with the Brooklyn Dodgers!

NOTES

[1] Howard Butt, conversation with the author.

[2] From the personal files of W.F. Howard. Used by permission.

[3] Charles Ashby, *31 Years of Texas BSU Happenings* (Fort Worth: BACA Publishing Company, 1978), 51.

[4] Ibid., 51.

Front (l-r) Jack Robinson, Bruce McIver, BO Baker, Charles Wellborn, Howard Butt Jr., Ralph Langley. Back (l-r) Bill Cody, Raymond Underwood, Earl Miller, Frank Bounds, Bob Harris, W.F. Howard.

The "First Wavers" at Samford University in 1999. (Seated: W. F. Howard. From left to right: Jess Moody, Jack Robinson, Howard Butt Jr., Charles Wellborn, BO Baker, Warren Hultgren, Reiji Hoshizaki, Foy Valentine, Bruce McIver, Ralph Langley, Dick Baker, Bob Harris, Frank Boggs, Asa Couch. Not pictured: M. D. Oates, deceased.)

Waco Youth Revival poster (1945)

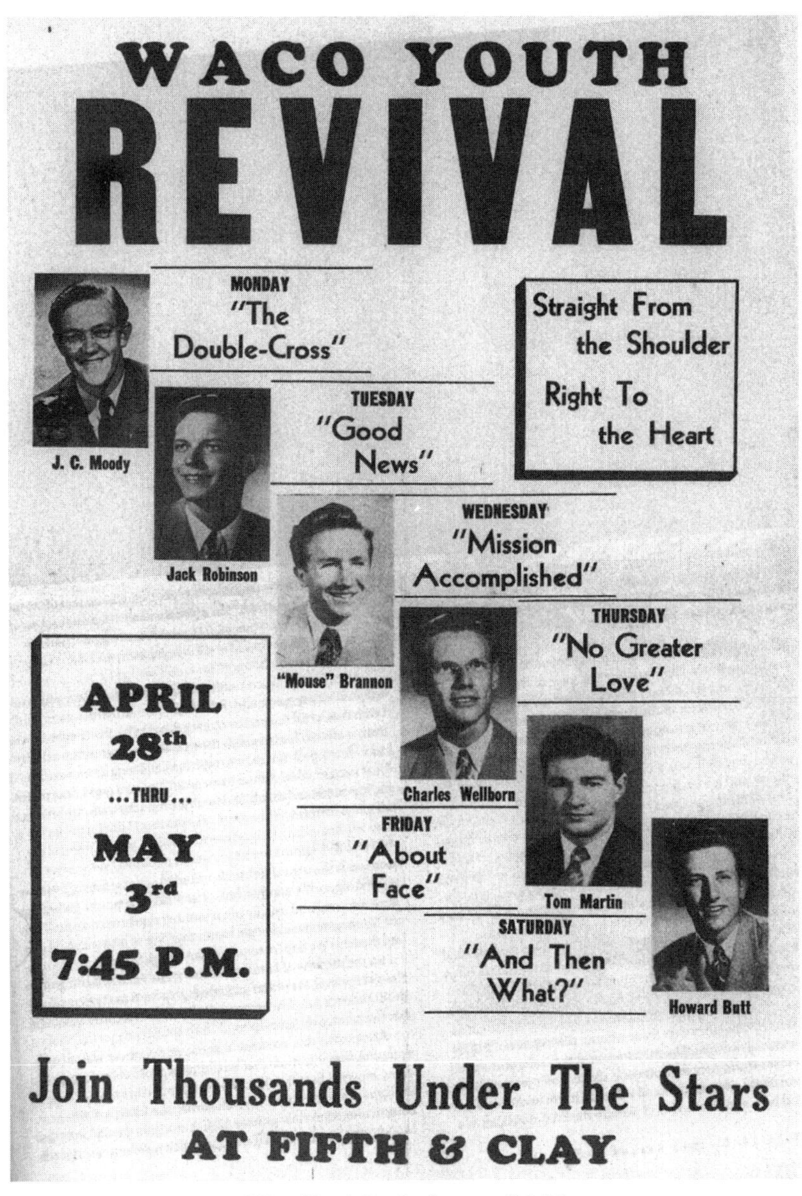

Waco Youth Revival poster (1945)

Bruce McIver

Howard Butt Jr.

BO Baker

Jack Robinson

ONLY 3 MORE NIGHTS

You Will Not Soon See
Another Meeting As Thrilling As

HOUSTON'S YOUTH
REVIVAL

--- TONIGHT ---

WONDERFUL
SINGING

POWERFUL
TESTIMONIES

Ch

Hear This Nationa
pion and Veteran

Speak on

1020 LAMAR

HOUSTON YOUTH REVIVAL

1020 LAMAR — 7:45 PM — JULY 1 THROUGH 6

MONDAY, JULY 1:
J. C. MOODY
"AREN'T YOU GLAD YOU'RE YOU?"

TUESDAY, JULY 2:
JACKIE ROBINSON
"NO, DEVIL!"

WEDNESDAY, JULY 3:
BO BAKER
"WAKE UP OND LIVE"

THURSDAY, JULY 4:
CHARLES WELLBORN
"FACE TO FACE"

FRIDAY, JULY 5:
HOWARD BUTT
"WHAT'S THE HURRY?"

SATURDAY, JULY 6:
BRUCE MCIVER
"ONE THING LACKING"

JACKIE ROBINSON

Former Southwest Conference Basketball star at Baylor. He was pastor of the Ninth Street Mission at Waco while attending Baylor.

BO BAKER

His home is in Farmersville. He is a graduate of Baylor and served two years as State B. S. U. Music Director.

CAPACITY AUDIENCES
Come Early to Take Advantage of Entire Service

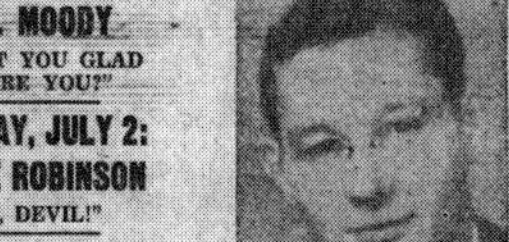

POWERFUL TESTIMONIES
Music That Thrills—
Vital Preaching

HOWARD BUTT

His home is in Corpus Christi. He is not a ministerial student but is planning on religious educational work.

CHARLES WELLBORN

Served with the Tenth Mountain Division Ski Troops in Italy. Is a member of the Baylor faculty.

BRUCE MCIVER

He is the retiring State B.S.U. president. His home is in Siler City, N. C. He expects to enter Southwestern Baptist Seminary this fall.

Howard Butt Jr. in front of a packed FBC-Houston

PRAYER LIST FOR HOUSTON YOUTH REVIVAL
July 1-6, 1946

1. Spiritual power; definite decisions for Christ(800).
2. Complete unity among workers, speakers, musicians, etc.
3. Finances.
4. Fair Weather.
5. Speakers:
   Jack Robinson..
   Howard Butt....
   Bruce McIver..
   Charles Wellborn.
   J. C. Moddy....
   B. O. Baker....
6. Music director.
7. Choir.
8. Special music.
9. Each committee chairman.
10. Each committee member.
11. School and church publicity.
12. Radio programs and spot announcements.
13. Airplane advertising.
14. Good newspaper spots.
15. Cooperation of pastors and city officials.
16. Visitation program.
17. Personal prayer list:
   a.
   b.
   c.
   d.

'I'd Rather Have Jesus.' How about you?

Prayer list for 1946 Houston Youth Revival

"FOLLOW THE LIVING CHRIST"
HOUSTON YOUTH REVIVAL
FIRST BAPTIST CHURCH AUDITORIUM
Lamar at Fannin
JULY THE 1ST THROUGH JULY 6TH

THIS IS THE PLACE
ODESSA CITY-WIDE
YOUTH REVIVAL
EVERYONE
WELCOME
8:15 P.M.
AUG. 15 – 20
PREACHERS BOB HARRIS and DAN RAINBOLT
SONG DIRECTOR BILL TANNER

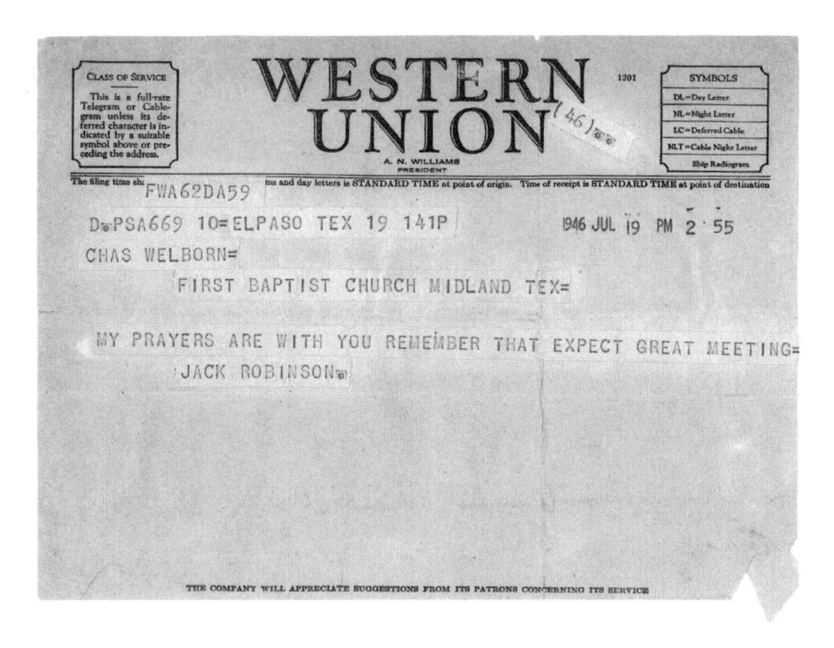

CLASS OF SERVICE
This is a full-rate Telegram or Cablegram unless its deferred character is indicated by a suitable symbol above or preceding the address.

WESTERN UNION

1201

(46)

A. N. WILLIAMS
PRESIDENT

SYMBOLS
DL=Day Letter
NL=Night Letter
LC=Deferred Cable
NLT=Cable Night Letter
Ship Radiogram

The filing time sh... ms and day letters is STANDARD TIME at point of origin. Time of receipt is STANDARD TIME at point of destination

FWA62DA59

D.PSA669 10=ELPASO TEX 19 141P 1946 JUL 19 PM 2 55

CHAS WELBORN=

FIRST BAPTIST CHURCH MIDLAND TEX=

MY PRAYERS ARE WITH YOU REMEMBER THAT EXPECT GREAT MEETING=

JACK ROBINSON.

THE COMPANY WILL APPRECIATE SUGGESTIONS FROM ITS PATRONS CONCERNING ITS SERVICE

Telegram from Jack Robinson to Charles Wellborn

Ninth Street Baptist Mission house, Waco, TX

Cole Park, Dallas Youth Revival (from back)

Cole Park, Dallas Youth Revival (from front)

You'll Enjoy . . .

Fort Worth's City - Wide

Youth Revival

★ You'll be Challenged by the Messages

★ You'll Marvel at the Enthusiasm

★ You'll Thrill to the Singing

8:00 P. M.

JUL

Poly

In S

"Youth

SPONSORED BY

Our team . . .

Bruce McIver

from San Marcos, Texas is a graduate of Baylor University.

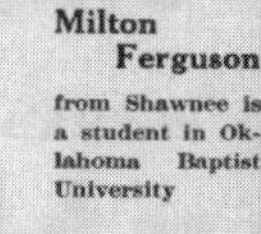

Milton Ferguson

from Shawnee is a student in Oklahoma Baptist University

C. A. Roberts

from Fort Worth is a sophomore at Baylor University

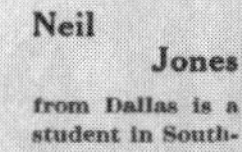

Neil Jones

from Dallas is a student in Southwestern Seminary

Milton DuPriest

from Temple is a graduate of Baylor University

Charles Wellborn

from Gladewater is a graduate of Southwestern Seminary

Charles Strong

from Fort Worth is a sophomore at Baylor University.

Dick Baker

from Farmersville and a graduate of Baylor, will lead the singing.

. . . among the finest

Youth Revival traning clinics. Bill O'Brien teaching and leading.

Howard Butt Jr. (second from right) and Bill Cody (far right) discuss plans for the 1947 Birmingham revival with (l-r) Charles Wellborn and BO Baker.

Birmingham crusade

Howard Butt Jr. (right) welcomes Jack Robinson to preach in the San Antonio Youth Revival. The Shield *was published by Jess Moody.*

"Spreading the Word" favorite publicity stunt. The car signs were designed by George Mostetly (above) and painted by art students on various campuses.

ELEVEN

MIRACLES!

You are the God who performs miracles. (Ps 77:14a)

I shook my head in disbelief and said to a friend, "We've just seen a miracle." A miracle it was. No question about it. Jack Robinson had just scored six points in ten seconds, and the Baylor Bears had beaten the Texas Longhorns in one of the greatest basketball games ever played. Jack scored two points on a beautiful shot from near the top of the circle. A deliberate foul sent him to the line for two more points. As Texas passed the ball in Jack intercepted it and quickly got off another shot. Perfect! Six points in seconds.

The capacity crowd that filled the Marrs McLean Gymnasium on Baylor's campus sat in stunned silence, as if disbelieving what they had just seen. Then, as if someone had pushed a button, unrestrained enthusiasm exploded, rocking the very foundations of the building. In that moment I didn't care if I never saw another basketball game; I had just seen it all! Nothing could top this. Baylor had lost every game in 1944, and recorded eleven losses and one win in 1945. Now it was on its way to winning the Southwest Conference Championship for the first time since 1932. How did this happen? The answer was simple: a freshman by the name of Jack Robinson.

Jack was an all-state performer at Fort Worth's Paschal High School, a team that won the state championship in Austin in 1945. He was an excellent student, a team leader, and a committed Christian — just the kind of student that Mr. Bill Henderson, Baylor's new coach, was looking for as he faced the challenge of rebuilding the basketball program after WWII.

"Come to Baylor," Mr. Bill, as he was affectionately called, said to Jack, "and we'll have a winning program. And bring any of your Paschal friends with you. We'll try to find scholarships for them." Obviously, Jack had scores of scholarship offers from colleges and universities across the nation, but there was a special tug about Baylor. He couldn't put his finger on it, but he felt it keenly. He enrolled in Baylor, bringing with him two high school teammates, Bill Johnson and Ralph Pulley.

Shortly after helping the team win the conference in 1946, Jack was asked to give his testimony in chapel at Baylor. A young Political Science professor, somewhat skeptical of the Christian faith, heard him and wrote an article for *Reader's Digest* on "The Most Unforgettable Person I Ever Met." Within a month of his speaking in chapel, Jack was asked to be one of the preachers in the 1946 Waco Youth Revival. During that week Charles Wellborn, the young Political Science professor, made his own commitment to Christ. Each became a major voice in the Youth Revival movement and in the years that followed.

"It's a miracle!" But behind that miracle was another miracle. Isn't that the way it often happens? Jack Robinson's grandmother was Ellen White, the mother of eight children. She was a gentle, kind woman who struggled as a single parent to provide for the children and to encourage them to make the best of every opportunity that came their way. This is why "Momma," as she was lovingly called, tried against overwhelming odds to send each of her children to Baylor University. Money was scarce, but there was no price tag on prayer, so she prayed each of her children through difficult times.

One Sunday before the turn of the century, young George Truett preached at the Lane Prairie Baptist Church, four miles north of Cleburne, Texas. Momma White was a member of that little church and listened with deep concern as the dynamic young preacher talked about the needs of "saving Old Baylor." The college was $92,000 in debt and faced bankruptcy. When the offering was taken for Baylor at the close of the service, Momma removed a ring from her finger and placed it in the collection plate. Through sacrificial responses like this, "Old Baylor" was saved and the doors of the college did not close. It was a miracle!

Momma White then began to pray for her grandson, Jack. Her prayer was that God would call him into the ministry. To her, this was far more important than his becoming All-State, or All-Conference, or All-American in basketball. The call was even more important than his playing on the US Olympic team.

One Sunday, Momma White arranged for her grandson to preach at Lane Prairie. It was a biting cold day, and the only heat came from a wood-burning stove in the center of the little church. Jack shivered from the cold; so did the nineteen others who had gathered for worship. Jack also shivered from the battle within, the battle over his life's work and the call to the ministry. He knew that his grandmother was praying about that, but he felt he had covered all bases. Like Gideon, the Old Testament character, he had bargained with God. "Lord, if anyone in that service makes a profession of faith, then I'll take that as a sign you want me to preach." He felt a lot of comfort in that prayer. This was a small church that met only twice a month. The weather had kept all but those deeply faithful at home, and surely none of the nineteen would be making a profession of faith. He was safe.

This was one of the first times that Jack had tried to preach, and he wanted to do it right. So he borrowed a large, impressive railroad watch and carefully put it in the vest pocket of his new Robert Hall suit. The watch had a hinge over the face of the dial and a long gold chain that looped through his lapel buttonhole. Three or four times during a sermon the minister would pause, remove the watch from the vest pocket, press a tiny button that caused the ornate hinged front to spring open, study the hour and minute hands carefully, clear his throat, close the face of the dial with a click, put the watch back into his pocket, and continue his message. Jack went through these motions four times in his

11-minute sermon, while every little boy and girl near the front watched in fascination.

He then looked at his watch for the last time, closed his notes, gave the usual invitation to the half-frozen congregation who huddled as close to the wood-burning stove as they dared. But, Jack was confident of one thing as the little group began to sing in unison the first stanza of the closing hymn: he had escaped the call that day. On the third stanza of the song, a woman in her 20s, with a baby on her hip, moved out of the pew and walked down the aisle, past the pot-belly stove, to the spot where Jack was standing. Her words were few and simple. "I want to give my life to Christ," she said. It was a miracle! No other explanation. A miracle.

And a few weeks later, Jack Robinson enrolled in Baylor University on a basketball scholarship, but also as a ministerial student. He had been called of God at Lane Prairie on one of the coldest days of the year. And Momma White was the only person who was not surprised.

During the fall of 1946 a weekend revival was scheduled for the First Baptist Church in Jacksboro, Texas. Even though Charles Wellborn had been a Christian for only a few weeks, he had already become one of the most gifted Youth Revival speakers. Fortunately, he was available for this particular Friday through Sunday engagement. The church was thrilled and the auditorium was filled the first night. Then, on Saturday morning, Dr. Howard received a call that Charles had become ill and needed to cancel his engagement. He went immediately to his list of youth preachers and began making calls to find a replacement. To his surprise, not a person he called was available. It was now noon and he was running out of names — and time.

Then Dr. Howard remembered a new student who had enrolled in Baylor named Buckner Fanning. After spending nearly four years in the South Pacific in the Marine rifle corps Buckner had returned to his home in Dallas. The week he returned he attended the Dallas citywide revival of 1946 and made a commitment of his life to the Lord. A few weeks later he entered Baylor University with a strong feeling that he should study law. During a Religious Emphasis Week on the campus, he shared his testimony in one of the sessions. Dr. W. F. Howard was in the service that night and was moved by what Buckner said and how he said it. He remembered all this as he called Buckner about noon that Saturday.

"Buckner," he said, "Charles Wellborn has been scheduled to preach a revival this weekend at Jacksboro, but he's become ill with some kind of virus. Do you think you could fill in for him? You'll have to preach only three times — tonight and twice tomorrow. I really need you." Obviously, this was unusual since Buckner had no experience preaching, but Dr. Howard, though nervous, still had confidence in him.

Buckner thought about it for a moment and then said, "I think I can do it. I'll get packed and head for Jacksboro within the hour." He also knew that he'd have to pull together something that resembled a "sermon." But he'd heard his friends preach and knew that two or three good points, an illustration and perhaps a poem would get him by.

The auditorium was packed when he arrived at the church that Saturday evening. After a rousing song service the pastor explained that Charles was ill and that Buckner would be taking his place. Buckner marched to the pulpit like a Marine in the rifle corps, went through his three points and closed with the illustration. He looked at his watch and realized that he had preached ten minutes. That's all. Ten. They sang a hymn of invitation and not a single public commitment was made.

The pastor made a feeble comment that "it doesn't take a lot of words to tell the gospel story. This young man has done it in ten minutes. Now, I know you'll want to be back tomorrow to hear him again."

Buckner went to his hotel room devastated. He felt that he had utterly failed. Throughout the night he wrestled with his notes, arranging and rearranging them, but they looked dead on paper — almost as dead as they must have sounded in the Saturday night service. He prayed most of the night, but when Sunday morning came he was still stuck with those same points. He did manage to come up with another illustration. But when he asked the people to stand and sing a hymn of invitation, grown men began to weep and people started down the aisles making their own commitments before the first note was sung. Buckner, like a spectator, stood back and watched God move in the hearts of the people.

On Sunday evening he shared the same three points, rearranged for the third time. He came up with another illustration, looked at his watch, and, sure enough, another ten minute sermon. He then gave an invitation and, to his amazement, watched dozens of people make decisions to follow Christ.

The weekend revival was over and Buckner drove back to Waco. Charles got over the virus and Dr. Howard's nerves settled down. The pastor ignored his own words that "it doesn't take a lot of words to tell the gospel story" and continued preaching long sermons. But a young Marine who had fought across the South Pacific learned that God can take us where we are — as we are — and "stand us up like miracles!"

Milton Cunningham, affectionately known as "Squirrel" to his friends, enrolled in Baylor in the summer of 1945. He was a short little guy with a heart as big as the world, but if you really got to know him, you sensed that his heart was warped and broken. He covered it well with a sense of humor, a winsome personality, and alcohol.

"I was the campus drunk, as you may remember," he said to me as we talked on September 1, 1998.

"Be careful what you say, Milton," I chided. "You know I'm writing a book."

"Put it in," he insisted. " It's the truth and everybody who was there knows it." I always liked Milton's honesty. Like the old cliché, "What you see is what you get."

His size kept him from playing football but he became manager of both the football and baseball teams. The athletes would have done anything for him, but most of the ministerial students, unfortunately, had no idea what to do for him, or with him. Squirrel's spiritual life was in a constant state of turmoil. In Squirrel's own words:

> When I came to Baylor, I didn't want anything to do with the church, and I didn't want to be around anybody that did. My mother died when I was born. My dad told me that it was her prayer that if she had a son, the Lord would use his life. I knew the Lord was calling me to preach, but I just didn't want anything to do with the church. The first time I went to church after I came to Baylor was in April of 1946. The youth revival was being held at 5th and Clay and Jess Moody was preaching. I didn't have a clue in the world about what he said, but I knew the Lord was dealing with my life. I made a decision to stay away from it.
>
> I had all kinds of problems at Baylor. I got kicked out of school three times and returned to my home in California. Dr. W. R. White, the president of Baylor, had always taken an interest in me and would say, "God loves you and cares about you. He wants to use your life."
>
> One night in California I woke Dad up about three o'clock in the morning and told him I was tired of running and he helped me and I committed my life to the Lord. I hitchhiked back to Baylor for Homecoming and met with the football boys I had been running around with. We gathered in some rooms upstairs on the third floor of Brooks Hall. I told them I had surrendered to preach. Sammy Pierce, a fullback, said, "Squirrel, if you mean what you said, we will all stick with you and we will help you. But, if you ever turn back, we won't have anything to do with you."
>
> Dr. White made arrangements for me to get back in school and also sent me out to preach. It was a miracle! I had made up my mind when I surrendered to preach that I would never look back. And I resolved I would never talk about how bad I was and how I had changed. I refused to use the pulpit to define

> what I had done and hadn't done. Keith Parks, Gene Turner, and I were in a youth revival in Galveston. I became restless in my heart and said, "I don't have anything to say. I don't know what to do."
>
> If ever in my life God spoke to me, that night I heard him say, "I want you to tell your story." So, I told my story publicly — for the first time. I finished my story, or the story of how God worked in my life, and gave the invitation. The first person down the aisle was the number one football recruit in the state. Eighty others followed him, surrendering their lives to Christ.
>
> The following week that young man's mother wrote me. She said, "When we walked up the steps to the church he said to me, 'This is the last time I will ever go to church with you. I'm leaving home and I'm going away and I will never go to church again. I hate you and I hate this church.'" The mother concluded the letter with the words, "I want you to know the change we see in our boy."[1]

Squirrel graduated from Baylor. He didn't disappoint his football friends and he became a friend to a host of ministerial students who later would become pastors. He served as vice president of a university until he and his wife, Barbara, went to Africa as missionaries. Later, he pastored churches and served as president of the Baptist General Convention of Texas. And, until his recent retirement, he served as chaplain of Baylor University. One other thing: When Dr. W. R. White — scholar, pastor, and educator — died, at his request his funeral service was conducted by Squirrel, now Dr. Milton Cunningham, who had been expelled from Baylor three times.

There were so many things that happened in those "Halcyon Days," as Katy Stokes describes them, that defy both understanding and explanation. In all sincerity and humility, we look back over the fifty ensuing years and say with awe, "God did something beyond us."

Ralph Langley and I were in a revival in a small West Texas town in 1947. When we arrived, the pastor thrust into our hands fifteen hundred church census cards, listing the names of people and families who did not belong to a church in the town. "Here," he said with a dour expression, "this is your work for the week. I'm expecting you and the youth of the church to visit each of these homes."

We looked at the stack of cards and struggled to conceal our feelings at the moment. Making visits was not the problem; Ralph and I had done that on numerous occasions. And, challenging the youth to assist was not the real problem. Our experiences had taught us that young people would rise to most any need if you loved and, sometimes, laughed them into it. But it was obvious that the gulf between the pastor and the youth in this church was so wide they would have difficulty responding to any challenge.

For three days the people went through the motions of "doing church." They gathered for the worship services, sang the hymns and choruses, and announced the schedule for the following day. The youth remained for the after-church fellowships and seminars. They were especially attentive as we led one seminar on "How to Know the Will of God." Meanwhile, Ralph and I began to count the days until we packed up and moved to our next engagement. This place was "Deadsville," and the quicker we could get out of town, the better.

Then something happened. The youth suggested that we cancel the fellowship scheduled to follow the evening service and that we meet in the basement of the church for a period of prayer. The youth invited the adults to meet with them. In the non-structured, informal service the youth prayed aloud, confessing their own needs, their concerns for the church, and their longing to experience a genuine revival in their hearts. The prayers, void of shallow emotionalism and seasoned in love, continued for more than an hour. Then an unusual thing happened. The pastor, who had slipped into the service unnoticed, rose and said, "Please, could I pray?"

"Father," he began, "you know I have been standing in the way of your work in this church. My attitude has been wrong. I have no joy in my work because I'm not where you want me to be. I'm not in your will, and I haven't been for a long time. Lord, I ask you to forgive me, and I humbly ask these people to forgive me." Quietly, those in the prayer service began to weep. What most of them had sensed had now been confessed. The pastor, in honesty and openness, had found peace.

When we gathered the following evening for the worship service, we didn't "do church"; we worshipped the Living Christ with joy and celebration. When the invitation was given at the close of the service for people to confess Christ as Savior or to join the church, the aisles were filled. This spirit continued throughout the remainder of the week. Revival had taken place throughout the church and in the community. The huge stack of census cards were forgotten as people shared joyfully their faith.

Two weeks later, still basking in the spirit of revival in that west Texas church, Ralph and I received word that the pastor had resigned and another door of opportunity had opened to him. He said he had "found God's will for his life."

There's nothing more difficult than trying to "do church" and not be in the center of God's will. There's nothing more satisfying than doing God's work, regardless how difficult it seems to be, knowing that you are where He wants you to be. It's a lesson that Ralph and I could not have learned in a seminary classroom, as important as the academic studies were. We learned it in a small west Texas town, where both the oilfields and the Spirit of God had dried up. The oilfields remain dry, but the Spirit of God flows again.

Buckner Fanning, Ralph Langley, Jack Robinson, and Frank Boggs were in a citywide revival in Knoxville in 1950. The revival services began in a local church, but the crowds became so large they were forced to move to the gymnasium on the campus of the University of Tennessee. "It was one of the most remarkable experiences of my life," Buckner observes. " It was truly a revival." Those in charge of arrangements wanted to continue the revival for another week. Both Jack and Ralph had other engagements, but Buckner and Frank remained for the second week.

The Tennessee School for the Deaf is located in Knoxville. One day Buckner and Frank were invited to conduct services there. Frank sang, and even though the students couldn't hear the music, the words of the songs were signed for them. Buckner preached, and again, his message was interpreted through signing. A couple of nights later two girls from the School for the Deaf attended the revival services at the gymnasium. When the invitation was given both girls came forward, indicating they were making some kind of commitment to Christ. There was not an interpreter with them so communication was practically impossible. Buckner went to a microphone and asked the crowd, "Is there anyone here who can sign for the deaf?" Someone responded, "Sure, I can do it." Through the interpreter the girls told Buckner that they had sensed deeply the presence of God. They knew, also, that God loved them and Christ died for them. They wanted to commit their lives to the Lord.

"This was an humbling thing to me," Buckner adds. "It reminded me that we try to 'preach the stars down.' We want to do the best we can. That's okay. But here were two people who didn't hear a word I said, and couldn't understand a thing I said. They just watched other people, and opened their lives to the Spirit of God."

Buckner paused, and then quietly said, "This is both reassuring . . . and humbling."[2]

Miracles!

NOTES

[1] Milton Cunningham, correspondence with the author.

[2] Buckner Fanning, correspondence with the author.

TWELVE

THE CALL TO EXCELLENCE

Whatever you do, work at it with all your heart.
(Col 3:23)

Dr. John Newport, an outstanding scholar, served on the faculty of Southwestern Baptist Theological Seminary for many years. Dr. Kenneth Scott Latourette, a Yale professor, pioneered studies in both Asian history and the global history of the church. He studied what he called the "advances and recessions" of the church, emphasizing that every advance brought unforeseen results that shaped civilization. In the late 1940s, the two scholars were crossing the Atlantic on the same ship, the Queen Mary. "I had seen Dr. Latourette in the Louisville Center of Southern Baptist Seminary," Newport said. "He came there while I was a student. We had lunch together two or three times on the ship. During our conversations we talked about what was going to happen to Christian work and to Baptist life."

Over one of those meals Dr. Latourette observed, "I think Southern Baptists will become the largest and most dynamic Protestant denomination in the United States because of what is happening. In the Youth Revival Movement and the Student Movement (the Baptist Student Union) you are not just getting numbers, you are also getting quality. The young people who are yielding to the call of full-time Christian service in your denomination — as I understand it — are not the 'second-rate fringe people.' They are the outstanding students on the university campuses. So you will not only have the largest number because of this dynamic movement, but you will have quality people."

Obviously, it will be left to history to define and interpret such words as "cream of the crop" and "brightest," but that was one of the goals that Dr. W. F. Howard had in mind as he enlisted and supervised those who served on youth revival teams. His standards were high, and there was no place for compromise. A student selected to preach, lead the music, preside over seminars, or direct fellowships was expected to be at his best at all times. From his first interview to his last written report by the pastor and local church where he served, the student was thoroughly evaluated.

Dr. Howard, a man of profound wisdom, sensed a deep stewardship as requests for youth revivals poured into his office. Weary pastors, who had walked with their congregations through both a depression and a war, were looking for a new day in ministering; battle-scarred veterans were hoping for different kinds of victories; parents were praying that their children and grandchildren would be spared what they had endured; victorious military leaders were asking for missionaries to be sent all over a world ravaged by the war; and youth were facing both challenges and options in Christian service never before available. New doors were opening, and students by the thousands were ready to walk through those doors.

The Department of Student Work kept careful statistics as youth revival teams were sent out and as revivals were conducted. A capsule of events from 1946 to 1962 is most revealing. During those 17 years, 1,560 revivals were booked through the department. When the invitations were given, 54,916 made public Christian commitments and recorded these on cards made available to them. Of that number, 3,681 committed their lives to some kind of Christian ministry (preaching, youth ministry, music, missionary work, etc.), and 10,024 made first-time professions of faith to follow Christ.

These statistics, of course, do not include hundreds of commitments made in revivals not officially sponsored through the Department of Student Work. There is no way to gather all this information, but more than fifty years later, we're still hearing about revivals, rallies, and commitment services where scores of young people responded to the challenge. While it's impossible to capsule the statistics of a movement, it's not hard to see the quality of their commitment lived out through the years.

For instance, I first met Pat in Lamesa, Texas, when he was 14 years of age and in the 8th grade. He was a leader among the students and he and his parents were pillars of the church. Later, Pat graduated from college and was accepted into medical school. He did his residency at Minneapolis and would often fly his own plane from Minnesota to Dallas, spend the night with us, and then fly on to Lamesa for a brief visit with his family. For more than forty years he has been in practice as a plastic surgeon in Austin. From the 8th grade his friendship has enriched me.

In a recent conversation with Pat I asked, "What did youth revivals do to and for you? What lasting impressions were left upon your life?"

Pat thought for a moment, and then said, "I sensed the integrity of living, and not just talking." There was another pause, and he added, "I also sensed the sanctity of vocation. I realized I didn't have to be a preacher to preach; I could serve the Lord through medical practice."

That's the kind of preaching Dr. Pat Beckham has done year after year in his office and in the surgical suite. This call to ministry also takes him and a group of other doctors to Central America each year as they perform reconstructive surgery on the faces and bodies of little children trapped in birth deformities. They do this, joyfully, at their own expense.[1] This was what the great Yale historian was talking about as he conversed on the deck of the Queen Mary with Dr. Newport: "Not just numbers, but quality." The kind of quality that spans nearly a century — a genuine respect for people, and a commitment through surgical skills to repair broken, malformed bodies so a person can feel whole again.

As the requests for Youth Revival teams flooded the office of the Department of Student Work, Dr. Howard was faced with the growing dilemma of finding students to staff the teams requested. Most teams consisted of four people: two preachers who alternated in presenting sermons; a musician who could lead congregational singing, direct a choir, and, hopefully, sing solos; and a young woman who usually planned after-service fellowships and directed seminars, or discussions, on current problems facing the youth. Of course, each team member shared some of the weight of the total program, including visitation and witnessing to those who were not Christians.

Those assigned to teams needed to be mature enough not to embarrass the church or the pastor, yet young enough in spirit to appeal to the young people. They needed to be professional enough to get the job done, but amateur enough to be refreshing. They needed to be strong in their convictions, yet respectful of the views of others. They needed to be secure enough to stand alone, but wise enough to work with others. And, they needed to dress appropriately, pick up their clothes, pay their phone bills, abide by policies, and learn to say "Thank you." The churches were asked to pay each team member — preachers, musicians, and leaders of fellowships and seminars — the same amount of money, usually $50 or less. Even in the '40s, thankfully, women were paid the same as men.

Finding students who measured up to these standards was a challenge, but the newness of the Youth Revival program, the success of several citywide campaigns, a call from General MacArthur in Japan to "send us a thousand missionaries," and the concern of veterans who had fought around the world that we go back into that same world and win people to Christ caused students to rise to the occasion. Many saw it as an opportunity to do something positive in a world still reeling from depression and war.

One of the stories often told at large student gatherings in the '40s concerned a pastor who was looking for a globe of the world that had been removed from his study. He was told an adult Sunday School department had borrowed it and somehow it had become misplaced. He sent a custodian to look for it. The custodian returned empty-handed and said, "Pastor, the adults said they've lost the world, but they've got some young people looking for it. When they find it, they'll bring it back to your office." Right or wrong, there was a feeling among some that the adults had "lost the world." It would now be up to the youth to find it and build it into something better. So, for the first time people could remember, doors were flung open and the youth were given major responsibilities in churches, and later, in denominations. Youth buildings, youth activities, youth directors, youth choirs, youth days, youth weeks, and youth conferences became familiar terms in many of our growing churches. And 18- and 19-year-old young people preached and sang and led conferences, while adults cheered them on. It was a new day — a day that demanded quality.

But who determined quality? How were the teams chosen? Who assigned them? What were the logistics? Early in the fall semester each year Dr. Howard, or one of his associates, began visiting campuses in Texas, interviewing prospective Youth Revival team members. Notices were posted on each campus announcing the visit and Baptist Student Union directors, or other responsible persons, helped set up the interviews. The task was challenging, often involving personal conferences with as many as 30 or 40 students in one visit to a campus. The task was challenging, also, because the brief conferences often determined if the students would be asked to attend a Youth Revival clinic held each year in the February. Attendance at the clinic was essential if the student planned to work in the Youth Revival program the following summer. It was the only focused training he or she would receive. Dress, appearance, manners, first impressions, grades, leadership on the campus, preaching and singing experience and letters of recommendations all became a part of the student's file. Obviously, strong leaders were discovered through this process; unfortunately, some were missed through human error.

For instance, while I was Dr. Howard's associate (1956–1958) it was my responsibility to oversee the Youth Revival program. I visited the campuses, interviewed the students, planned the Youth Revival clinics and sent letters of invitation to those selected to attend. I also scheduled the revivals and assigned teams to the churches. We had a policy — for good or bad — that no student would work in Youth Revival without a personal interview, a face-to-face encounter with those of us responsible for sending out the teams.

Bill Pinson, a student from North Texas University, had already been chosen to preach the following summer in the program. He wrote me several letters about an "outstanding" young man, also from North Texas. "He is an excellent communicator, the most gifted student on any campus, and one who should not be overlooked," Bill insisted. The problem was that the young man was in graduate school in Edinburgh, Scotland, and would not be returning to the States in time for a personal interview prior to the summer schedule. So, I thanked Pinson every time he contacted me about his friend, explained our policy, laid the letter aside, and muttered something about "rules are rules" and should not be broken. I learned in the process that Pinson had run for president of the student body and that his friend, a young man named Moyers, had been his manager. Pinson, of course, had won the election, but I turned *Bill Moyers* down, because "rules are rules."

Several years later I attended a Christian Life Conference in Washington. Bill Moyers had become the chief aide to President Johnson who invited the group to the White House. While standing in the Rose Garden I whispered to Bill, "You know, Bill, the greatest favor I ever did for you was to turn you down for youth revivals!" And, to this day, my friends will not let me forget my wisdom and insight in rejecting one of the sharpest minds and best communicators on the American scene!

Out of the scores of students interviewed on campuses, about 120 were invited to the youth revival clinic, usually held over a long weekend at Mt. Lebanon, an encampment about twenty miles from Dallas. The retreat was a time of instruction, inspiration, and fellowship. Interestingly, many of the speakers for the program were older students who had themselves participated in youth revivals. For instance, a notebook for the 1963 clinic lists the program guests: Jimmy Allen, James Barber, Kenneth Chafin, Louis Cobbs, Lester Collins, Harles Cone, S. L. Harris, W. F. Howard, T. B. Maston, Bruce McIver, Bill O'Brien, and Britton Wood. Many of these could share straight from their own experiences in working with pastors and churches in youth revivals. Some on the program could tell the youth revival story from the early days in 1945–1946. This gave a personal touch to the movement and caused new team members to feel that they were a part of something very special.

When the clinic was over and the evaluations were in, sixty or seventy students were chosen to participate in revivals for the coming summer. From February until June requests from local churches were processed, student leaders were assigned according to ability, experience, and availability, and confirmations were returned to pastors. Those students who were not chosen to work in revivals usually found other opportunities for ministry and often worked on revival teams the following year.

The program guide for the 1963 Youth Revival Clinic, like those for each year, spells out in simple language guidelines for conduct, practical problems, and the building of lasting relationships. A section under "Do's and Don'ts" is as timeless today as it was then.

> **DO:**
> Notify the pastor about the time and means of your arrival. Plan to travel in such as way as to guarantee your arrival and departure according to this schedule.
>
> **DON'T:**
> Travel by plane when some other means of transportation is possible — even if the cost is relatively the same. This will prevent much criticism.
>
> **DO:**
> Seek to know and honor the pastor's plans for the meeting, to counsel with him, and to magnify his leadership in every possible way . . . .

Be considerate and thoughtful with other team members — even if it hurts!
Differences of opinion will arise...but remember that there is A CHRISTIAN WAY to do everything that should be done.
Begin the service on time . . . .
Be careful with your relationships with the opposite sex . . . be courteous and respectful to all . . . dating during the revival is out!
Spend some time alone each day.
Be clean and neat in your appearance.
Keep your conversation on a high plane . . . in private as well as public.

DON'T:
"Take over" the church office during the revival.
Consider yourself a missionary for the school you attend.
Be lazy.
Invite your girlfriend or bring your wife to a revival.
Ride personal jokes to the extreme.
Openly disagree with team members on controversial issues.
Be critical of your colleagues or of local people.
Succumb to the temptation of professionalism. Maintain that fresh "amateurishness" which reflects the youthful sincerity of your heart.

DO:
Respect the plans the local youth committee has made.
Write "thank you" notes to the pastor, staff, and those who entertained you.
Look for ways to strengthen any decisions which were made during the revival.

DON'T:
Be proud or boastful when you return to your campus.
Leave the city without making arrangements to pay for personal toll charges, laundry, cleaning, and so forth.[2]

It was not unusual for Dr. Howard to receive 125 to 150 invitations from churches asking for Youth Revival teams for the summer months. In addition, many churches scheduled weekend revivals, beginning on Friday night and concluding on Sunday night. With these demands, it was impossible to send the best youth preachers and the finest musicians to every church. There is a sense in which the clinics became crash courses, helping students prepare for their work in the churches. It is amazing how quickly they learned, and how fast they grew.

Obviously, the "Do's and Don'ts" were essential as the potential team leaders were brought together. These provided guidelines for discipline, established accountability, and created moral and ethical responsibility. One errant team member could wreck team unity, embarrass those who sent him out, and hinder the Spirit of Christ. The greater contribution, however, came in the heart-to-heart sharing.

One year, a student who had just finished his first year in the seminary was invited to be a clinic leader. He had been converted in a Youth Revival and had preached in scores of them. He was a delightful person, an excellent communicator, and one of the most sought after Youth Revival preachers anywhere. Standing before an open fireplace, he shared a discovery he had made during his busy year at the seminary. With the daily academic demands and the continuing invitations for him to conduct weekend revivals, he had neglected his own personal devotional life. He made a commitment during this hectic time that he would rise each morning at 5:00 and spend an hour in Bible study and prayer. It had changed his life. It made a profound impact on everyone at the clinic. Dr. W. F. Howard, our leader, slipped out of the lodge that night and was gone for an hour. Later, he shared quietly with me that he had been down in the woods, searching his own heart, and making a vow to practice the same discipline in his own life. I knew the man well — very well — and, for the next 50 years, I never knew of a day when his alarm clock did not signal him to Bible study and prayer. Dr. Howard didn't talk often about his own spiritual discipline, and he didn't include it in his list of "Do's and Don'ts," but his spirit rubbed off on those who knew him. And that same spirit touched the lives of more than a hundred students who attended that clinic. This is one student sharing with others, in honesty and openness. It's excellent teaching, and, occasionally, even the best of leaders are taught!

Late in the spring months the requests for revivals were reviewed, the abilities of those chosen to attend the Youth Revival clinic were evaluated, and maps of Texas and surrounding states were studied. Then, letters and schedules were sent to the sixty or seventy who would serve on the teams. The pastors and churches also received a letter naming the team assigned to their church. Of course, special requests were honored when possible.

Through the years, literally thousands of students were involved in this process: the initial interview, the Youth Revival clinic, the responsibilities in churches and in cities, the education of working as a team, the experience of working with mature, seasoned pastors, and the fellowship of sharing with other students. There is no doubt that the thorough approach given to this selection process helped develop the quality people Dr. Latourette had mentioned.

Bill Tanner, long-time pastor, denominational leader, and president of the Home Mission Board for Southern Baptists observes:

> I didn't realize it at the time; I wish I had, but those of us who worked on teams were recipients of an uncanny trust level from the youth in the churches where we ministered. I think the experiences of youth revivals gave an opportunity for the participants to observe first-hand how strong, solid churches operated. I have often said that it put me ten years ahead in ministry, and I really believe it did. We saw the leadership style of the pastors; they were different. We saw the effect of a team, in some instances, of called professionals working together. We saw how programs for the areas of work were devised and organized and decided upon and put into effect. And often, we were informed of their success or failure. Occasionally, we even met with some church committees. All in all, I conservatively calculate experience-wise, my three years in the Youth Revivals put me ahead a decade in the ministry, and not only in ministry, but in churchmanship.

> . . . I know this is true — I lived through it at Westend Baptist Church in Houston, Texas. I went to the church at age 22. They had an unhappy situation. It was an inter-city type church, not yet in transition as it would become. We built a building; we were averaging about 1,100 people in Sunday School; and one year, we led all the Baptist churches in Houston in the number of baptisms. There is no way someone who is 22 years old, who never pastored anything but a half-time church at Whetlock, Texas, could live through five years of that experience without being burned in effigy! We did it in part because of the experiences and things I had seen, observed, and heard in those 40 or 50 Youth Revivals in which I participated.[3]

Cecil Sherman, former head of the Cooperative Baptist Fellowship and now a professor at the Baptist Theological Seminary at Richmond, reflects on the clinics and the contributions that youth revivals, in general, made upon his life:

> Youth revivals were a schoolmaster to me. I listened as W. F. Howard instructed us in how we were to act while on assignment. Mainly he addressed manners and ethics. Those instructions have served me well the past 50 years.
>
> I watched pastors in the churches where I was sent. They affirmed me; they coached me. Never did they put me down or diminish my efforts . . . though often they must have been weak. I learned some humility. Not all ministerial students are born equal. Some have more ability than others. Some are good when they are 22. Some will not get good until later. Some are still waiting.
>
> I learned the politics of life. Not always did the people I thought best qualified get the first assignments or the desirable assignments . . . . Life has been much like youth revivals. Much later some were asked to important churches and others were not. Dealing with those questions and dealing with them in a way that leaves the soul intact is a pretty important lesson for a young man to learn.

> I learned some social skills. A hundred times I was a guest in a home. Some dear woman had gone to some trouble to feed the youth revival team. Talking to her (and others), saying thank you, eating with good manners . . . in all these things I was blessed and hurried toward some maturity. Such would serve me well when I became a pastor.
>
> Youth revivals marked the way I measured evangelism. I saw good evangelism; I saw bad evangelism. Until I was in youth revivals I don't think I knew the difference. While in youth revivals I began putting what I saw in those revivals alongside what I read in the New Testament. That has been helpful to me . . . . I came to a lifelong commitment to New Testament evangelism.... We are assigned to go and tell. Youth revivals helped me see the Bible base for this work.[4]

George Mosier uses the word "awe" repeatedly as he remembers the Youth Revival Clinics. Listen as he shares his memories:

> Freshly equipped with release papers from the Marine Corps, a Scofield Bible, one sermon plagiarized from C. Roy Angel and twenty-five dollars, I entered Howard Payne College . . . . I became active in the Baptist Student Union and was asked to speak (or give a sermon) on several occasions. I now had memorized Vance Havener's sermon, "Empty Hands."
>
> During my sophomore year Dr. W. F. Howard took an interest in me and suggested I apply to attend the Clinic for Youth Revivals. By now I had personalized those two sermons and divided them into four, having met Chester Swor, the popular student speaker, who suggested I "outline simply and illustrate profusely." I packed for the trip to Mt. Lebanon for the Clinic. Shiny shoes, heavily starched shirts and a sharkskin suit that glowed in the dark was my total list of gear.
>
> Awe was my first impression. Awe lingered throughout the meeting while I lingered near the back of the room. No one has ever believed me to be shy or to feel inadequate. But I did that day . . . .
>
> We were told at the close of the Clinic that assignments would be made soon. I expected making one revival. When the letter arrived, I carried it to the prayer chapel. Finally, I opened

> it and saw a blinding array of large and small churches. For five summers my schedule was full.
>
> Looking back, I still get hit by awe — awe that I had the opportunity to preach, awe that I worked with some great team members, and awe that God used us with some degree of effectiveness. Forty years later I still pick up Vance Havener's book, recall great things God did through all of us and say, "Thank you, Lord."[5]

In 1970, my wife, Lawanna, and I were in Israel. We drove to the top of Mt. Carmel, located near the port of Haifa, hoping to visit briefly with one of my "heroes," Dwight Baker. Dwight and I had preached together in youth revivals in the late '40s and now he and his wife, Emma, were missionaries to Israel. Unfortunately, they were not home that day and we were on a typical tight travel schedule. It would be 25 years before I heard his full story. He recently shared it with me in Dallas, Texas.

Dwight was a paratroop chaplain in Germany in 1947. A group of servicemen started a Saturday night rally and asked him to be their sponsor. Dozens of young men and women from various branches of the armed services came to Christ at those rallies. Dwight also became a friend of the pastor of the First Baptist Church in Frankfurt. The church had been badly damaged by bombs. Windows were shattered and there were gaping holes in the roof. Through Dwight's efforts and the approval of senior officers, the windows and the roof were fixed. No heat was available, but the people flocked to the church in the cold winter months, filling it beyond capacity on both Sundays and Wednesdays.

Dwight shares his story:

> One day Pastor Gronenberg asked if I would like to visit the church's orphanage for children who had lost one or both parents in the war. There at the back of the church and into a small courtyard some thirty children were at play, being gently herded by two starched, white-capped deaconesses. Came snack time and they were given water and a bit of unidentifiable substance. I got together with some of my leaders and described the make-

> shift orphanage and its paucity of supplies. They immediately declared a panacea. We would bring all our weekly rations of candy, cookies, and fruit juices and take them to the orphanage. These wonderful service men and women adopted this group of war orphans and cared for their many needs. We found a second orphanage run by Lutheran Sisters and opened a similar pipeline to their children.
>
> In the course of ministering to more children than we had supplies for, we alerted friends and families back home to the plight of our kids. Soon boxes of food and clothing began arriving, creating two happy groups: our service people who reveled in the joys of giving, and the thankful children and surviving parents who were the recipients . . . . These grateful German people, working in the churches and orphanages, dubbed our small band of Christian serving people, "The Angels of Frankfurt."

Dwight's tour was over and he returned to Texas — the "Angel of Frankfurt" and a hero to all who knew of his work in Germany. Invitations came for him to speak throughout the nation. There were rallies, parades, and overwhelming expressions of gratitude. During these "halcyon days," as he describes them, an unexpected letter came from a strict Baptist denominational leader, criticizing him and chastising him for giving his time and energy to an "outside group." The insensitive writer argued that Dwight should be giving his time and energy working through the local church and through established programs in the local church.

The "Angel of Frankfurt" (now with clipped wings!) continues:

> I was pretty dismayed over this rebuke which I didn't believe was fair or deserved After wrestling with it for a few days, I visited with W. F. Howard, head of Texas Baptist Student work. He listened as I expressed my sense of disillusionment for I considered myself a loyal Baptist and not an ecclesiastical adventurer on an egoistic roll. Then without a word of criticism, he asked if I would participate in Texas Baptist youth revivals that by this time were reaching out to young and old

> alike in Texas and in southern states. Would I ever! A good word from Foy Valentine enhanced the interview and glory descended!
>
> For many months I joined hands and hearts with teammates made up of friends from earlier Baylor and Southwestern Seminary days, preaching, praying, and playing (believe me, we had fun!) from the deep valley of the Rio Grande to the plains of Oklahoma: Charles Wellborn, Bruce McIver, Foy Valentine, Ralph Langley, young Doug Dillard (freshly out of high school) Helen Jean Bond (now Mrs. Keith Parks), Dorris Cummins, Ross Coggins, Dennis Harris, Leeta Bean and others. The joy of winning souls to Christ, seeing commitments made to the Lord's service, bonding with pastors and their flocks — to say nothing of frolicking with other youth revival team members was unspeakable!

Dwight closes his letter with a provocative question and sobering observation:

> Some will ask, "Will there be another authentic, Spirit-fed movement for Christ like the Texas youth revivals of the 1940s?"
>
> Others advise, "Don't pray, Lord, do it again; rather wait and pray for a totally new out-burst of Spirit revelation."
>
> Is it up for silly debate or vote? Whatever form, shape, or magnitude it may take there will be some of the same elements that exploded Texas youth revivals over and within the hearts of many Texans: prayer and more prayer, expectancy, and the enthusiastic belief that there is another one out there and God is waiting to turn it loose, again and again and again.[6]

Dwight Baker, who with his wife, Emma, spent most of their adult lives as missionaries in Israel and India, is right: "God is waiting to turn it loose, again and again and again."

But the key now is the same as the key then. In the words of Latourette: "Quality." God's quality stamped upon our lives.

NOTES

[1] As I was typing the above paragraph the postman came with the annual Valentine letter from Jo Beckham, Pat's 95-year-old mother. She gives piano concerts for senior citizen groups and urges her friends to master the computer, especially e-mail. Listen to her words: " My health is blessed of the Lord and my days are brightened by the e-mail my computer brings from missionaries and family scattered around the world . . . . I send weekly e-mails, called 'Footprints,' that carry a short encouraging devotional with scripture, praise, and prayer. They go to the far-away ones as well as family and friends at home. As their replies thank us for our prayers and tell of needs, we send scriptures that give strength. Jo Beckham."

I read Jo Beckham's annual "love letter" and remembered with gratitude her hospitality and her prayers for those of us on Youth Revival teams assigned to Lamesa for a week's revival every summer in the late '40s and early '50s. I smiled as I thought of Windy, her late husband, and his down-to-earth sense of humor and his encouragement to the Youth Revival team members. And then the words of their physician son hit me, "integrity of living" and "sanctity of vocation."

[2] From 16th Youth-Led Revival Clinic Booklet, 1963.

[3] Bill Tanner, conversation with the author.

[4] Cecil Sherman, correspondence with the author.

[5] George Mosier, correspondence with the author.

[6] Dwight Baker, correspondence with the author.

THIRTEEN

SERENDIPITY

The wind blows wherever it wishes. (Jn 3:8)

One of my favorite words is "serendipity." The dictionary defines it as the "faculty of making happy discoveries by accident." The research and the writing of this book has been filled with such serendipity. I'd look under one rock in my research and find another. I'd chase a particular story and discover three others in the process. Almost daily, I'd find myself saying, "I didn't know that" or "Look what I found." One revival led to other revivals; one commitment led to dozens of other commitments; one decision for Christ led to unbelievable experiences around the world. And, when the last page of this book is written, the half will not have been told. The wind of God's Spirit does blow where it wishes, and wherever it blows there is another serendipity. Here are a few:

KEITH PARKS: THE MISSIONARY ILLITERATE WHO BECAME A MISSIONARY STATESMAN

"I was a missionary illiterate," Keith Parks said to me as we lunched at a quaint little hideaway restaurant in Dallas called "Sweet Temptations."

"A missionary illiterate?" I questioned. "Tell me about it."

That was all the prodding needed as Keith opened up and shared his story.

"I grew up on a farm in a remote area of Arkansas, "he began. "We had a little church in the area that had 'preaching' once a month, whether we needed it or not! Usually some student from the seminary in Fort Worth would come out and preach to us. There was no Sunday School, no mission activities or education, no training, no youth programs — just preaching once a month.

"When I graduated from high school," Keith continued, "my family moved to Denton, Texas, where I attended North Texas State University. Before long, I met some students on the campus who belonged to the Baptist Student Union (BSU). Word reached us all the way from Waco that a revival had broken out among the students at Baylor and hundreds were making commitments to follow Christ. This impressed us deeply, and we said, 'If the Baylor students can do it, so can we.' We began planning immediately for a revival in Denton."

I listened in fascination as Keith relived those days.

"We found a church on the outskirts of Denton that was about to close its doors. The building was practically falling down and the little congregation had no pastor. We shared with them our dream for revival services to be conducted on a Friday though Sunday and they gladly gave us use of the facility. With a great deal of excitement we scrubbed the building, cleaned it up and, in some cases, propped it up. A chaplain who had just been released from military service was enlisted to preach the revival. Students were enlisted to serve on committees, publicity saturated the campus, and we were all set to begin the services."

Keith paused, took another sip of coffee, and continued, "Then the chaplain bailed out. I don't know what happened," he added, "but we found ourselves with a revival scheduled and no preacher. We called an urgent meeting of the student leaders and they came up with a unanimous decision."

"And what was that?" I asked, sensing the plot of his story deepening.

"They voted that I should be the preacher."

I smiled, but Keith shook his head in disbelief, even after 50-plus years.

"I'd never preached a sermon in my life," he protested as if still pleading his case. "I didn't know what to say and had no idea what I'd do when it came time to give an invitation. How do you do it? What do you say? And what happens if someone responds?"

"Well," he continued, "I didn't want to let my fellow students down, and I sure didn't want to let the Lord down, so I told them I'd try to get a sermon or two. With that, I went to my room and began to write my first sermon ever. I used every theological word and expression I'd ever heard. I scripted an outline that should impress anyone, but as I read it out loud, it sounded flat, absolutely flat. And, the more I read, the flatter it became. From the beginning, I had been drawn to John 3:16. But who wants to hear a sermon on John 3:16? It's so elementary. So simple. Everybody knows about John 3:16. Why, I heard about John 3:16 in that little rural church in Arkansas."

Friday night came, and Keith, filled with fear and trembling, stood to preach. To his own surprise he laid his carefully prepared notes aside and began preaching on (you guessed it) John 3:16. When he had finished his brief message he found himself giving an invitation and meeting people at the front of the little church. "It felt so warm and natural," he said. "I had a feeling that I was standing there watching God do His work."

When the weekend emphasis had concluded, thirteen people had given their lives to Christ and John 3:16 became alive in their hearts. And just as important, something new and wonderful came alive in Keith's heart that later would touch the entire world.

His story was not finished. During his second year at North Texas someone said to him, "Keith, you should apply for summer mission work next summer."

"What's that?" Keith asked sincerely.

"Well, it's a new opportunity for students from campuses here to go to other parts of the world and do mission work for the three-month period between the spring and fall semesters. The idea originated in Hawaii after a citywide youth revival in

Honolulu, but students are now going to other parts of the world. You apply for the work and are then interviewed by other students and student leaders from across the state. If you are selected, they send you where the needs are the greatest and where your skills match those needs. There is no salary, but your expenses are paid and you'll have a view of mission needs that will make a profound difference in your life."

Keith followed the procedures and was selected to go with three other young men to San Andreas, a small island off the coast of Venezuela. When they landed they discovered a breakdown in communications and no one met them. They finally established contact with missionaries who told them to check into the airport hotel for the night. The missionaries had never worked with "summer missionaries," but they assured Keith and his friends they would find something for them to do the next day.

"We walked to the hotel, dragging our luggage behind us," Keith continued. "The manager took one look at us and must have sized us up as four 'rich Americans.' I could almost see the dollar marks in his eyes. He immediately showed us the penthouse while I protested in broken Spanish, 'No dinero. No dinero' (No money! No money!). To underscore this I added, 'muy probres, muy probus' (very poor, very poor!). Slowly and painfully he got the message as he led us down the stairs and showed us our rooms — in the basement where we spent a miserable night. Insects were everywhere. The big bars on the windows kept the large mosquitoes out," he said with a grin, "but the smaller ones got in and kept us awake all night.

"The next day the missionaries picked us up and we were off to begin a Bible School for the children. There had been no preparation and no promotion, but kids came from everywhere to attend. After the morning Bible School we knocked on doors throughout the day, gathering information and sharing our faith with people. In the evenings we had revival meetings. I've never worked so hard in all my life, but I loved every minute of it. Before the summer was over I began to say to myself, 'I think I'd like to spend the rest of my life doing this around the world.'"

That, of course, is exactly what he did. After graduating from the Seminary he and his wife, Helen Jean, left for Indonesia in 1954 where they served as missionaries for 14 years. He then accepted the position as Area Director for Southeast Asia where he worked for eight years. He returned to the States in 1976 and became Director of the Mission Support Division of the Foreign Mission Board for Southern Baptists. In 1980 he became President of the Foreign Mission Board, a position he held until his retirement in 1993.

The young man who was a "Missionary Illiterate" had spent 38 years serving as a missionary around the world. But he was not through. He then gave another six years as Coordinator of Global Missions for the Cooperative Baptist Fellowship.

The lunch hour had come and gone, and Sweet Temptations was empty of customers — except for the two of us. We continued to sit in silence as I tried to absorb what I had heard and experienced from this statesman. There remained one more question to be asked.

"Keith, if there had been no youth revivals, and if there had been no summer mission programs, would you have spent your life as a career missionary?"

Without a moment's hesitation, he replied. "No. It was through these that the doors to missions for me were opened."

Two weeks later I ate again at Sweet Temptations. The food was good; the memories were better.

BILL AND VETA SHERMAN: THE GENTLE BREEZE OF THE CARIBBEAN

Bill and Veta Sherman were asked to serve as summer missionaries in Jamaica in 1954. It was unusual for a husband and wife to be sent as a team in those days, but the gifts of the Shermans matched the needs facing the churches there. It turned out to be a wonderful marriage for everyone. Read and listen as Bill shares their story.

I preached in the Baptist church in Oracabessa, a small town on the coast, for the first five weeks we were there. The pastor, Rev. O. T. Johnson, was doing missionary work in Belize for the Jamaica Baptist Union. While he was away, we stayed in the pastor's house high on a bluff overlooking the blue Caribbean. In addition to preaching on Sundays we held a Vacation Bible School in two of the churches of Rev. Johnson's circuit of churches. It was during the VBS in Oracabessa that we became acquainted with a shy seventeen-year-old teenager, Vinston Clemetson. He lived with his grandmother. His dad had disowned him. In short, he was the town hell-raiser, but we did not know it. He came to Bible school, was in my class of teenagers, took us to get bamboo, took us "sea-bathing" (the Jamaican term for swimming) and what have you.

On Friday night after the commencement exercise around 10:05 p.m., he showed up on the front porch of the parsonage. Mrs. Johnson vehemently denied him entrance. She said, 'No one of your character can set foot in here.' I was startled. He wanted to speak to 'one of the students.' I told him I would talk with him. So we went down by the shore of the Caribbean and this is what he said: 'I've tried all the ways of my friends and they have not led me to happiness. I have seen happiness in the lives of your students. Tell me what it is so I can experience it, too.'

I asked him if anyone had ever explained to him in language he could understand how to become a Christian. He said, 'No.' I shared Christ with him and he made a commitment. I asked him to come to church Sunday and confess Christ as Savior. He said, 'I don't have any shoes.' I told him to take mine for I had another pair. He came forward the next Sunday (all the way from the back row). I presented him to the congregation. You have never seen so many hard looks in your life. I explained what had happened the previous Friday night. They hesitantly accepted him into the church.

'Vinny,' as he was often called, began to follow us for the next five weeks. We had Bible schools in Bogwalk, Linstead, Savannah la Mar, and Oxford. He rode his bicycle and slept on porches. He was truly a changed young man. He adopted his

> illegitimate son that his father was rearing in Kingston. His father accepted him back. It was a great story.
>
> When we came home we sent 'Vinny' money to go to Bible college in Mandeville. He graduated and went on to get a degree from the British Baptist Seminary in Kingston. He married and began to pastor Jamaica Baptist Union churches.[1]

Now, if the story stopped here, it would be a thrilling one. But, like the gentle breezes of the Caribbean, it moves on, reflecting both the sovereignty and grace of God.

Several years later I was pastor of the Wilshire Baptist Church in Dallas. Bob Harris, the advance man for so many of our youth revivals in the '40s, was a missionary in Bermuda. He called me and told me about a man named Vinston Clemetson. Vinston, he said, was chairman of evangelism for all of the Caribbean. He had a problem. His teeth had deteriorated through years of neglect and he needed immediate medical treatment. This treatment was not available in Jamaica or on any other of the islands in the Caribbean. He also mentioned that the crooked teeth had become an aesthetic problem since Clemetson was before audiences almost daily leading conferences and preaching revivals.

"Do you think," Bob asked, "that some of the dentists in your church could help him if he could get to Dallas?"

I assured him that we would do all we could. I then shared this with a few in the dental field and they quietly took it on as a project. They gave their own time, used their own staff and equipment and paid for materials needed out of their own pockets. The laypersons accepted the challenge and reconstructed his entire mouth.

Several more years passed, but the story continues.

In 1997, I received a call from a young man, Jonathan Clemetson, who had moved to Dallas. He asked if we could visit briefly and I arranged to meet him at the Tom Landry Center on the campus of Baylor Medical Center.

"My father is Vinston Clemetson," he began. "He was known as the 'bad boy' of Jamaica until Bill Sherman led him to Christ.

He wanted me to thank you and those of your church who fixed his teeth."

Then Jonathan added, "I've just graduated from North Texas State University. I have a sister who will finish there in a few weeks. I'm enrolling in the dental school here. That's one way I can minister to my people in Jamaica and also to those on the other islands."

He paused and we sat in silence for a moment. Then he quietly said, "That's also a way to say 'thank you' for the help your people gave to my father."

The wind blows where it wishes and from generation to generation.

Postscript: In reviewing this story with Bob Harris on July 2, 1998, he shed additional light on it. It is true that Vinston Clementson, who became the evangelism chairman for the Caribbean Baptist Fellowship, was converted through the ministry of Bill and Veta Sherman. It is also true that two others, destined to become outstanding leaders in that part of the world, became Christians through the same Summer Mission program.

The first is Virgil Taylor, pastor of the leading Baptist church in Kingston, Jamaica, and, according to Bob, is "considered by many people to be the outstanding Baptist leader in the Caribbean." The second is Dudley Stokes, a missionary of the Jamaica Baptist Union, who now ministers on the Turks and Caicos Islands, located north of Haiti in the Caribbean. "Bill (Sherman) told Vinston (Clementson)," Bob said, "that all this was an overflow from a revival that started in Waco" on the campus of Baylor University.

Then Bob Harris concluded our conversation and the Caribbean story with the words, "There are probably spin-offs like this all over the world. But I know definitely my life was changed in that Waco revival. I know my ministry was changed. And, I believe God alone knows of all the fruit from that revival."[2]

RON HILL: IN THE COURT OF THE KING

Ron Hill was a fellow "Tarheel" from North Carolina. We were roommates during my senior year at Baylor. We had been classmates at Mars Hill College prior to our moving to Texas and there was something about his presence that did me good. He was "full of life" with a delightful personality; yet, he was a serious student. He was involved in numerous campus organizations; yet he found, or made, time for study. His example helped bring balance in my own life.

Ron had been active in the Waco citywide youth revival in the spring of 1946. He was a leader in the "fan-out club" that resolved to visit every house in Waco prior to the actual revival services. Day after day, he and a disciplined corps of students pounded the streets — block after block — sharing a positive word about Christ and urging people to attend the revival. Without question, this disciplined witness was one of the reasons for the overwhelming numbers who came to the meetings.

Ron's commitment did not slacken or waver when the revival services concluded. On several occasions I would awaken at 4:00 or 4:30 in the morning and find him at his desk studying his Bible and praying. He read the Bible as though every verse had his name on it, and often, in spite of the hour, he could not resist sharing some new "discovery" he had just found in a verse of scripture.

We graduated and went our separate ways. Ron attended Southern Baptist Theological Seminary in Louisville. He met and married a beautiful girl named Evelyn, also a "Tarheel." When their studies at the seminary were over they left for Thailand, one of the first couples ever to be appointed by the Southern Baptist Foreign Mission Board to serve in that part of the world. Listen as Ron shares his reflections on youth revivals and how they paved the way for his lifetime of mission work in the Far East.

> There were many things that led to a great movement of God in those youth revivals. Perhaps the prayer meetings were paramount. I remember those prayer meetings in the Sunday School rooms at Seventh and James (Baptist Church). The Spirit really

moved among us. There were times of confessions and tears — even some leaving the meeting to go find someone and get something right . . . . I remember B.O. Baker leading singing and then reading a Psalm that seemed to speak to all of us in that moment ("Ten thousand shall fall at thy right hand, but it shall not come nigh thee"). I remember the night when Charles Wellborn slipped into the meeting while we were on our knees in the dark and the surprise and thrill when I heard him begin to pray, "Lord, whatever you want me to do, I will do it." Those prayer meetings were a spiritual milestone for me.

One great thing that may have helped produce this revival's long-term effectiveness and continuation was that it was turned outward toward reaching others and not inward for our own enjoyment. So many movements on campuses tended to stay turned inward.

The BSU (Baptist Student Union) was active and a factor enabling the revivals to happen. W. J. Wimpee gave support. We had a large group of students involved in Friday night missions all over Waco. They led in services, prayed, visited in the homes of people, and kept moving out to discover new areas of ministry. My call to missions began in attending those meetings.

Looking back, I'm amazed at how many friends made lifetime career mission decisions that grew out of youth revivals and mission programs. There were scores of these, but a few come to my mind as I write you today: George and Veda Ray Lozuk, Venezuela; Ralph and Laverne Rummage, Africa; Mary and Bill Culpepper, Japan; Ross and Doris Coggins, Indonesia; Harold and Rose Reeves who joined Evelyn and me in Thailand; and many more that will come to my mind."

Ron then shared in detail an amazing story of how the Lord used summer student missionaries to minister to the King of Thailand.

In 1961 the Baptist Students of Texas organized a choir of about 20 to give concerts in the far eastern part of the world. Louis Cobbs, Associate Director of the Baptist Student Union for Texas, was the coordinator of the mission project called

> "Project Understanding." Dan Pratt, an outstanding vocalist, was the choir director, and Bill Lawson, a wonderful black Baptist Student Director from Houston, was the preacher/speaker. The choir's itinerary included concerts in Hawaii, Japan, Philippines, Indonesia, Hong Kong, Thailand, and many other nations in that part of the world. While in Thailand they were invited to sing for the King and Queen and about 200 members of the royal family. During tea time the King began to play the piano. He invited the choir members to come up and they ended up having quite a session, ending with the singing of "When the Saints Go Marching In." Bill Lawson did "The Creation," from James Weldon Johnson's *God's Trombones.* The King loved it. The King kept us so long that we were late for a big concert at the Immanuel Church that night. It was Sunday, and you don't leave until the King says you can leave.
>
> A few years later, Baptists in Thailand were trying to buy land for a Baptist Student Center. A great piece of vacant land was found at a major intersection in Bangkok. It looked perfect, but it was not for sale. It was royal land, the place where a consort of a former king had been murdered some years before. We prevailed on the prince who was handling the land to talk to the King about our interest in purchasing the property. He agreed, and when he mentioned "Baptists" the King asked if that was the same group as the Baptist choir who had sung for him a few years earlier. When assured it was, he said, "Sell it to them!" We got a prime piece of land in the heart of Bangkok for about $60,000. Today, at that intersection in the heart of Bankok, there is a highly visible Baptist Student Union Center with facilities to accommodate Bible studies, conferences and gatherings of leaders from throughout the nation.

Ron Hill concluded his letter with the simple affirmation, "True story."[3]

BILL O'BRIEN: THE WONDER OF A BACKWARD LOOK

Bill O'Brien has a special place in my heart. He was the first staff member to join our team when I became pastor of Wilshire Baptist Church in Dallas, Texas, in 1958. Although I didn't realize it at the time, one of his goals (self-appointed!) was to find a wife for his pastor. My first wife, Jean, had died in 1956 at the age of 30, leaving me a widower to take care of a little four-year-old girl. Bill and his wife, Dellanna, played it cool, but you could almost see the wheels turning in their minds.

"Bruce, there's a girl at the seminary..."

"Bill, I don't want to hear about some girl at the seminary," I would protest.

"But just a cup of coffee with her won't hurt!" He'd argue.

"Bill, do me a favor. Just take care of the music ministry at Wilshire and stop trying to play Cupid. I've already got a thousand members here trying to do that. Do me a favor, and stay out of the middle of my personal affairs."

But he didn't stop. There was a cup of coffee . . . and a dinner . . . and *serendipity!*

A few months later, Lawanna and I married, and Bill O'Brien sang and cried with joy at our wedding.

During his high school days Bill was introduced to the Youth Revival movement through his brother Chester. Chester and his wife, Bonnie, students at Hardin-Simmons, were both involved in revivals. Bill met many of the revival team members, including Frank Boggs, who stayed in the O'Briens' home in Abilene during one revival. All of this made an impression on his life.

Shortly after joining the staff at Wilshire, Bill was invited by Dr. W. F. Howard to lead the sessions for the musicians who attended the Youth Revival clinic. He describes his experience:

> Those annual events became a defining moment in my own pilgrimage. I was in the process of integrating theology, ecclesiology, and music/worship in my own heart and mind. I desperately wanted these students to live and lead beyond any

fads of the moment and be serious representatives of the Kingdom of God.

Seminary, Wilshire, and Youth Revivals became intertwined in my experience . . . . God used all this to get our attention about openness to serve God through arts in other parts of the world. Keith Parks, a missionary to Indonesia, preached at Wilshire on his first furlough in 1959. He and his wife, Helen Jean, described the Indonesian people and the need for someone to work with them in the field of music. This was a "heart-opener" for Dellanna and me. The next year, Ross Coggins, a missionary to Indonesia, and one supported directly by Wilshire, preached a renewal week for us.

Serendipity! Bill and Dellanna were appointed by the Foreign Mission Board of the Southern Baptist Convention in October of 1962. Bill continues:

I did not know what a music missionary was supposed to do. I did have strong feelings about what not to do. I did not want to recreate a USA Southern Baptist church music program halfway around the world. It was important to ascertain what God was up to in that context, and to listen to the culture. Even as the Youth Revival movement was marked by prayer and openness to the leadership of the Spirit, so should our service in the Indonesian context be marked by openness, flexibility, and creativity.

The deeper levels of cultural creativity were reached with the ancient five-tone scale music, especially accompanying the folk dances and shadow puppet plays. The greatest sense of creative fulfillment came in the utilization of the folk dance forms to tell the Good News of Christ's love for all. Working with one of Indonesia's leading choreographers, we were able to provide on stage and national television the works of art that reflected God's willingness to be communicated through Indonesian culture.

When did it all begin? When listening to Dick Baker sing his own composition of "His Way — Mine?" and the haunting words: "I place my hands in the hands of God, those hands so scarred now outstretched for me. Wherever it may be, over

> land, over sea . . . ?" I don't know exactly when or how things begin. But I know that God intertwined music, Dellanna, Youth Revivals, Wilshire, and Indonesia together in such a way that the continuum goes unbroken to this day.[4]

Bill and Dellanna spent twelve years as missionaries in Indonesia. The Foreign Mission Board of the Southern Baptist Convention then asked him to return to the States and become the Vice-President of overseas mission work. Later, Dellanna became the Director of the Woman's Missionary Union of Southern Baptists in Birmingham, Alabama, and Bill joined the faculty of Samford University in that same city, serving as director of its Global Mission Center.

Serendipity!

The Wind blows where it wishes.

NOTES

[1] Bill Sherman, correspondence with the author.

[2] Bob Harris, conversation with the author.

[3] Ron Hill, correspondence with the author.

[4] Bill O'Brien, correspondence with the author.

FOURTEEN

THE BONDS OF FELLOWSHIP

Jonathan.... loved David as much as he loved himself. (1 Sam 20:17)

On June 18-20, 1999, 17 of the earliest Youth Revival team met on the campus of Samford University in Birmingham, Alabama, for a delightful reunion. Those present were Howard Butt, Jack Robinson, Ralph Langley, Reiji Hoshizaki, Bob Harris, BO and Dick Baker, Frank Boggs, Charles Wellborn, Asa Couch, Bob Harris, Jess Moody, Foy Valentine, Warren Hultgren, Bruce McIver, and Dr. W. F. Howard.

The gathering, hosted by Samford University and President Thomas Corts, was designed as an opportunity for members to reflect on the revivals of the late 1940s and early '50s, share lasting impressions out of those remarkable experiences, renew friendships, and prayerfully ponder another spiritual awakening among students. We were wired for recording when we arrived and more than 30 hours of video taping was left as a legacy for future generations. These are on file at both Samford and Baylor Universities.

As we gathered for the first session, Jess Moody said, "Well, fellows, as I was saying 50 years ago . . . ."

Then we hugged and cried and laughed.

Charles Wellborn, who had flown in from London where he now lives, greeted me with the question, "Have you fallen into any garbage cans recently, Bruce?"

"Nope," I replied. "Have you experienced any broken ribs recently?"

Then we hugged and cried and laughed again. And remembered . . . .

After a pressure-filled day in a citywide crusade back in 1946, the revival team usually went out to eat. It was our chance to relax, unwind, and release tension. We weren't on stage and we didn't have to impress anyone. You can imagine the horseplay and practical jokes that came out of these sessions. A sensitive person with thin skin didn't last long in this group. For instance, one evening, in the middle of our "after-the-service" meal, Charles Wellborn and I disagreed on some inconsequential issue. Wellborn, a national debate champion with a brilliant mind, carefully set out to prove his point. I resisted and held my ground, not out of strong convictions, but out of stubbornness that hated to lose an argument. As we walked out of the restaurant and down the street, we passed three empty garbage cans neatly arranged in a row. Wellborn lifted the lid off one of them and suggested that a person with my attitude would fit nicely in a garbage can. "Come on, fellows," he urged, "let's put the lid on McIver!"

Charles then grabbed my shoulders while two other "friends" lifted my lower body off the pavement. They then flipped me upside-down in mid-air. I dangled there for a second, looking into the chasm of the empty can. I wasn't thinking of Charles' great sermon, or BO's dynamic leadership as he directed congregational singing, or Cody's excellent pre-revival preparation, or Jack's Olympic Gold Medal. I was thinking only one thing: survival — my own survival! Mustering all my strength, I freed one leg from the grasp of those who held me, and kicked with a force that made me feel proud. As my right heel landed on Charles's chest I heard a "crack!" followed by a groan. My aim had been perfect. His cracked rib took months to heal; the relationship needed no healing, for nothing had been broken. We laughed all the way back to the hotel. And, more than 50 years later, our first greeting was punctuated with laughter.

What was the issue that started the "garbage can incident?" I can't remember; neither can Charles. That's friendship.

It was Monday, April 1, 1946. Most of the plans were in place for the opening service of the Waco Youth Revival. Some students were busy setting up 2,000 seats, others were checking the public address system, and still others were making sure the pianos were in tune. We had prayed and planned for nearly 12 months. You could feel the tension, the expectancy, and the hope. Now, there was nothing else to do but wait — wait five hours until students lined up to march from Baylor's campus and through downtown Waco to 5th and Clay, where the huge tent had been erected.

Five or six of us who were preaching in the revival that week were sitting around, getting more and more nervous. "Let's get away from the campus for a couple of hours," someone suggested. "We need to clear our minds and go to the service tonight fresh and relaxed."

"Good idea," everyone resounded.

"How about we drive out to the Bosque River and go swimming?"

The Bosque River runs into the Brazos River at a perpendicular angle, or 90 degree turn, just outside Waco near Cameron Park. In months gone by we had found the perfect spot for skinny-dipping. In fact, some of our most creative thinking and planning for the revival had taken place on the muddy banks of the Bosque. And some of the best fellowship ever experienced took place there, even if the water was cold.

We all piled into Howard Butt's car and left without telling anyone where we were going. After an hour of splashing in the chilly water, and then lying on the bank soaking in warm sunshine and silence, it was time to head back to the campus. Meanwhile, Jess Moody had "popped-off" about something, and one of the guys felt he should be taught a lesson, so he hid Jess's clothes in the trunk of Howard's car.

"Okay, wise guy. Who's got my clothes?" Jess asked.

No one spoke up. Silence.

"If someone doesn't come up with my clothes, and do it quickly, no one is going back to the campus," Jess mouthed to no one in particular.

More silence.

At that moment Jess reached into the car, grabbed the car keys, yanked them out of the ignition and said, "I mean it! My clothes, or you guys walk home!"

"No way, Jess," we tried to reason. "It's 10 miles back to the campus; besides, you're preaching in the revival tonight. You can't be serious."

But to our consternation Jess was serious. Without another word he hurled Howard's keys over the car and into the woods. To make matters even worse, the leaves were at least four inches deep under the trees. Searching for the keys was a challenge, not unlike the proverbial looking for a "needle in the haystack."

Imagine five guys, sans clothes, crawling around on hands and knees in the woods, digging and rooting under piles of leaves, saying things like, "I think they hit the limb on this tree"; or, "No, he threw them further into the woods"; or "Dear Lord, if you've ever helped us, help us now. Please lead us to the keys!" Or, the concerned whisper 30 minutes later, "We're in deep trouble, and I realize you'd like to baptize Jess again, and hold him under the water, but we can't let this ruin the fellowship on the first day of the revival."

Just when we were ready to give up the search, our prayers were answered as someone miraculously found the keys. We dressed quickly — everyone except Jess. We felt he needed to be "humbled" so we refused to give him his clothes. But by then Jess couldn't have cared less. He had enjoyed seeing everyone else worked up and panic-stricken. Instead, he grabbed a skimpy towel, wrapped it around himself and leaped into the back seat. We drove quickly from the Bosque River, through the heart of Waco, and to a little house near the campus where Jess and his mother lived. As we drove up and stopped in front of his house he reached to open the car door. We told him we loved him and that we'd be praying for him as he preached the opening message in less than two hours. Jess smiled at us, leaped out of the car wearing only the towel, dashed across the lawn, singing some gospel song at the top of his lungs, threw open the front door of his house . . . and stumbled into a Woman's Missionary Meeting being hosted by his mother! Two hours later he showed up at 5th and Clay streets, well-dressed, and, believe it or not, well-prepared to preach!

What bound us together? What kept us together? What got us through the rough places? What made it so easy to forgive, and laugh, and cry? What saved immature students from jealousy, resentment, and criticism? What caused us to rejoice when someone else preached or sang better than we could? What drove us to pray for one another even more than we sometimes prayed for ourselves?

Without trying to sound pious, the answer obviously begins with the grace of God. We were sinners, each one of us. Howard Butt had money, Charles Wellborn had a keen mind, Jackie Robinson had unusual athletic ability, Jess Moody had a winsome personality, Ralph Langley had a dramatic preaching style that held an audience spell-bound, BO Baker had a stage presence that could lead 10,000 in singing like a choir, and on and on. But we were sinners, and we were where we were only because of the grace of God. Through endless hours of prayer we were reminded of that, and in genuine concern we reminded one another. This understanding of *who* we were and *why* we were refused to let anyone take himself too seriously. If he did, there were always garbage cans with removable lids, car keys that could be lost, and towels that could replace clothing!

Dr. W. F. Howard observed: "Those old boys would pray for each other; they would sit up half the night praying for each other. They would meet in the afternoon, and they would pray until supper, and during the services some would get down under the platform and pray for the person preaching that particular night. They had a genuine burden for the person who was preaching."[1]

In 1982, Dr. Dan McGee interviewed Bill Cody. McGee observed: "In any movement you have a small group working together. As it grows and becomes significant, different ones go off on their own thing but are still associated with the movement. Was there any sense of tension in the larger group of some of the folks demonstrating more loyalty to their own enterprises than to the communal effort of the revival?"

Cody, who knew the group better than most anyone, replied, "I think there was some tension in the larger group, but the exciting thing to me is there was next to none in the smaller (or core) group. There was a kind of bonding in relationship between the guys who were in that small group of 1946 that caused commitment on our part to each other that is really unlike almost anything I have known in my whole life . . . . It is absolutely incredible to realize the way in which we can move back into conversation and into relationship and into trust levels . . . . To me, that is a witness to a kind of commitment we had to each other. Were there differences of opinion? Yes. Were there different interests? Yes. Different styles? Yes. But (there was) an intense kind of loyalty to each other and commitment to each other and trust of each other."[2]

The loyalty, commitment, and trust that the core group had for one another went a step further. There was also a healthy accountability to each other. It was not unusual to hear the group critique a sermon in a spirit of genuine love. Everything from the length of the sermon, to the contents, to the illustrations used (especially if they were "borrowed" from someone else in the group!) was under scrutiny. And anything that threatened the unity of the group, or the clarity of the purpose of the group, was dealt with up front. Instead of estrangement, this led to deeper devotion and genuine fellowship. Persons who love can handle truth if it is spoken through love and grace, and if it is shared to help, not hurt.

Again, the late Cody, wise beyond his years, observed: "There were times when we were presumptuous . . . and egotistical. There were some things we did that were seen by our peers and by some persons in authority over us as being sacrilegious. I don't believe for a moment they were for us, in the moment, sacrilegious. Those events were for us, in the moment, the release of tension and the touch of our own humanity that kept us sane . . . . We made mistakes, true; but we did a lot of things right, and some of the things we did right, I don't really think we knew we were doing right. I think God's hand was on us."[3]

In 1946, the entire team was invited to stay in the home of Mr. and Mrs. O. P. Emerson during the Dallas citywide revival. The Emersons had two lovely daughters, Joanne and Jackie, who were away for the summer. The entire upstairs was given to us for the week. This was the revival that made front-page stories in the *Dallas Morning News,* that had as many as 10,000 attending nightly, and that attracted the attention of people throughout Texas and beyond. The magnitude of built-up emotions was overwhelming for a group of teenage boys. One afternoon, when we were supposed to be resting prior to the evening service, Howard Butt began to sing the old gospel song, "Lord send the power, the old time power." The Emersons were not at home, so he sang louder and louder. Soon he had all of us joining in. Then Howard began changing the words, "Lord, send the power, the *atomic* power." Other words were changed and the voices grew louder and louder. You could have heard us a block away. By now, Howard, clad only in boxer shorts (expensive ones, I might add!) was really *with* it! He began bouncing on the bed, and then he climbed on the headboard, and did a swan dive into the middle of the bed, not missing a note. There was a "crack!" as the frame of the bed spit to pieces. The concert was over immediately, and we rushed around trying to tie the frame together, or brace it up on bricks or boards. We didn't have the nerve to talk with the Emersons about it, or to try to explain the circumstances that broke the bed.

The revival was over, we left the city, and the broken bed was forgotten . . . until 15 years later when I moved to Dallas and became the Emersons' pastor! Again, the bed was never mentioned by this dear couple as long as they lived. But, a hundred times I wanted to do what my little grandchildren do. I wanted to say to them, "I didn't do it, *Howard* did!"

Childish? Yes. Immature? Perhaps. Sacrilegious? No. As Cody put it, we were releasing tensions in order to keep our sanity.

Laughter also helped us keep our sanity. And our humanity. The writer of proverbs speaks plainly to this, "A cheerful heart is good medicine" (Prov 17:22a), and, "A cheerful look brings joy to the heart." Our late friend, Grady Nutt, put it this way: "Laughter is the hand of God on the shoulders of a troubled world."

So, we played together, prayed together, wept together and laughed together.

Several of us were in Corsicana, Texas, for a citywide youth revival. As was the custom, team members took turns preaching. It was Buckner Fanning's night to preach, so the rest of the team left the historic old Navarro hotel to give him space and time to prepare his message. After about two hours I returned, stepped off the elevator, and heard a familiar voice crying out, "Help! Somebody help me now! Quick!"

That's Buckner, I thought, and he sounds like he's in serious trouble. I quickly opened the door to our room, looked in, and saw no one. Then, from the bathroom came a moan and a cry, "Somebody help me!"

I thrust open the bathroom door, and there he was — all 200 pounds of him. He was in the tub, but his body was arched about three inches above the waterline. His feet were braced against the front of the tub where the faucets were, and his arms were against the other end of the tub. Every inch of his suspended body, from head to feet, was lathered in shampoo, and broken glass covered the bottom of the tub. I stood there and studied the situation for a second, grateful that Buckner had gone through basic training with the Marines, and feeling certain that no military exercise was no more demanding or challenging than the one he was now experiencing.

"What is the world happened?" I asked.

"Isn't it obvious?" he answered in a not-so-reverent tone. "I was shampooing my hair, dropped the jar, and glass slivers are covering the bottom of this tub. I can't sit down, and it's so slippery I can't get out."

"Just relax," I interrupted, "I'll get you out."

"Relax! How do you think I can relax in this position? If I relax, my bottom will be cut to pieces with broken glass."

"And, furthermore," he added with a touch of sarcasm, explain to me how *you* plan to get me out! I can't remain in this position much longer. My arms are about to burst with pain."

At that point I got tickled. He looked as slippery as a greased pig. I studied the situation, trying hard to wipe any trace of a smile off my face.

"What are you doing just standing there?" Buckner yelled. "Do something, and do it now!"

"I'm trying to," I answered, "but I can't seem to find a handle anywhere." For some reason, he saw no humor in my words.

Thankfully, the door opened and other team members called out, "Where's everybody?"

"Back here," I yelled. "I need help. We've got to get Buckner out of the bathtub!"

"Isn't he old enough to take a bath by himself?" someone asked with a chuckle.

"Careful," I cautioned. "He's not in a good mood, and he preaches in a couple of hours."

The three or four of us stood in the tiny bathroom like so-called friends of the Old Testament patriarch, Job — discussing, analyzing, speculating, and projecting opinions.

"This is a first," someone said. "In the history of youth evangelism we've never faced a problem like this." Another grinned and suggested, "Maybe we should discuss it at our next youth revival clinic when we talk about the problems we've faced." Still another opined with a hint of a smile, "Buckner is guilty of vanity; he should have been preparing his sermon."

It didn't take but about 10 seconds for Buckner to vent his feelings and get our attention. The man suspended in the bathtub was no longer a youth evangelist; he was in the Marine rifle corps, and we felt like an unarmed enemy on a South Pacific island. The tub was quickly drained; old towels were used to gather up broken glass; new towels were gently placed under him and he lowered his body ever so carefully to a sitting position, whimpering with every move. Each of the four friends surrounding the tub found a "handle," and we finally yanked and strained until we pulled him out of the soapy tub. For some strange reason, Buckner's patience was exhausted. With a few choice words, not appropriate for the pulpit, he rejected our offer to dry him off and "talc him down."

In spite of the debacle of broken glass, the service was a success that evening. The rest of the team made it through our assignments with straight faces. But we almost lost it in the heart of the sermon when one of the guys leaned over and whispered, "Buckner smells good tonight!"

NOTES

[1] W.F. Howard, Oral History, 1982.

[2] Dan McGee and Bill Cody, Oral History, 1982.

[3] Ibid.

FIFTEEN

WORKING TOGETHER

We are God's servants, working together. (1 Cor 9)

"ALL THE WONDERFUL WOMEN"

In my last conversation with W. F. Howard, shortly before he died, we were talking about Youth Revival teams we had known. Then he said, "What would we have done without all the wonderful women!" One of his last statements was an affirmation of the role women had in the Youth Revival Movement.

In the 1946 Waco revival, they prayed, worked on committees, hauled benches, sang, and marched through the streets. On the day the revival was to begin, April 1, we discovered we had no electricity. The fellows stood around and discussed the problem, analyzing it and fretting over it. One of the women said, "Go get Hazel!" Hazel Kramer had just returned to the campus from the WACs. Fifteen minutes later she showed up, dressed in work clothing, including heavy, spiked boots. She strapped her leatherwork band around her waist, scaled the light pole, and five minutes later . . . lights! That soon became the battle cry for problems we couldn't seem to solve. "Somebody get Hazel!"

Lillian Wheelis Brown was a remarkable woman who left her mark on the whole Youth Revival movement. When Lillian was five years old she had diphtheria and lost her voice. "Nevertheless," she says, "I had music in my soul and in my ear." That music showed in everything she did. Her husband was in the army overseas and she enrolled in Baylor to complete her education. An elderly lady lived with her to help with her two little boys. Life was a struggle, and the schedule was tight, but she found time to participate in the Friday Night Mission Program sponsored by Baylor students and then attend Singspiration following the mission activities. She was a gifted pianist and played for all the services in the Waco revival.

One night, Lillian arrived early and began to play the piano quietly. There was a special burden on her heart that night. As she played, "Teach me to pray, Lord, teach me to pray," other words came to her, and she began to sing softly:

"Baylor for Thee, Lord; Baylor for Thee.
Souls bound in sin, Lord, give power to free.
Search Thou my heart, Lord, dwell Thou in me;
Baylor for Thee, Lord, Baylor for Thee."

BO Baker arrived for the service, and Lillian "croaked out the words" (as she put it).

Quickly, someone raced to an office on the campus and the words were typed and duplicated. Thirty minutes later, the revival choir sang those words to a deeply moved audience. Gradually, the audience joined in, and it seemed the whole campus was singing as a prayer, "Baylor for Thee." For the next 10 years, those words, slightly altered, were sung wherever there was a Youth Revival. "Dallas for Thee, Lord . . . Fort Worth for Thee . . . Houston . . . Birmingham . . . ."

There's a beautiful postscript to that story. With tuition to pay, two boys to feed, and a husband overseas, life became a financial struggle for Lillian at times. One month, there was a mix-up in the mail delivery, and no check came from her husband. She was broke and down to canned tomatoes and corn bread. A Waco businessman sought her out and said, "I go in hunches. There's something in me that says you have a need."

Lillian bristled. "I'm doing fine," she insisted, reflecting her independence.

"I've been meaning to do this for quite a while," the businessman continued, "because you were a blessing to me at that great Baylor meeting." He then handed her an envelope and added, "This is something between me, the Lord, and you. I give it to you in gratitude for the blessing I received at the revival." Inside the envelope was a check for $150 — just what Lillian needed![1]

Most local Youth Revival teams consisted of two preachers who alternated preaching responsibilities, a singer, and a woman. The contributions the women made were invaluable. They participated in visitation, led seminars, conducted fellowships, gave testimonies, and graced the ministry of the entire team.

Leta Beene Woodfin shares her experience:

> I was blessed to be one of several dozen who, for about twelve weeks, went into churches all around Texas in teams of four. I am aghast at my audacity: an awkward teenager with no similar experience and virtually no talent. But possibly that was the essence of the whole movement. Students offered what they had, and God multiplied it like loaves and fishes. Certainly many who worked on the teams had magnificent natural ability, but even those were lifted beyond themselves and their abilities were glorified beyond their wildest dreams.
>
> When Ralph Langley preached, "Don't Die on Third," for example, no orator in history could have surpassed that young seminary student. When Dick Baker sang, "Longing for Jesus," he wasn't just the son of a small-town candy maker, but the son of a King who gave him songs to surpass the angel choirs. When congregations sang, "He Lives! You ask me how I know He lives? He lives within my heart!" the world vibrated with the love we felt for Him and for each other because we knew something phenomenal was happening. Dozens of magnificent young men and women were in the right place in God's time to be used, but if they had not been willing, I believe God would have raised others because it was His miracle.
>
> I firmly believe that half a century of strong Southern Baptist leadership emerged from this explosion of faith and commitment in a generation of students, who, my husband observes, were not afraid to ask God for miracles.

> Two human blessings also occurred in my life related to the movement.
>
> First, in the First Baptist Church of Monahans where I worked with S. L. Harris, Foy Valentine, and Bob Feather, a staunch supporter was an elderly, uneducated widower, Mr. Hill, who had become wealthy in the oil business. His great joy in life was to help young people get the education he had missed. A generous loan from him enabled me to complete my degree at Baylor.
>
> Second, in the late summer of 1946, while visiting in Fort Worth, I went to a citywide Youth Revival at Will Rogers Auditorium where a young man's earnest testimony touched my heart. He had a very odd name that I had trouble remembering, but over the next few months I heard it often enough from a dear friend he was dating. When their relationship ended sometime later, I was waiting in the wings and chased him until he caught me, and I became Mrs. Yandall Woodfin. Again, God took this gentle, soft-spoken, humble young man and made him a college religion professor, missionary, seminary professor, and artist, and I was blessed to be along for the ride.[2]

The pioneers among the women on Youth Revival teams were Treysa Seely McKinney and Dorothy Gilbert Pettit. They spent the summer of 1945 as team members working in churches across Texas. Others on this historic team were Ralph Langley, Asa Couch, and Foy Valentine. Later, Ardelle Hallock Clemons, Eunice Parker Means, Billie Russell Templeton, Faye Wellborn Robbins, Grace Westmoreland Langley, Bonnie O'Brien, and Doris Cummings Moody — to name only a few — worked on revival teams.

Faye Wellborn was a superb seminar discussion leader, but, like others, she had difficulty keeping the kids focused on deeper issues, such as, "How to know or find God's will for my life?" The young people would inevitably bring the discussion back around to "Is it right to kiss on the first date?" or, "When am I old enough to date?" or, "What about mixed bathing?" ("mixed bathing" in East Texas; "mixed swimming" in West Texas!) or, "What's wrong with dancing?"

"As I think of it now," Faye writes, "there was so much innocence in it. There's something kind of wonderful about that because these youngsters were wanting to live a holy life. They wanted to separate themselves, if necessary, from the world; yet, they were not otherworldly. They just wanted to live the Christian life in their world, and they wanted to do it with a clear witness. So we listened, and wound our way through some of that, and then tried to talk about what the Lord really requires of us in our lives."[3]

By the way, one revival team was discussing the dancing question. Someone asked, "Really, what's wrong with dancing?" There was silence until one of the football guys said, "Well, I think it would mess up your suedes." End of discussion.

On November 8, 1947, Baylor University conferred on President Harry Truman an honorary degree. It was a special day for Baylor, all of Waco, and for Doris Cummings (Moody). Doris, a student at Baylor, worked in the dining room in Burleson Hall where the President was to be served lunch. In preparation for the event, they practically remolded the entire dining room. They brought in china, crystal, and silver from the socially elite in Waco. They also secured beautiful serving pieces and linens for the occasion and moved in new mahogany dining tables and chairs. The changes were so dramatic that Doris hardly recognized the place. The Secret Service had been on the scene for two weeks. They practically camped in the kitchen until one of the black cooks shook a big spoon in the face of one of the agents and said, "Get out of the way, and stay out! I wouldn't poison the President. I'm a Democrat!"

Doris was asked to serve as hostess for the head table and to personally serve the President. The wife of one of the administrators of Baylor arrived early. She was a small woman and wore four large orchids on her jacket. The poor woman had difficulty getting seated and needed assistance. When Doris got her in her proper place, the woman's jacket slid off and fell to the floor under the table. Doris tried gracefully to crawl under the table and retrieve the jacket. While she was down there she noticed that the woman, slightly senile, was wearing black rubber galoshes, and there was no rain in sight! Doris struggled under the table until she removed the galoshes, and then raced to the kitchen to wash her hands just as President Truman walked into the room.

The Secret Service quietly insisted that the meal be served quickly since the President was behind schedule. Doris did a fast trot back and forth to the kitchen, making sure there was a smile on her face every time she served President Truman. Halfway through the main course the signal was given for Doris to bring the dessert, a huge serving of strawberry shortcake with ice cream. The President had taken one bite when the agents pulled his chair from the table, and lifted him to his feet. They half-led and half-carried him out the door. As he made his exit, Mr. Truman looked back and licked a strawberry from his lips. With that, he was gone. Poor Doris studied the fiasco, laughed, and then sat down and ate the President's dessert.

And that experience helped prepare her for work on a Youth Revival team!

COME BEFORE HIS PRESENCE WITH SINGING (PS 100:2B)

To paraphrase the words of Dr. W. F. Howard, "What would we have done without those wonderful singers!" In looking back over the years, names and faces come together of those singers who led us into His presence through music: Dick Baker, Frank Boggs, Asa Couch, Wayne Philpott, Billy Ray Hearn, Stan Howard, James Franklin, BO Baker, Bob Feather, Bill O'Brien, John McLaughlin, and Beryle Lovelace. These, and dozens more like them, were team members in every sense of the word. They participated in visitation, assisted in seminars and fellowships, prepared the order of service daily, led Booster Bands and revival choirs, and endured more half-baked sermons than one should have to hear in a lifetime. And they did it with smiles on their faces and prayers in their hearts.

In 1947, Milton Cunningham and I were the preachers in a revival in Springdale, Arkansas. This was either Milton's first or second revival. To put it mildly, his sermons were created on the go. The first night he was to preach in Springdale was an overwhelming challenge for him. When it was time for the service to begin, he asked the team to pray for him, and then suggested he would like to be alone in a little room adjacent to the choir loft for a few minutes. We knew he was having a tough time, so we insisted that he take his time and come to the platform when he was ready. Stanley Howard was the music minister for the revival. He led us in singing all the songs he had selected, and then sang a solo. No Milton. Stanley sang a couple more hymns. No Milton, but eyes began to focus on the closed door through which he was to enter. Two more songs were sung by the congregation, and then there was a crack in the door. Milton whispered to me, "Have him sing two more; I'm on the third point." Poor Stanley had sung through half the hymnal when Milton opened the door and marched out as though he could tackle the whole world. Believe it or not, he preached an excellent message, but Stanley limped back to his hotel room exhausted.

In 1947, Jimmy Allen, Jess Moody, Billie Russell, and Dick Baker conducted a revival in First Baptist Church, Laredo. It was a difficult week for the team, and everyone was discouraged. Dick Baker returned to his room after the service one night, "longing for a fresh glimpse of anything holy." The yearning in his heart cried out for answers.

"I had a longing for Jesus," Dick said. "I had never written a song, but I got out of bed, turned on the light, and wrote the first stanza and chorus. It was so simple," he added, "I didn't have the nerve to even introduce it or to say anything about it there in Laredo. But I kept working on it, and the following year at Ridgecrest, North Carolina, I finished another verse and put it down."

Months later, Dr. B. B. McKinney, head of the music department for Southern Baptists, visited the campus of Baylor University. Dick approached him and asked what he needed to do with the song. Dr. McKinney took the song and carried it back to his office in Nashville, Tennessee. He had it set on a metal plate, free of charge, and sent it back to Dick.

"That great man encouraged me," Dick said, "and he personally began to promote and use what began as a 'longing' in Laredo." The song, a favorite with young and old alike, has been translated into Chinese, Portuguese, Spanish, and German hymnbooks. Since then, Dick Baker has written over 400 songs and choruses, but none speak to the heart better than "Longing for Jesus."

Teamwork. What's it all about? It's working together even if someone else gets the credit. It's praying for one in his or her achievements and suffering with him or her in failures. It's exercising patience in difficult situations and holding one's tongue when it would be easy to speak. It's discovering the joy of diversity and understanding that God "gives gifts to whom he chooses." It's learning to hammer out problems in a back room, perhaps on your knees, and presenting a sincere, solid front in places where you're called to witness. It's minimizing differences and maximizing unity. It's working together with God, and you don't care who gets the credit — as long as God gets the glory.

The year before Dr. W. F. Howard died he thought about lessons learned by high school students because of the ministry of Youth Revival teams. These are his conclusions.

• They learned about God's correct address. He is not up there, or out there. He's in your heart . . . where you live every day.

• They learned to tell God the whole truth about themselves. They do this because He forgives and loves.

• They learned God is on their side. He is their friend.

• They learned to use their own vocabularies without loss of reverence.

• They learned to omit some of their "amens." The prayers continue.

• They learned to be quiet and to listen while God is speaking to them.

And I believe Dr. Howard would add one other to the list today:

• If the world is won to Christ, it will not be won by individuals insisting on their ways and their rights. It will be won as we work together — with God.

The "with God" was the most difficult part at times. We wanted to do it ourselves. We felt at times that our answers were the best.

A case in point. In 1947 Milton Ferguson, a graduate student in theology at Southwestern Baptist Seminary, and I were part of a team in a citywide revival in Fort Worth. Tom Norfleet, a Fort Worth boy, was in charge of arrangements and had done an excellent job making sure every detail had been given attention. Creative plans had been made and people who had expressed interest in the revival had been cultivated.

"Fellows, here's the name of a man who has just returned from active duty in the South Pacific," Tom said. " I've been told he's ready to make a commitment to follow Christ. Could you visit him at his apartment this afternoon?" We drove across town, found his room, climbed the steep outside steps, and knocked on the door. Quickly, the door swung open and we were greeted with, "Come in this house! Come on in now!" He was dressed in casual clothes, his handshake was firm and strong, and he smiled from ear to ear. He told us he had been in the thick of naval battles for more than three years. The truth is, he was so warm, so open, so gracious that I wondered if he could be really searching for anything.

"Er," I stammered, "someone gave us your name and said you might be interested in the youth revival at the Polytechnic Amphitheatre. It begins tonight."

"Wonderful," he replied. " I'd like to attend."

"And we'd like to talk with you about your Christian life," Milton added.

"I'd like that very much," he said sincerely.

At that moment I really don't know what happened. For some reason I'll never understand we stood to leave and told him we would be back the next afternoon at the same time.

Neither Milton nor I said a word until we got in the car and prepared to drive off. "I'm not sure that man is being honest with us," I finally mumbled.

"What makes you think that?" Milton asked.

"Well, he's just so eager, so warm, so anxious." It was about the dumbest answer I ever gave anyone.

The next day we drove back to the apartment and were met with an enthusiastic, "Come in!" We read a verse or two of scripture, shared our testimonies and knelt with our new friend to pray . . . With joyful tears he gave his life to Jesus, and then said to us, "I've been praying for a month for someone to come by and tell me how to become a Christian. And, I told the Lord, if no one could come by, then please send me a postcard explaining what it means to be a Christian."

He joined a local church. I was told months later that every Sunday for a year he walked the aisle of that church with someone he had led to Christ during the week. Now, looking back, I take full responsibility for dismissing our first visit with him. I take responsibility for saying, "We'll be back tomorrow." I take responsibility for "working together," but not "with God."

Hopefully, I'm a wiser person today. We are workers together *with God.*

NOTES

[1] Lillian Wheelis Brown, Oral History, 1981.

[2] Leta Beene Woodfin, correspondence with the author.

[3] Faye Wellborn, Oral History, 1986.

SIXTEEN

TEARS AND LAUGHTER

A happy heart makes the face cheerful, but heartache crushes the spirit. (Prov 13:13)

Bill Tanner, a student from Houston, was in a revival in Tallahassee, Florida, with Jack Robinson and Jack's brother, Bryan. Bill was the youngest member of the team and was conned by Jack and Bryan into taking an early morning radio broadcast. "They told me what a great preacher I was," Bill said. "I was 19 and enjoyed hearing them say that."

"We want you to have this opportunity of speaking on the radio," they insisted as they rolled back over in their beds. They further encouraged him by telling him that the pastor himself would pick him up in time to be at the station at 6:00 in the morning. He believed them and was grateful that the two brothers were doing him such a big favor. Bill observes:

> I had run out of sermons, so I borrowed a book written for young people by an older man, R. L. Middleton. I had planned to read one of his brief messages on the air, and, like any wise youth preacher, I thought I'd scan the book the next morning before the pastor picked me up. But the next morning I overslept and had no chance to look at the contents of the book. "Oh, well, it will work out," I reasoned as I walked toward the car to meet the pastor. I'll just find a chapter when we get to the radio station and read through it on the air. Jack and Bryan

both said I was a good reader. There's nothing to worry about, not at all.

Time moved swiftly and the program director gave me a signal that I was on the air. My opening words were, "My sermon for this morning comes from a chapter in my book." The words were out. That's not what I meant to say, but there I was claiming to have written a book — at the grand old age of 19! I was shaken by what I heard myself saying, but I wasn't about to give up. I closed my eyes and remembered what a good preacher Jack and Bryan said I was. So I moved bravely on to another paragraph, and read aloud Middleton's words. "What we fathers need to do . . . . " I paused and swallowed hard, for I was nineteen years old and not married. But I was determined to get through this radio assignment, so I read on. "What we need to do," Middleton wrote, "is to stoke the fires of evangelism." I gulped, while most of those in the station chuckled and coughed silently. I had never seen the word, "stoke the fires of evangelism," so I read, we need to "stroke the fires of evangelism." By now, the devotional service was just about out of control, and, thankfully, just about out of time.

The devotional closed with a wonderful story about a little boy who got hit by an automobile. He had been selling newspapers to earn enough money to buy his mother flowers for her birthday. The little boy was not injured seriously, but it was a touching story. Watching the others in the studio who were almost out of control made it doubly difficult for me. I tried to keep a straight face, but it was nearly impossible.

What experiences had been pressed into a less than 15 minute radio program? I had claimed to have written a book, insisted that "we fathers should stroke fires," and laughed about a little boy who was hit by an automobile — all at the grand old age of 19!

We got to church that night. I led the singing and Jackie and Bryan preached. At the close of the service a lady came up to me and said, "Brother Bill, I heard your program this morning on the radio. You brought a tremendous message, and the thing that impressed me the most was that you were so moved when you told that last illustration about the little boy, you just

> broke down. And, Brother Bill, I just pulled my car over to the side of the road and cried with you."[1]

John Woods and Russell Dilday, Baylor students from the Wichita Falls area of Texas, preached most of one summer together. The format was simply one that was often used in Youth Revivals. Russell would preach one night, and John would preach the next. They made a pact at the beginning of the summer. The one who was not preaching on a particular day would help the other one in the preparation of his sermon for the evening service. It was a workable plan, and each grew through the suggestions and criticisms of the other. John, a cheerleader at Baylor, had a line that he often used to "rouse" the crowd. At some special point he would exclaim, "Why, I'd rather be here in this revival tonight than to be the King of England!" The people loved it. They would often break out into applause and laughter as the cheerleader cheered them on.

One night, when things seemed to be moving slowly — too slowly for John — he dramatically declared, "Why, I'd rather be here tonight than to be the King of England!"

Silence. No response at all. John didn't understand why there was no reaction, but he braced himself and moved on in his sermon delivery. When the service was over, he asked Russell, "Man, what happened to that line about the King of England? They always respond positively to that."

"John," Russell said, weighing each word, "*The King of England died yesterday!*"

Jimmy Allen, a Howard Payne student and an extremely gifted speaker, preached with fervor one night on the Old Testament strong man, Samson. It was a great sermon, except Jimmy called him "Tarzan" all the way through his message.

Richard Brannon, known to his college friends as "Mouse," declared one night in a sermon, "I can see old Gabriel now, putting the trumpet to his ear and sounding the end of the world."

And who can forget the night Ross Coggins gave the congregation a bit of wisdom in reminding them, "You can bring a horse to drink, but you can't make him water! "

Richard Brannon, Ross Coggins, Billie Russell, and Buckner Fanning were in a citywide Youth Revival in Odessa. Buck tells the story:

> It was hot as blazes out there in West Texas! Each day we would have our noon meal in the homes of various people who were providing hospitality for the team. As we reached the home where we were to eat, I'd call the husband's wife aside, and say, "Billie is a wonderful girl and she has a beautiful voice, but she has one difficulty."
>
> They would look at me with concern all over their faces, and whisper, "What is it? Is there anything we can do to help?"
>
> "She's hard of hearing," I'd say. "Just speak loud and distinctly to her and she'll do fine."
>
> Then we'd take Billie aside and tell her that the hostess was hard of hearing. Of course, neither had hearing difficulty, but what we did have was a complete fiasco.
>
> Billie would smile sympathetically and yell, "THIS IS A WONDERFUL MEAL. I DON'T KNOW HOW YOU'RE ABLE TO DO THIS WITHOUT HELP."
>
> "THANK YOU, BILLIE , I ADMIRE YOU SO MUCH. YOU MUST HAVE OVERCOME A LOT TO MAKE IT THROUGH THE UNIVERSITY." The hostess would holler back.
>
> And on and on it went, back and forth, until Billie, knowing the team better than the hostess, figured it out. The host family enjoyed it more than the team.[2]

In 1947 several of us preached in a citywide San Antonio revival. The meetings were held in Sunken Gardens, a beautiful, natural amphitheater located near the heart of the historic old city. Jess opened the meeting and was the first to preach. I preached on Tuesday and was followed by Howard Butt and Jack Robinson. Frank Boggs was in charge of the music for the week. Each night, Monday through Friday, the Gardens were filled to capacity.

On Tuesday evening I planned to preach a sermon that normally lasted about twenty-two minutes. About 12 minutes into my sermon I was aware of a restlessness near the back of the outdoor theater. They were no longer looking at me; they were looking back over their shoulders to a cliff above the gardens. Once, when there was a natural pause in my preaching, I heard voices coming from the cliff. I moved back quickly to the heart of the message, and for a couple of minutes I seemed to have their undivided attention, until a blood-curdling scream reverberated throughout the Gardens. The scream followed the form of a body hurling downward and downward through space from the top of the cliff into the rear of the Gardens.

Now, I saw all this and was about to stop preaching, when someone on the platform whispered, "Bruce, don't stop. Hold the crowd together. Stay with it."

I did my best for the next eight minutes, barely pausing to catch my breath, and working the hardest I ever worked trying to keep people focused on the service and the sermon. Obviously, I had no idea what was happening, on the cliff, or under the cliff. But I knew that whatever it was, I wasn't in a position to do anything about it in that moment. Thankfully, the crowd remained focused, and when the invitation was given 32 made commitments of their lives to Christ, and dozens more rededicated their lives.

The leading San Antonio paper cleared up the mystery the next morning. On the front page there was story and a picture, "Dummy thrown off Cliff." The article went on to say that this was a ruse, a trick, played by gangs on groups meeting in the Sunken Gardens. Fortunately, it didn't wreck our meeting — not at all. Instead, it gave us good publicity in the daily paper, and, somebody said, "If we count the dummy, we had 33 conversions!"

The next morning I woke up early with a migraine headache. I rolled over, dialed Jess's hotel room, and pleaded, "Jess I've got a headache this morning, and I'm supposed to be on the radio in 30 minutes. Will you take the radio spot for me?"

This would have been no problem at all for Jess. He had a daily radio program in Waco and was completely "at home" behind the microphone. "Bruce, I'm tired, too," he answered. "Why don't we just forget it?"

"Forget it?" I asked in disbelief. "Forget it, while some pastor or local team member wonders where we are? No way."

I wasn't trying to show Jess up, or to set an example for others. I wanted to get out to the radio program more than anybody. In that moment, for me, I saw no way out but to roll out of bed and stagger to the station. So, like a faithful martyr, I threw on my clothes and walked a couple of blocks down the street to the radio station. When the announcer gave me the cue, I said a few words about the Youth Revival, invited others to attend, and thanked everyone for their support. In 15 minutes I was out of there and on the way back to my hotel room for the rest of my morning sleep.

Just as I dozed off, the telephone rang. With effort I lifted it from the cradle and heard a voice say, "Hi, Bruce, let's go flying."

"Jess? Jess? Are you crazy, or what? You know I have a headache. I begged for your help, and you turned me down. Now, you have the nerve to wake me up and ask me to go flying with you!"

"Don't worry," he said with a laugh. "You need the fresh air. You'll like it. And it will give us a chance to talk some more about the revival, and — "

"Shut up, Jess. Where do I meet you?"

"Downstairs in 10 minutes."

Why do I let Jess do things like this? I moaned. *Why do we let him get away with it? It's simple,* I thought. *We love the clown! And he's fun to be around.*

Jess's plane was a two-seater Luscombe Silvaire, powered by a Continental engine. It was given to him by a group of businessmen from the Houston area. He confesses that he tried to learn to fly in record time, and crashed on his solo flight. "It was then," he says, "when I learned you're supposed to use those pedals down there." He was once in Laredo in a revival, and he needed to get back to Waco for a Greek class. He set the plane on autopilot, began studying his Greek lesson, and went to sleep. Thirty miles into Mexico he woke up and realized where he was. He got back on course and headed for San Antonio, where he was greeted by the border patrol. They questioned Jess at length about who he was, where he had been, and where he was heading.

"Well, I was in a revival in Laredo, and needed to fly to Waco for an afternoon Greek class at Baylor University," Jess began. "After I took off and had reached a good altitude I set the plane on autopilot and began studying my Greek textbook. I guess I went to sleep and drifted off course."

The patrol officers looked at each other, shook their heads, and said, "That's so ridiculous it has to be true. Let him go."

That's the same Jess I was flying with 10,000 feet over San Antonio. Billowy clouds surged all around. Visibility was zero. And then . . . a flash off the right wing . . . and another flash off the left wing. Planes! Planes all around us, and they don't know we're up here!

"Jess, what's that? Where are we?"

"Oh, we're over Randolph Air Field, and those are military fighter planes on practice."

Trying my best to remain calm, I asked, "How much gas do we have?"

"We're in good shape," Jess said. "Why, we've got a 10 minute supply."

"Put this thing in a nose-dive, Jess, and get us down!"

As we landed and taxied toward the hanger, I realized for the first time how weak I was. But I didn't have a migraine!

One Thursday in San Antonio, both Jess and Jack had to leave. Jess had an engagement in Waco, and Jack was due to preach that night in Hearne, Texas.

"Just fly with me, Jack," Jess invited. "Hearne is on the way to Waco. There's a good little landing field there. I'll drop you off, and then be on my way."

"Are you sure you know the directions to Hearne?" Jack asked.

"Of course I do," Jess answered impatiently. "Besides, we'll fly low and catch the road signs."

All of us had a few hours off before the Thursday evening service, so we decided to drive out to the airport and see them off. The plane was small, but Jack finally succeeded in getting his luggage on board. He left out of his baggage a fresh white shirt he would need for the evening service, a tie, and a big ham that some friend had given him. As Jackie, always a meticulous dresser, tried to get his lanky body into the passenger seat, he promptly stepped on his freshly laundered white shirt. This irritated him, and he dropped both the ham and the tie. It was quite a scene. Jess was now in the cockpit.

Jess leaned out the window, and hollered, "Hey, Butt, give the prop a spin." The older modeled planes did not have self-starters. You started the engine by having someone crank, or spin, the propeller. The pilot turned the switch to the "On" position, and then called out, "Contact!" when he was ready for the spinning to begin.

Howard walked up, and reached for the propeller, just as the manager of the airport ran out yelling, "Don't touch that prop! Don't touch it!" The manager gave Jess a dirty look, and then said to Howard, "Son, you can get your head cut off spinning that prop if you don't know how to do it. It's tricky. You gotta spin it and then step away from it quickly. Now, git back out of the way and let me do it." With that warning, he reached up, shouted "Contact!" and pulled down on the propeller and took two steps backward.

The engine started on the first spin of the prop, dust blew in circles, we waved good-bye, and they were off. We slowly made our way to the car to drive to the hotel. The service at Sunken Gardens was still before us. We laughed about Jack and his ham, Jess and his maps, and a two-seater plane dropping down just above the ground to read the road signs.

The closing service in the Sunken Gardens was a wonderful experience. We were both thrilled and exhausted as we made our way back to the hotel. It had been a good week together, but in a few hours each would move on to his next revival responsibility. Every Friday night brought a note of sadness.

We had no sooner entered our room at the hotel when the telephone rang. Howard answered and whispered to us, "Someone is looking for Jack. They're calling from Hearne."

In as calm a voice as possible, Howard said, "Jack left several hours ago, flying to Hearne with Jess. They planned to land at the airport in Hearne."

"That's one of our concerns," the caller stated. "There is no airport here now. They've torn it up and have made into a new housing development. There was no way they could land there."

Howard covered the phone with his hand and whispered aside to us, "Jess and Jack are down. They're either lost, or they've crashed."

The shock was beyond comprehension. Not Jack. Not Jess. Two of our favorites. We knelt for prayer and tearfully asked God to help them get through this situation. This praying, wondering, weeping, and not-knowing stayed with us another two hours. Then another phone call. Howard answered. The relief on his face announced good news.

"It's Jack," he said as he turned to us. "Where are you Jack? What happened?"

Briefly, Jack told him the story. They had followed the highway signs without difficulty. They made it to Hearne on schedule. They got the landing field in sight and started the long approach to the field. As they got nearer and nearer, they realized something was wrong. There were no terminal buildings, no runways, and no planes on the ground. The Hearne Airport was now a new housing development.

"Get this thing out of here!" Jack yelled at Jess. "Pull up! Now!"

"Take it easy, Jack," Jess said. "We'll have this thing back up in no time." He pushed the throttle and the 65 horsepower Continental engine did the rest as Jess headed for Waco.

"Where're you going?" Jack asked with concern. "I've got to speak down there."

"You don't speak anywhere if I can't land." Jess answered in a matter-of-fact-tone.

There was silence. Then Jess began to sing, and Jack pouted.

About 15 miles from Hearne they spotted a beacon. "What's that?" Jack asked.

"That's an American Airline beacon. It's a signal there's a small landing strip there for planes in trouble," Jess answered.

"Put it down!" Jack ordered. "Put it down right now!"

By now, the sun had gone down and there was little light. But Jess was determined to do what Jack wanted.

"How will you get to Hearne?" Jess asked.

"I'll walk!"

Jess helped him out of the plane, loaded his long arms with his Bible, the ham, and the now-crumpled shirt. He waved to him and watched him walk off into the dark woods.

Jack said later he fell into a creek, brushed against a tree, and bumped into a cow. He came upon a little house out in the woods, and knocked on the door. A lady came to the door, looked out, and Jack said, "I'm Jack Robinson."

"Jack Robinson, the athlete?" she asked as her children gathered around.

"Yes ma'am."

"Well, boy, you sure has paled!"

The family laughed, then put the Baylor Basketball star, not the Brooklyn Dodger baseball player, in the car and drove him into Hearne. The congregation had been waiting . . . and praying . . . and singing . . . and hoping. Jack spoke at the church briefly, gathered up his ham, and found someone to drive him to Waco.

In the telephone conversation with us at the San Antonio hotel, we rejoiced that he was safe (and that his ham was secure!). Then Howard asked a logical question, "Where's Jess?"

Instantly, Jack said, "I hope he's dead!" And then he added, "The last time I saw him, he was speeding down the emergency landing field where the American Airline beacon is, singing at the top of his lungs, "God will take care of you!"

It's amazing that He did. God did take care of all of us, through tears and through laughter.

NOTES

[1] Bill Tanner, Oral History, n.d.

[2] Buckner Fanning, correspondence with the author.

SEVENTEEN

THE SECOND WAVE

One generation shall praise your works to another.
(Ps 145:4a)

One of the characteristics of the Youth Revival Movement was the way each revival seemed to produce new leadership for the future. For instance, Charles Wellborn made his commitment to Christ in the 1946 Waco Youth Revival. Two nights later, he gave his testimony in that same revival, and two months later he preached in the citywide revival in Houston. Buckner Fanning made his commitment in the 1946 citywide revival in Dallas. In 1947, he preached in the second Dallas citywide revival. Bailey Stone was converted in the Houston revival in 1946. A few months later he was a student at Baylor and was preaching on revival teams throughout the state.

This spirit of immediacy did two things. First, it kept the original team members from becoming "pros." Obviously, experience is a valuable asset, but no one was assigned a revival responsibility because of tenure. Second, the constant request for revivals from across the nation presented opportunities for younger team members, providing they had the ability to lead. Some of those who followed the 1945–1946 revivals called themselves "The Second Wave." Their experiences are inspiring.

Doug Dillard writes:

> As a "second wave" Youth Revival team member I was paired as a song leader for "first-stringers" like . . . Warren Hultgren . . .

> Ralph Langley . . . Foy Valentine . . . Jack Robinson . . . Eunice Parker . . . Faye Wellborn . . . and Doris Cummings. It was an incredible experience for one who had just finished his sophomore year at Baylor and was not to turn 19 until mid-summer . . . . I was rarely a headliner, and then only in smaller meetings. My story is not about the great things I contributed, but rather how I am a product of which the Baylor phenomenon was only a part.

Doug was a member of a small neighborhood church in Temple, Texas, 35 miles south of Waco. In the summer of 1944, a spiritual awakening began in the hearts of the young people. Three young men surrendered their lives to preach on three successive Sundays, there were 83 additions to the church in less than a month, and the youth moved from the back rows to the front rows for the worship services! The youth also fanned out across the county, preaching and singing in abandoned buildings, dying churches, and anywhere else a few would gather. Out of this, two missions were started which resulted in permanent churches in Temple.

In 1946, several of the youth from Doug's church drove to Waco for the Waco Youth for Christ revival. They watched as over 100 made commitments to Christ at the end of the service. The group drove home, convinced they needed that same kind of revival in Temple. A steering committee was formed, and Doug was elected general chairman. Jess Moody, who had preached in the Waco revival, was invited to be the preacher.

Doug continues:

> We had quickly fleshed out a complete organization of committees and started raising money by going one by one to the leading businessmen in town. When we got a $100 gift from the bank president on our first visit, it never occurred to us that we would not raise the $2,800 we had set as our budget goal. So we opened an account with the $100 and ordered the tent, the same tent used in the Waco crusade. Scores of other details were handled, each in turn, by kids 15, 16, and 17 years old.

All of this had happened so fast, and with such excitement, that the pastors of the community had not been included in the plans. Clay Burns, one of the young people, said, "You know what would be great? We ought to let the pastors in on this."

When Milton DuPriest, representing the youth, presented the matter to their pastor, he "came up over his desk."

"You want to do WHAT?" the pastor responded. "Why…why…why, you can't do THAT! Do you know how much it would COST?"

"Mmmm, yes sir," said Milton, pulling out his bankbook. "We figure it will cost $2,864."

"How in the world do you think you're going to raise $2,864 in less than a month?" he gasped.

"Er . . . We already have the money on deposit in First State Bank," said Milton.

Doug continues:

> By then, every act of preparation was another expression of the movement of God in that high school and town. Laymen began to step in . . . . They helped us get lumber donated for the platform and choir risers, showed us how to build them, and donated many hours of their own labor. They helped convince pastors from across the country to lend benches and then donated trucks for us to go after them . . . .
>
> Each activity involved new young people and their parents and friends and heightened anticipation for the event. Sleepless nights painting banners, distributing posters, and stenciling sidewalks were not work; instead, they were part of God's plan to focus our dedication, increase our faith, and prepare us for his blessing.
>
> By the time the Temple Youth for Christ opened under the tent at American Legion Field, there was nothing we thought to be impossible for God . . . . During the six nights of services, there were 503 decisions for Christ, including professions of faith on the part of 11 of the Temple Wildcats football team. Three of the team members were among many young people who surrendered to preach.

What Doug Dillard has shared so beautifully in his story, "The Second Wave," is the story of what happened in Texas and beyond in the late 1940s and early 1950s. One revival led to another (or was each revival a part of the whole?), one commitment inspired another, and one act of faith paved the way for even more faith.[1] And one wave produced another and another and another.

In 1947, Clark Scanlon, a high school senior from San Antonio, Texas, faced some of the toughest decisions of his life. He was at a crossroads that would determine directions for the rest of his life. Clark had just received an appointment to the West Point Military Academy. He had just taken the admissions test and had been accepted. This was enough to thrill any young person, but Clark was confused. He had just attended a Youth Revival at the Riverside Baptist Church in his city. He listened as Bob Feather, Charles Downy, Faye Wellborn, and Bailey Stone shared their own experiences and talked about the importance of finding God's will in your life. For the first time, Clark, a typical fun-loving high school student, saw something in the Christian faith that was not "stiff and straight-laced," as he put it. He saw a group of Youth Revival leaders, much like himself, "loving the Lord and having fun at the same time."

To further complicate matters, Clark also received within the month an appointment to the United States Naval Academy. This was more than he knew how to handle. Late in the spring of his senior high school studies, he served as a counselor for a Boy Scout retreat held in the Hill country west of San Antonio. One night he slipped away from the group, climbed to the top of a hill, and sat in prayer. Two impressions came to him. First, he remembered the fresh vitality demonstrated in the lives of the Youth Revival leaders. Whatever it was they had, he wanted it. Second, he reviewed the "sameness," the dullness, and the lack of joy in his own life.

Clark climbed down from that hill late that night with a clear-cut sense of direction. He declined his appointments to both academies and wrote Baylor University for admission papers.

Those closest to him couldn't understand why he had made these decisions. To them, he was throwing away the gift of a lifetime. His father, an Irish Catholic with little understanding about Baptists, said, "If you're fool enough to go to that Baptist college, I'll never help you with a cent!" But Clark was determined. He "sweated" in a cotton gin his first year in college to make enough money to get by his freshman year. By the second year, two uncles came to his aid and helped some with his future finances.

At Baylor, Clark found a fraternity of young men also interested in the mission fields — George Lozuk, Sam Canata, Bill Dyal, and Justice Anderson. On one occasion, Clark said in jest, "If you fellows don't stop making decisions to be missionaries, I won't have anybody to support me when I go!"

Clark and Sarah Scanlon spent nearly half a century serving in Guatemala, the Dominican Republic, and in administrative responsibilities at the Southern Baptist Foreign Mission Board in Richmond, Virginia. I tried to call him recently, and he was out. He's a volunteer with a hospice program in Richmond. The agency had asked him to visit two patients who speak no English — only Spanish.[2] The commitment made in one night on a lonely hill west of San Antonio continues.

Justice Anderson arrived on the campus of Baylor University in the fall of 1946. He was "a scion of a staunch Baptist family, converted at an early age, called to preach as a teenager, and had attended the citywide Youth Revival in Houston in the summer of 1946." He was a graduate of Bay City High School, where he excelled both in athletics and academics. Justice shares his own story:

> The "second wave" of the Youth Revival Movement permeated the campus. I threw myself, naively and enthusiastically, into the athletic and religious activities . . . . On the basketball taxi squad I met Jack Robinson, Ralph Pulley, Mouse Brannon; through living in the athletic dorm I met Buckner Fanning and several of the Christian football players, all leaders in the revival

movement. I fell under the influence of several "first wavers" like Ron Hill, Howard Butt, Charles Wellborn, the Baker brothers, Frank Boggs, Bill Cody, Dan Rainbold, and Bruce McIver . . . . A tent revival was held in Minglewood Bowl on the campus, and I was asked to preside at the services. This led me and my fiancée to make decisions to be "maximum Christians," the term in vogue at the time.

During those years at Baylor I was invited to preach in a number of Youth Revivals around Waco. In the summer months I preached in churches near my home church in Bay City, Texas. During my junior year, under the influence of Youth Revival leaders who excelled in academics, plus the challenging teaching of Dr. A. J. Armstrong, Sara Lowery, and several Bible professors, my own academics "took off." My later missionary calling was nurtured by the Movement and its strong emphasis on foreign missions.

After receiving his BA and MA degrees from Baylor, Justice joined many of his Youth Revival–Missions friends and moved to Southwestern Baptist Theological Seminary for additional studies. While there he received his MDiv degree and his ThD degree. He continues to reflect on his journey and the influence of the "Second Wave."

In retrospect, after 9 years as a Texas pastor, 17 years as a foreign missionary professor, and 27 years as a Professor of Missiology at Southwest Baptist Theological Seminary, I find the Youth Revival Movement at Baylor as the most formative period of my life. The healthy balance between the "intellectual-devotional," "evangelistic-discipleship," "local-world missions" emphasis, which have characterized my ministry, were discovered and forged during those years. Thousands of other ministers point to the same period as the seedbed of Baptist ministry and mission.[2]

Charles Lee Williamson served for 23 years as Missions Division Director for the Baptist General Convention of Texas. He knows as much about missions as anyone in our state. More than that, he is the kind of person who "practices what he preaches." In reflecting over his life and ministry, he observes:

> My first touch with the Youth Revival Movement came in 1947. I was discharged from the army in January and returned to Port Arthur, Texas, where my father was pastor of Fourth Avenue Baptist Church. That summer, First Baptist Church hosted a citywide Youth Revival. Foy Valentine was the preacher. I attended one night. His sermon title was "The Cords of the Cross." During the invitation I felt for the first time that God was calling me to preach.
>
> Subsequently, my father led Fourth Avenue Baptist Church to have a Youth Revival each year well into the '50s. Some of the teams included Doug Dillard, Faye Wellborn, the Sherman brothers (Bill and Cecil), and Chester O'Brien. The impact of those revivals, together with the godly influence of my father, resulted in many decisions for full-time Christian service. Fourth Avenue Baptist Church averaged 400 in attendance. In the early fifties there were twenty-five young men and women from the church in colleges and seminaries preparing for Christian service.[3]

Jack Robinson, the Olympic basketball star, was definitely a part of the "first wave." But his influence, like the influence of so many of the early youth revival teams, has rippled like waves to the next generation . . . and the next. Bobby Bowden is a good example. When the famous Florida State University football coach was in high school, he attended a youth revival in his hometown of Birmingham, Alabama. He was immediately attracted to a lovely girl who played the piano. That was enough to bring him back and keep him coming back.

But there's more. One of the youth revival preachers for the week was Jack Robinson. Bobby Bowden was deeply impressed by Jack's message. A few years ago, *Sports Illustrated* carried an article on Bowden under the title, "His Time Has Come."

> Bowden's reputation as a fair man and as a man of his word precedes him throughout Florida, where the Seminoles get about

> 85% of their recruits. In addition, it does not hurt that Bowden's strong religious faith is common knowledge in the state. Bowden, who begins staff meetings, practices, and games with a prayer, has been a lay speaker in churches throughout the South. He still remembers a Sunday when he was a teenager and heard Jack Robinson, a member of the US Olympic basketball team, speak at the Ruhama Baptist Church in the East Lake section of Birmingham, where Bowden grew up. "Back then, I always sat in the back row and cut up during church," says Bowden. "But this guy was so impressive, I just said, 'Boy, I wish I could do that.' Now when I speak, I try to have the same positive influence on kids that he had on me."[4]

The psalmist was right, "One generation shall tell another..."

NOTES

[1] Doug Dillard, correspondence with the author.

[2] Clark Scanlon, conversation with the author.

[3] Justice Anderson, correspondence with the author.

[4] *Sports Illustrated,* 30 April 1993.

EIGHTEEN

LISTEN TO THE WIND

The wind blows where it wishes. (Jn 3:8)

In 1949, there was a growing feeling on the part of Southern Baptist leadership that a youth night service should be held at the annual meeting of the Southern Baptist Convention. Dr. R. G. Lee, pastor of Bellevue Baptist Church in Memphis, Tennessee, was the president of the convention that year and enthusiastically endorsed the idea. The convention met that year in Oklahoma City, Oklahoma, and Howard Butt was asked to be the speaker for the occasion. Jack Robinson, the Olympic Gold Medal winner, was asked to give his testimony. It was a tremendous success, with thousands of young people attending and scores making commitments of their lives to Christ. Records show that these Convention youth nights continued for at least another decade and proved to be one of the best attended of all convention activities. Pastors and convention leaders were beginning to see that the youth had a message — even for a routine Southern Baptist Convention meeting!

When the services were over in 1949, Dr. Lee, a tall, physically strong man with wide shoulders and white hair, towered over Howard and showered him with expressions of gratitude for his message. Then, unexpectedly, the great pastor, looking like an Old Testament patriarch, reached down, picked Howard up, lifted him off the floor, and for a moment "danced a jig of joy" as he spun him around with Howard's feet never touching the floor. That one act symbolized the spirit of so many pastors and leaders as they opened their hearts and their pulpits to a bunch of 19 and 20 year old kids.

One of the young people attending that particular service was Phil Briggs, a teenager from Oklahoma. Recently Phil wrote a letter to the editor of the *Baptist Standard*, Texas Baptists' weekly publication, a letter about the youth night service and what Youth Revivals had meant to him personally.

> You resurrected many wonderful memories and heroes out of my past. My heroes were many and still give me challenge: Jess Moody, W. F. Howard, Howard Butt, Bruce McIver, Jack Robinson, and Buckner Fanning. Fifty years ago at the 1949 Southern Baptist Convention in Oklahoma City, I sensed God's call to ministry as a teenager and responded.
>
> Later, in my freshman year at Hardin-Simmons, W. F. Howard enlisted me to join the youth revival teams, something that continued for me over 10 years. Our teams went beyond Texas to conduct revivals. Some of the people I was privileged to work with were Jimmy Draper, Charlie Osburne, Bill Sherman, Britton Wood, Buddy Johnson, Ann Vinson, C. A. Roberts, Browning Ware, Andy Odom, Veo Gray, Hal Potts, Ginger Moon, Rhea Gray, and Bill O'Brien. We were a second wave, inspired by the heroes and others. All this came from the support of the Baptist General Convention of Texas. W. F. Howard, a dear friend and later a colleague, permeated the spirit of evangelism and missions among the revival teams.[1]

Today, Dr. Phil Briggs is the Distinguished Professor of Collegiate and Youth/Student Ministry, Southwestern Baptist Theological Seminary. In addition to his daily contact with students in the classroom, he writes articles and speaks to youth leadership groups all over the world.

It's been a long and happy journey from a campfire at Latham Springs to the platform of the Southern Baptist Convention; from a few students on one campus praying, to students on every campus praying for spiritual awakening; from Waco on the Brazos, to

Honolulu in the Hawaiian Islands; from several committed to Christian ministry, to 30, 000 (as Dr. Latourette has suggested) moving into full-time Christian work; from praying for a miracle, to witnessing more miracles than one can count in a lifetime; from a revival on a campus, to hundreds of revivals across the land.

How did it happen? I don't know. Really, I don't. And neither do the others who were deeply involved in the Youth Revival Movement. Of course, we could offer platitudes, list ten answers, project impressions, and speculate, but honesty says the Movement was beyond our doing. We were only spectators, only witnesses. As has been suggested, we were like the little boy who brought the loaves and fish to Jesus, then stood back and said, "Wow!"

When I set out on this project to tell the story of the Youth Revival Movement, I asked Charles Wellborn, a product of the revivals and later a participant in them, for his impressions. They are worth repeating here:

> In thinking back over the youth revival phenomenon, several major reflections intrigue me.
>
> First, the way in which the atmosphere of the entire Baylor University campus — faculty, administration, students — was markedly affected and changed by the revival and its aftermath. Anyone on the campus — in classes, chapel, or otherwise — could not have helped but see and feel the difference.
>
> Second, the way in which the appeal and influence of the revival extended, not just to young people, but to all types and ages. Recently, in going through some old papers, I came across a letter written to me after the Waco revival by an elderly retired Waco banker, who out of curiosity had attended the services. He was an Episcopalian and did not make any kind of public decision, but he wrote to tell me that the revival experience had renewed his Christian faith in "the most remarkable religious experience that I, and I believe others, have ever had."
>
> Third, the lasting influence of the revival. Through the years I have frequently encountered people, both ministers and lay people, whose lives were changed in meaningful ways by the revivals. But I especially have reflected on the fact that, to my

> knowledge, all the young revival preachers — most of them almost totally inexperienced in planning, preaching, etc. — have continued, each in his own way, in fruitful Christian service.
>
> Looking back, I can find no viable human explanation for what happened in Waco and in Houston, Dallas, Fort Worth, Birmingham, etc., in those [years]. Looked at from a hard-nosed secular viewpoint, the revivals should never have happened. The organizers and preachers were naïve and inexperienced; many mistakes were made in plans and operations, but the revival still happened. I have no explanation except to attribute what happened to the power of God.[2]

Can it happen again? That depends . . . .

This book is one of stories — stories that happened to people in Youth Revival days. They are stories about a small slice of time in the vast record of church history. Let me share one more story with you, not out of the revivals, but out of the Bible.

In 1 Kings, chapter 19, we encounter a prophet named Elijah. Sadly, this great man was tired, discouraged, depressed, somewhat angry, and had given up on the possibility of God doing anything redemptive in a world made up of kings like Ahab, queens like Jezebel, and gods like Baal. So he ran all the way south through a desert and ended up in a cave on a mountain named Horeb, or Sinai. There he hid.

> Then the LORD spoke to him: "Elijah! Why are you here?" . . . There was a mighty windstorm, but the LORD was not in the storm. Then there was an earthquake, but the LORD was not in the quake. And there was a fire, but the LORD was not in the fire. (See vv. 9, 11)

After all that (and the Hebrew translations vary here), "there was a quiet, gentle whisper," or "a still, small voice," or "the sound of nothingness" (v. 12).

And in the silence, Elijah listened . . . and heard.

Could the Youth Revival Movement happen again? Yes, but it will not be in the gale forces of life, or the dramatic quakes, or the fires of organization. It will begin when there's a genuine "Longing for Jesus" (as Dick Baker puts it), and we gather around our own "campfires," and pray, and dream, and listen.

"The wind blows where it wishes" (John 3: 8).

Listen . . .

Listen . . .

Listen.

NOTES

[1] Letter to the editor, *Baptist Standard*, 9 July 1999.

[2] Charles Wellborn, correspondence with author.

Bruce McIver asked God for enough time to complete this important ten year researched writing project. God's grace was sufficient. That prayer was answered. Though Bruce did not live to see the publication of this book, he did live to complete the manuscript, . . . and then lept into Glory, December 22, 2001 . . . riding on the Wind of God.

Lawanna McIver

NINETEEN

REVIVAL MOVEMENT EXPANDS TO SOUTHEAST

John D. Pierce
Executive Editor, ***Baptists Today***

A NEW GENERATION OF LEADERS

In an editorial titled "Southern Baptists look for new leadership," Georgia Baptist editor O. P. Gilbert wrote that "the death of Dr. (George W.) Truett in 1944 marks the end of the most aggressive and far-reaching constructive period in Southern Baptist history."[1] He wondered from where the next generation of leadership might come.

While Southern Baptists certainly found leadership in many places in the late '40s and early '50s, it is unlikely anyone of that era expected a significant revival movement focused on youth to sweep across the land. Even more doubtful would be that those prominently leading the movement would be inexperienced college students—one coming out of Truett's First Baptist Church in Dallas.

Revival was already in the air among Southern Baptists as the nation began its recovery from the war years. Gilbert's predecessor at *The Christian Index,* John Jeter Hurt Jr., who became editor of the *Baptist Standard* in Texas, acknowledged in late 1945 that the recent "Centennial Evangelistic Crusade of Southern Baptists has revived the spirit of evangelism which has been in process for some years."[2] Gilbert, like other observers and commentators on Baptist life, was not completely surprised by the growing role of young people in both leading and responding to evangelistic efforts, however.

Two weeks before asking who would fill Truett's great leadership shoes, Gilbert's paper carried an editorial titled "Values of the Youth Revival." Contributing editor W. S. Smith recalled how the "golden voice of Dr. Truett" would often quote Melanchton's words: "Fitly to train one single youth is greater achievement than the taking of Troy." Smith added that the churches of America had a great opportunity to "win and train the youth of our land for Christ." He noted estimates upward of 20 million youth between ages 16 and 24 living in the United States. Another five million persons ages 12 through 14—"who are, roughly speaking, young people as the term is commonly used"—could be added as well, noted Smith.

"Now that it is 'Good-by G. I.' and young men and women of the armed forces are returning, the churches are confronted with their biggest opportunity and gravest responsibility," Smith wrote. "Here at our door is a mission field of the first magnitude." Smith suggested that churches willing to face this challenge "will find definite values in the Youth Revival . . . as a means of reaching, enlisting, and training young people, and of bringing to the vital problems of youth the light of Christian experience and teaching." Holding youth revivals during the war years was difficult "because of the scarcity of youth and the scarcity of workers," Smith wrote. He concluded, however, that those conditions no longer exist and that "for the first time in several years, our churches have a real chance with youth." [3]

Such a chance was not lost on the pioneers of the Youth Revival Movement.

BEYOND TEXAS

Early American history tends to flow from east to west. With the establishment of the first colonies on the eastern seaboard, and western expansion coming later, one routinely reads of how educational ventures, cultural influences, and even religious movements came from established cities in the east to the frontier regions of the West during the nation's developing years.

After the United States was settled from the Atlantic to the Pacific by a variety of immigrants, however, unique regional influences strongly emerged. Then advancements in travel and communications allowed these influences to move both directions across the nation.

The Youth Revival Movement in the middle of the 20th century had its roots firmly planted in southwestern soil. More specifically, as indicated earlier in this volume, the movement was clearly birthed by Baptist students at Baylor University in Waco, Texas. While true pioneers, these Baylor students were not the first Southern Baptist students to do youth evangelism. Bob Denny, the respected Baptist Student Union director at Baylor—who encouraged and supported the successful Waco revivals in the mid-'40s—later wrote that "youth evangelism in the Southern Baptist Convention began as early as 1931."[4]

In the early 1930s, college students began conducting youth revivals under the auspices of the Mississippi Baptist Student Union, according to Denny. He identified several Baptist missionaries and church leaders who served on these early student revival teams during the years leading up to the start of World War II. Among them were Leo Green, Leo Eddleman, Claude U. Broach, W. O. Vaught, Hugh Brimm, A. L. Gillespie, John Allen Moore, Robert C. Norman, Pope Duncan, Charles Roselle, Polly Hargis, and J. R. White.

The war years of the early 1940s interrupted many college careers, though some local churches continued to sponsor youth revivals, according to Denny. By 1945, he asserted, there was also a widespread feeling that mass evangelism was fading out in America. "Just as this feeling was reaching its peak, students at Baylor University were praying that God would lead in a great revival of evangelism," wrote Denny. "These fires of evangelism, which were kindled in the hearts and prayer lives of scores of students, broke into open conflagration in the spring of 1945 in a youth revival on Austin Avenue of Waco, Texas."

While the Baylor students had not originated youth evangelism services, they had revived the efforts and taken the concept to heights not previously imagined. Such a phenomenon was destined to spread. So it is not surprising that the young student evangelists soon were invited to lead revival meetings in other places. Even Texas—as big as it is—could not hold the movement within its sizable boundaries.

The young revivalists accepted an invitation to hold evangelistic services in Hawaii in December 1946. That effort proved to have multiple significance. First, these young Baylor evangelists were taking the Youth Revival Movement well beyond the Texas border. Second, the context of ministry was vastly different than in Texas towns where Baptist churches had great influence. Third, and certainly unknown to participants at the time, this project was the impetus for another significant movement: the Student Missions Program.

The young evangelists were so well received that Hawaii Baptists requested a second student revival team come to the islands the following summer. To fulfill this request, however, a 14-member team of Baptist Student Union (BSU) students from several states was selected and sent in June 1947 to the U. S. territory just a few years removed from the 1941 attack on Pearl Harbor. Their experience launched a missions program that has sent out thousands of students from college campuses for more than half a century. Many career missionaries, ministers, and active lay persons point to their service in student missions as a significant life-changing experience.

SOUTHEAST CONNECTIONS

Not all of the Baylor students leading the early revivals were Texans. M. D. Oates and Reiji Hoshizaki were from California, and others, like Bruce McIver of North Carolina and Ralph Langley of Alabama, were from the southeast.

Langley and McIver had already preached much smaller youth revivals in North Carolina churches in the summer of 1944, just prior to the Baylor retreat that sparked the first Waco crusade and the ensuing revival movement. So it is not surprising that word of the successful Baylor crusades reached students in the colleges and universities well beyond Texas, especially those in Baptist-laden states of the Southeast.

Student revival leaders and observers point to one particular event—1946 Student Week at Ridgecrest Baptist Assembly in North Carolina—as providing the greatest impetus for motivating students from schools throughout the Southeast to plan and pray for similar revival experiences to come to their campuses and towns. The first-wave Baylor evangelists brought their energy, passion, and strategies to fellow students in what could be considered the most important and far-reaching year of the movement.

The year 1946 was a significant one for the student revival movement in several ways, both in Texas and beyond. The revival team conducted the "explosive" second Waco crusade in the spring and then expanded the student-led revivals to other Texas cities. Invitations to lead revivals in other places soon followed, including the unprecedented invitation to come to Hawaii at year-end.

In June of 1946, between the second Waco revival and the Christmas crusades in Hawaii, the student revivalists shared their testimonies of the phenomenon at Ridgecrest and were well received by their peers. Southern Baptist student ministry leader Kearney Keegan, a former pastor in Los Angeles, California, urged Howard Butt, Bruce McIver, and other first-wavers to tell the students how God had led them to carry out these first crusades. Keegan and his two associates, William Hall Preston, who had accompanied the Baylor team on their mission trip to Hawaii, and Bob Denny, who had been the BSU director at Baylor during the first revival in 1945 and later led the Baptist World Alliance, were crucial in moving the youth revivals into the Southeast. Howard Butt described these men—Keegan, Preston, and Denny—as "huge enthusiasts and supporters" who gave the revival movement additional exposure outside of Texas by arranging Saturday night youth events for several years just prior to the annual Southern Baptist Convention meeting.[5]

Nowhere though could a more receptive audience of Baptist college students be found than at Ridgecrest. So even while preparing for an upcoming crusade in Houston, the young evangelists agreed to travel eastward to tell the assembled students of the impact of the previous Waco revivals. Their words fell on attentive ears and stirred more students to pray and plan for similar gatherings when they returned to their respective campuses that fall.

"As quickly and contagiously as its theme song, 'I'd Rather Have Jesus,' has been caught up and sung by college students, the idea and the power of the Texas youth revivals have spread at the southwide retreat of Baptist students at Ridgecrest, N.C., during the past week," is how Winnie Dudley, editor of the *Baylor Lariat,* wrote of the account. Dudley quoted veteran missionary to China, Martha Franks, who heard the student testimonies, as proclaiming: "This is what I have waited a generation to see—a real revival in America—and now I can return to China satisfied." According to Dudley, the first-wave evangelists were among 400 Texas students—"the majority from campuses where the first youth revivals were held"—making an impact at Ridgecrest. "They had a story to tell and they lost no time in telling it," Dudley added. "They had been at the beginnings of the Texas youth movement and had seen the power of God—they were there." [6]

"Ridgecrest served as the catalyst in taking (the revival movement) south wide," recalled Frank Boggs, whose musical skills were in great demand for the large student gatherings. "So many young preachers and musicians would catch this vision; this is really how it spread."[7] BO Baker, who often led a 500-600 voice choir and an audience up to 10,000 in music and occasionally preached at youth revivals, also credited the experience with the 2,600 students in western North Carolina to the movement's expansion. "At Ridgecrest the students of the Southland heard about it and they said we can do (this) up and down the land," said Baker, reflecting on the event in 1999. "We were just an early part of a wonderful, moving wheel of God that made a difference in that world."[8]

Bob Denny recalled in a 1952 article how the Texas revivalists "were swamped with invitations from the various state groups for more details" of their successful crusades.[9] The young revival leaders and other Texas students would attend the smaller state meetings each night and encourage the various campus leaders to take the revival spirit back with them. The meetings would often run late into the night as the students asked questions and held lengthy periods of prayer.[10] In her report from Ridgecrest, Dudley offered a similar assessment. "In prayer meetings, in state groups, students from university after university rose to pray and to ask for prayer for a youth revival on their campus. Students pledged to do all within their power to have one on their campus, to prepare themselves by removing everything from their lives that would hinder a revival."

At the close of the Sunday morning service—following a message by Marshall Craig, pastor of Gaston Avenue Baptist Church in Dallas—some 400 students made their way to the front of the Ridgecrest auditorium to make public decisions, Dudley reported.[11] Surely it can be assumed that many of those commitments involved plans to take what they had learned from the Texans about the impact of the student revivals back to their campuses and towns across the land.

This was not a one-time experience, according to one participant. Musician Frank Boggs said that for several years when students gathered at Ridgecrest, "the youth revivals would be the talk of the whole encampment."[12] These dynamic students and their leaders provided moving testimonies and modeled genuine commitments to reaching their generation with the gospel of Jesus Christ. In addition to such spiritual motivation, they provided fellow students from other states with practical strategies that involved highly organized structures and intense pre-revival preparations.

INTENSE PREPARATIONS

A prime example of how students would extensively organize, plan, and recruit for the highly-promoted and well-attended crusades featuring leaders of the Waco revivals was evident in Atlanta. Two large series of revival services were held in that city in the spring of 1950 and 1952.

Howard Butt and Jack Robinson were preachers at the 1950 youth revival, and Dick Baker served as song leader. Bill Cody and Tom Norfleet made advance arrangements, working closely with local committees, on behalf of the revival team. Services were held May 15-21 at Baptist Tabernacle in downtown Atlanta with 629 decisions recorded including 58 professions of faith.

An itinerary—divided into morning, afternoon, and night segments—of that week-long citywide revival at Tabernacle showed the young evangelists did far more than lead nightly services. On Sunday morning and evening, they spoke and sang in local churches and did the same for a Monday morning pastors' conference. Each weekday afternoon the schedule called for them to lead a 3 p.m. "Georgia Tech revival." While some time slots would state an "indefinite" assignment due to pending civic or church engagements, only Sunday afternoon was marked with the words: "You guys can just loaf." With loaded schedules and intensive planning, loafing was not really on the agenda of anyone involved in preparing for and conducting the 1950 Atlanta crusade that resulted in over 600 public decisions. Robinson stayed in the Atlanta area and led a youth revival at the First Baptist Church of Hapeville, Georgia, then adjacent to the Georgia Baptist Children's Home campus, May 21-28.

A "BSU Handbook for Atlanta Schools," produced in 1951, claimed a second revival was being planned even before the 1950 Atlanta City-wide Youth Revival was complete. That planning for the 1952 Atlanta Youth Crusade for Christ occurred over two years is quite conceivable considering the elaborate organizational charts and committee assignments from that event. Hank Greer, Atlanta's City BSU Director from 1948–52, compiled a large notebook of materials from that second crusade. Included are detailed organizational and promotional materials from the eight-day campaign that involved over 700 local youth on various committees.

In addition to the work by these committees and by co-directors D. J. Evans, pastor of Atlanta's Gordon Street Baptist Church, and Greer, Baylor's Jarrell McCracken made several preliminary trips to make sure that plans were in order. McCracken, founder of WORD Records, was listed on the crusade letterhead as "organizer," but Greer referred to him as the "advance man" who kept the planning on track and assisted with promotional efforts. Howard Butt recalled that McCracken offered to help organize the second Atlanta revival if he could have access to the decision cards in order to use the data in research related to his graduate studies at Baylor.[13] McCracken also spoke at one of three pre-crusade rallies designed to encourage students to faithfully promote and attend the upcoming services. Georgia pastors spoke at the other two rallies.

For well over a year, students worked tirelessly to prepare for the May 4-11, 1952 crusade that brought Butt and others to lead services that drew 2,000-3,000 nightly to the city auditorium. Long before Butt arrived at the airport to a warm welcome from hundreds of students and Atlanta Mayor William B. Hartsfield, however, local students held numerous prayer gatherings, committee meetings, and the three pre-crusade rallies.

McCracken's effort to have the Atlanta mayor meet Butt's plane was still fresh on Howard's mind in 1999. "To this day, I'm ashamed that I didn't treat the mayor with the proper dignity," said Butt. "I think about it every time I fly into the Atlanta airport"—that is, Atlanta's William B. Hartsfield International Airport.[14]

Proper political etiquette aside, the second big Atlanta crusade had been soundly planned and the long-anticipated event got underway with high expectations. "We started on Sunday afternoon and went every night of the week and ended with another service the following Sunday," Hank Greer recalled.[15]

The meticulously planned 1952 crusade also featured music leader Frank Boggs; gifted cartoonist Jack Hamm, who would do nightly chalk drawings; and local pianist Frances Schum. A familiar accompanist on the *Baptist Hour* broadcasts by the Southern Baptist Radio Commission in Atlanta, Schum played at every service and was listed in some promotional materials as "pianist extraordinary."

Although organizers sought to tie the crusade closely to local Atlanta congregations, and enlisted Pastor Evans as co-director, Greer said support from local ministers overall was not good. Pastors were asked to recommend youth from their congregations for leadership roles, and those making decisions during the crusades were directed to local churches for membership and follow-up. At one point during the planning, Greer sent a letter to each minister indicating that "We are in a fog . . . because only nine of the 112 pastors in the Atlanta Baptist Association have sent us their recommendations for Youth Crusade Chairmen in their church." This situation was in contrast to the support youth revivals usually got from local pastors. In 1999, Butt called pastors "the heroes of the youth revivals" because they were willing to "risk it for a bunch of green, untested kids."[16]

That was not the case with the 1952 Atlanta crusade, however, said Greer. "They just didn't get behind it at all, but the youth did."[17] The success of the revival was clearly tied to months upon months of prayer and planning. Promotional materials stated that the crusade was "sponsored by the Baptists of greater Atlanta for the youth of today." As the start of the revival neared, an Atlanta newspaper reporter wrote: "Atlanta's Baptist young folks are tirelessly distributing leaflets, holding prayer meetings and rallies, as they make plans for the Atlanta Youth Crusade for Christ.[18]

Promotional efforts were well planned and abundant. Press releases were sent to all media, advertising space was placed in all local newspapers, and spot announcements were provided to radio and television stations. Posters were everywhere. One of the most visible methods of announcing the crusade was accomplished by placing rooftop signs on automobiles. Though it was rare for students themselves to have cars in the 1950s, they found many volunteers willing to spread the word along Peachtree Street, Ponce de Leon Avenue, or wherever they drove or parked.

One amazing aspect of the Youth Revival Movement of the 1940s and '50s was the youthful leadership present in every city. There was no denominational model or professional ministry instigation for what took place among the young students who sensed a divine calling to pray, work, and lead in order to see a spiritual awakening. It is not surprising that journalist Tom Brokaw has deemed them "the greatest generation."
Because of World War II, they knew the precious value of life, relationships, and faith. They were always a generation ready and willing to work hard and cooperatively to achieve a goal.

The "crusade headquarters" for the 1952 Atlanta revival was listed as 365 Ponce de Leon Avenue. That building itself was a testimony to the tenacity of students to minimize obstacles and maximize opportunities, as were the highly planned—if not overly planned—crusades. Students themselves had raised $2,000 to buy the lot on Ponce de Leon Avenue and, with Georgia Tech students in the lead, built the BSU center with funds raised from local churches. The center out of which the revival was planned was affectionately and accurately known as "the house that students built."[19]

Therefore it should have surprised no one when Atlanta readers learned that "approximately 300 (young) people have definite jobs as chairmen of committees in their own churches and many more folks are active on these committees," all in preparation for the 1952 crusade.[20] As the beginning of the revival neared, Butt mailed a letter from his home in Corpus Christi, Texas, to each of the volunteer committee leaders in Atlanta. He thanked them for the "excellent work" that had been done in preparation for the crusade and reminded them of the source of spiritual renewal.
"We all know that genuine spiritual awakening does not come through the efforts of any one speaker or team," Butt wrote. "Instead, it comes from God as we together follow His recipe of

concern, expectant faith, prayer, tireless work, and personal cleansing."[21]

It was a lesson the Atlanta students had taken to heart as they met, planned, prayed, and promoted what they believed to be a divine mission—an opportunity to make a significant spiritual impact on the youth of their city.

"This was big stuff," Greer recalled, "and it was all organized by students."[22]

BIG CROWDS IN BIRMINGHAM

On Friday, June 10, 1949, the youth of Birmingham, Alabama, were invited to "Come and bring a date" to a rally at the city's Southside Baptist Church. Exactly one week later, at Birmingham's First Baptist Church, another rally was held featuring Howard Butt and Frank Boggs, two of the four Baylor evangelists set to lead Birmingham's second city-wide revival.

"Plans for a great City-wide Youth Revival are being pushed towards completion," reported the *Alabama Baptist* newspaper. "With 121 Baptist churches taking part in the movement, and with four of America's most outstanding young evangelists doing the preaching and singing, the revival promises to make a real spiritual impact on Birmingham and surrounding cities."[23]

Jack Robinson, Charles Wellborn, and Howard Butt did the preaching, while Frank Boggs led the music throughout the week. It was the second Birmingham crusade for some members of team. During an earlier revival in 1948, Robinson had spoken at Ruhama Baptist Church prior to the larger meeting and made a profound influence on a teenager named Bobby Bowden, who later became the highly successful football coach at Florida State University.[24]

By all accounts, the Birmingham Youth Revival of 1949 lived up to its high expectations. Local arrangement leaders Earle Trent and Roy Johnson worked with "advance agent" Tom Norfleet to have a well-organized and highly prayed-over meeting.

Beginning and ending with Sunday afternoon services—and with nightly gatherings in between—young people flocked by the thousands to the City Auditorium for each of the sessions held June 20-26.

"Much of the crowd came via chartered bus," reported the *Alabama Baptist*, noting that "every available bus of the Birmingham Electric Company was in use." A photograph of the packed auditorium for the final service was spread across two pages of the state Baptist newspaper.[25]

"Banners were everywhere," recalled Jack Robinson, one of the speakers, of that final "jam packed Sunday afternoon service that drew more than 6,000 persons in spite of the rain. "I remember Birmingham most of all for the...heartfelt, life-determining decisions," said Robinson. He also noted that Charles T. Carter, longtime pastor of Shades Mountain Baptist Church in Birmingham, had "cemented his desire to preach" during a youth revival service there. [26]

"The cooperation of churches and pastors, and liberal use of newspaper publicity," along with much prayer and preparation, resulted in an average attendance of over 5,000 per service. Team members visited 20 local churches on the first Sunday of the revival and Norfleet, who had come in early, had spoken to about 20 different congregations in three weeks. Reported decisions included 39 professions of faith, 83 rededications and 23 commitments to full-time ministry. Even the financial figures looked good. The expenses of $4,200 incurred were covered by offerings totaling $4,661.59. [27]

The young evangelists were receiving a modest $75 per week, plus travel expenses, at this time. Butt covered his own costs and did not accept honoraria. Earlier the revival leaders were given $50 per week, leading Charles Wellborn to quip during the Samford University symposium in 1999 that "Dr. (W. F.) Howard made certain none of us preached for material gain."[28]

In 1951 Butt and Boggs returned to the Birmingham City Auditorium, July 29 through August 5, to hold another mid-summer City-wide Youth Revival. Joined by Buckner Fanning, they led services under the theme "Longing for Jesus."[29] Leading up to the revival start, the *Alabama Baptist* noted that "Youth revivals in this city during the last few years have seen the youth of Birmingham come out by the thousands to attend the services."[30] The positive impact of the earlier meetings and the detailed pre-planning assured another successful crusade.

By this time the young leaders were becoming well known. In addition to speaking at an earlier revival in Birmingham, Butt had been featured along with Roy Rogers and Dale Evans at the recent Southern Baptist Convention meeting in San Francisco. Boggs was described as "a young man who is known and loved in Birmingham for his deep bass voice and his ready smile."[31] Just three months after Birmingham's successful third crusade, Butt and Boggs brought their ministry gifts and high reputations back to Alabama to lead the State Baptist Student Conference in Tuscaloosa.[32] The Youth Revival Movement had a strong presence in Alabama during the 1950s, and the impact of those meetings has extended through the years.

In 1954 Butt also conducted an eight-day revival at Ladd Memorial Stadium in Mobile, sponsored by the local association of 65 churches, that drew total nightly crowds exceeding 10,000 and resulted in hundreds of decisions.[33] The largest crowd of the week, "a throng of 15,000," attended the final service on Sunday evening and "surpassed anything ever held in Mobile in the form of a religious campaign,' according to a front-page story in the *Alabama Baptist.*[34]

CHATTANOOGA—THREE IN A ROW

For three years in a row beginning in 1949, large youth revivals featuring teams of first-wave Baylor revivalists were held in Chattanooga, Tennessee, with tremendous results. The first event featured Howard Butt, "a young evangelist from Corpus Christi, Texas," as speaker and Frank Boggs, "a graduate of Baylor

University and . . . a student at Southwestern Seminary," as music leader.[35]

Much was happening in Chattanooga in November, 1949. F. W. Woolworth Company had just opened a "bigger, better" store on Market Street that was drawing big crowds, two major entertainment ventures—the Ringling Brothers-Barnum and Bailey Circus and the Skating Valentine show—had hit town.[36] Also, local Southern Baptists and other Christians rallied to fight the legal sale of liquor in Hamilton County. However, the Nov. 8 prohibition vote narrowly failed. An end-times prophet had erected a tent on a vacant lot in town to dispense his message of urgency, and many Independent Baptists gathered at Highland Park Baptist Church for a missionary conference, sponsored by Tennessee Temple College, in support of World Wide Faith Missions.

But over at the First Baptist Church—then located at the corner of Oak Street and Georgia Avenue—the two Baylor boys were holding the first of three annual city-wide youth revivals. The November 6-13 crusade, began on Sunday afternoon. One newspaper advertisement promised "songs you'll remember; testimonies that thrill; messages to challenge; music which uplifts; (and) a gospel that saves."[37] As the services neared completion, another local paper told of the revival's impact on the community beyond the nightly services: "These two young men have attracted enthusiastic support from young people all over the city as they have led in daily chapel services at McCallie School, Chattanooga High School and the University of Chattanooga . . . . "[38]

In addition to school programs and nightly services, an interactive forum was held each night to discuss the topic, "The Christian and his amusements."[39] The term "amusements" was widely used—even as a heading in some newspapers—for what would more commonly be called "entertainment." *The Chattanooga Times*, for example, promoted a variety of entertainment options on its "Amusements" pages including motion pictures, live performances at the Tivoli Theater and Memorial Auditorium, and both "round and square dancing." The nightly forum that addressed the appropriate Christian response to such activities, one journalist reported, "has been informative and helpful to the group composed entirely of young people."[40]

Apparently, the enthusiasm from the 1949 revival motivated local youth to plan an even larger event for the following year. Howard Butt, "well known in Chattanooga and in other large Southern cities for his dynamic preaching," as one promotional piece put it, returned for a second crusade held August 6-13, 1950.

A large tent was erected on the playground of East Side Junior High School, and Butt was joined by fellow Baylor first-wavers Charles Wellborn and musician Dick Baker. The revival was sponsored and promoted by the Hamilton County Baptist Association—formed that year when a larger association was divided.

Wellborn, already gaining a good reputation for his preaching on the *Baptist Hour* radio program, was touted as a national debate champion and "decorated ski-trooper in the Italian campaign of World War II." Baker was called "one of the most talented young musicians in the field of revival music" and Butt deemed as "one of the most sought-after speakers in the South."[41] Tom Norfleet, another Baylor graduate, helped organize the event.

Like many cities, Chattanooga had two daily newspapers. The *Chattanooga News-Free Press* covered religious events more closely than *The Chattanooga Times* and was openly sympathetic to Christian evangelism. Writer Kay Ray, reporting on the 1950 revival, led with the words, "Christ glows from their eyes, His words fall from their lips," to describe the "Texas quartet of young evangelists" leading the city-wide tent meetings at East Side Junior High School. Ray wrote that the "clean-cut young men with southern accents"—ranging in age from 21 to 24—were "individualist(s), but the ultimate and immediate goal of each is service for Jesus Christ, their professed Savior." She recorded Butt's comments that, although his family's business success provided great opportunities, "I have found a lot more satisfaction in giving testimony for my Lord than in anything else in life."[42]

During the Tuesday evening service, Wellborn said the "destiny of the United States of America is dependent upon what God's people are willing to do, to give, and to be for Him." In a sermon titled, "The Kind of World We Live In," Wellborn emphasized the urgency of spreading the gospel in a era when "it is possible to wipe out the whole human race in a very short time." "What worries me is not the lack of guns, men, tanks or the presence of hoarders or the lack of economic balance—but something more serious," Wellborn told the youthful listeners. "Do we as individuals and a nation have the spiritual resources to withstand the coming events?"[43]

Crowds of 3,000 to 4,000 packed the huge tent each evening according to news reports. An editorial titled, "Inspiring Youth Revival Meetings," appeared in the Saturday August 12 issue of the *News-Free Press*, commending the event in which "many of our Chattanooga young people are rededicating themselves, in the face of this challenge, to higher purposes in their spiritual living." The editorial noted that "the appeal of the revival to young people is three-fold: it is conducted by young people, sponsored by young people and, as the leaders have pointed out, young people should lend their strength to Christianity during their youth and at the same time receive the strength and guidance of Christianity into their lives."[44]

Enthusiasm over the revivals continued to mount and plans were made by Chattanooga youth for yet a third consecutive crusade. Initially, the East Side playground was selected once again as the site,[45] but the event eventually was held in a huge tent erected at the popular Warner Park.

The Associational Youth Revival, held August 9-18, 1951, featured the return of musician Dick Baker and the preaching of Buckner Fanning and Ralph Langley. Bill Cody served as organizer.[46] Fanning preached the first service that, according to reporter George Burnham, drew 3,500 young people. Many "sat outside the rolled-up edges of the tent, which was comfortably cool throughout the service." Burnham added that Fanning challenged his listeners to seek the "solution" found in 2 Chronicles

7:14—"If my people, which are called in my name, will humble themselves and pray . . . . " "The decision for World War III," said Fanning, a veteran of the recent Second World War, "does not rest with the Kremlin, nor does it rest with China or the United States politicians; the decision for the next world war rests with you, the Christian people of America." Described by Burnham as "a fiery young evangelist," Fanning called the assembled youth to be humble, resist evil, and spend time in prayer. "We have thousands of people attending church now who won't even close their eyes when prayers are offered," said Fanning. "They won't humble themselves enough to bow their heads." Fanning said his grandmother used to tell him of Christians who got down on their knees to pray. "But I'll tell you now, if you get one good look at the holiness and righteousness of Jesus Christ you'll go down on your knees crying 'My Lord and my God.'"[47]

This message was not only recorded by Burnham, a reporter for the *Chattanooga News-Free Press*, but was taken to heart. As he covered the nightly services at Warner Park, Burnham became convicted about his own spiritual needs. He made his way to the downtown Read House hotel where the revival team was staying. There he found Fanning and the others and told of a life controlled by alcohol that often hindered his work and relationships. Langley said Burnham told them of being sent to cover the University of Tennessee football team in the latest Orange Bowl, but was too drunk to climb the stairs to the pressroom. Instead, Langley said, Burnham listened to the end of the game by radio on a train back to Chattanooga so he could write the story and save his job.[48]

The four talked with Burnham for about an hour before asking if he would like to accept Christ. "He did!" recalled Fanning, "and we all knelt in prayer and thanked God." That night during the service, Burnham publicly professed his newfound faith in Christ.[49]Fanning had no further contact with Burnham until he visited LaGrange, Georgia,in the late 1990's and preached at the First Baptist Church. Burnham attended the service and approached Fanning to see he if would be recognized. After hearing one clue—"The Read House in Chattanooga"—Fanning knew he had reconnected with Burnham. The reporter told Fanning: "My life has been totally different since (the Chattanooga revival)." Burnham later used his writing skills to pen a story about the ministry of Billy Graham, titled *To the Far Corners*, Langley recalled.[49]

A nearly full page ad in the newspaper's Saturday religion section welcomed visitors to the week-long "Chattanooga Youth Revival" in the big tent at Warner Park to hear "messages that are dynamic!" Ralph Langley, described as the "youthful pastor of University Baptist Church in Coral Gables, Florida," preached the second service and alternated with Buckner Fanning throughout the week while the popular Dick Baker, "remembered from last year...as song leader, soloist, composer and pianist," led the music.[50]

As the week progressed, Burnham gave detailed coverage in the *News-Free Press* of the protracted meeting. In one rather unusual story, he told of an elderly black man who would sit on the railroad bank near the Warner Park tent each evening to hear the singing and preaching.[51]According to Burnham, the man was noticed one night by a visiting evangelist who lingered after "practically all of the estimated 6,000 people had gone home." Dr. Fred Garland, described as having conducted some of the biggest revivals and Bible conferences in the nation, but was not a member of the youth revival team, reached out to the older man.

Burnham's account would likely be considered patronizing today. He emphasized how the busy evangelist delayed his plans to "meet the head of a college and a church editor at an ice cream parlor shortly after the service" in order to give attention to "an old Negro who wanted to hear some more about the Word of God." In very sensitive and descriptive terms, however, Burnham told how Garland engaged the old man in conversation about his faith. "Tears began streaming down the wrinkled cheeks of the old man after he had been talking with the preacher for some 10 minutes. Then the evangelist put his arm about the Negro and they got down on their knees. One prayed and then the other. The

Negro asked forgiveness of his sins and professed his faith in Christ."[52]

While journalists are taught to stay personally detached from stories in order to provide balanced coverage, it is interesting to consider how the reporter in this case was actually part of the news that he covered. In this particular account, Burnham painted a much more vivid picture of the scene outside the large tent than on the inside. He wrote of the old man "sitting off by himself in the quiet solitude, which was interrupted occasionally by a passing train." The man "evidently wasn't particularly interested in religion, because he occasionally took a pull on his bottle," Burnham wrote. It was something to which the reporter could apparently relate.

Perhaps the overflow crowds caused Burnham to keep his own distance at the services, but usually press members are afforded good seats. More likely it is that Burnham intentionally started covering the revival services from a distance and never gave up that unique perspective.

In 1999 Langley recalled how Burnham had told the revival leaders that he too sat along the railroad bank in hopes of getting enough information to write news stories, but not so close as to risk conviction.[53] But the message he heard coming from the tent made it out to the tracks and into his heart that week. Burnham probably wrote so vividly about the elderly black man kneeling in prayer to profess his faith in Christ, because that is exactly what he had just done as well in Chattanooga's Read House hotel.

The youth revival was deemed "a great success" with "a total of 238 decisions" and many pastors reporting that "the spirit of the meeting carried over into their churches" the next Sunday.[54] "Chattanooga!" Langley exclaimed, thinking back over nearly five decades. "I can never drive through the place...without remembering what God did at old Warner Park."[55]

KNOXVILLE—'DOUBLE PENTECOST'

In 1948 Udell Smith, BSU director at the University of Tennessee, reported that "the first effort along the line of a citywide youth revival in the city of Knoxville was attempted." Speakers were students from area campuses including Webster Carroll of Carson-Newman College, who served on the second Hawaii team and became a career missionary.[56]An additional Sunday service was added and young people from many denominations participated, according to Smith. He expressed surprise that among the 120 public decisions were a large number "who were saved after membership in churches for many years." It was not unusual, Smith reported, to see groups of students on campus kneeling in prayer after the services.[57]

Reflecting back several decades later, Smith—who left Knoxville to lead student work in Louisiana for many years—said, "These youth revivals just broke out" and "came along at the right time and filled a need." [58] Students in the Knoxville area planned a larger meeting the following year, and brought in Howard Butt and Frank Boggs.[59] But it was the third youth revival, held in May 1950, that participants are still talking about over half a century later.

First-wavers Ralph Langley, Buckner Fanning, and Boggs were enlisted as leaders. Jack Robinson—who often juggled his basketball and preaching duties—came in for one service. Response was so strong that the meeting had to be relocated to a larger facility and was extended for four additional services, making it an 11-day event. "The carryover from two previous meetings added to groundwork laid well in advance of the third meeting, helped to make the Knoxville revival the most successful Baptist youth revival yet held, as 1,105 young people made decisions for Christ in the eleven day meeting," claimed one report.[60]

Smith recalled how Broadway's pastor, Ramsey Pollard, had gone to Alaska and "had no idea what the results would be."[61] The results were that the church sanctuary could not hold those attending and overflow space had to be used. Smith recalled how lots of decisions were made by those unable to get into the sanctuary. Services were first held at Broadway Baptist Church in Knoxville until the overwhelming crowds required eventually moving the revival to the gymnasium on the University of Tennessee campus. [62]

The revival spirit took a little time to build despite the crowds, recalled Langley. At the first service—though well attended—"nothing happened," he said. But by Wednesday, "the thaw began." Langley described the Thursday night service as "Pentecost," and "Friday night it was double Pentecost."[63]

Incredible planning for the revival had obviously paid off. A general planning meeting had drawn 300 local youth and Langley had come in two months earlier to speak three times. Round-the-clock prayer meetings were held at the Baptist Student Center, and a major scheduling conflict for the revival leaders was finally worked out. "If the opposition of the Devil has anything to do with the success of a meeting," W. F. Howard, was reported to have said, "then this will be the most successful ever held."[64]

While true revival is hard to measure, the 1950 youth services in Knoxville had every sign of success. A total of 1,105 decisions were made including 170 conversions, 863 rededications, and 72 commitments to ministry. Youth from 14 denominations other than Baptist recorded decisions.[65]

Enthusiasm was so high that "scores of young people met at a downtown cafeteria for breakfast together and an earlier morning worship service. At noon, a room was set aside in the UT cafeteria for a panel on specific phases of youth life in modern America .... UT faculty attended one day, county pastors another as daily attendance ran near 100."[66]

Revival planners and leaders put a strong emphasis on local high schools. Many students from Rule High School attended the citywide revival and held their own services when the event finally concluded. More than 1,000 students attended chapel sessions at Knoxville High School during revival week. A program for cross-town rival Young High School resulted in three conversions and "nearly every boy on the football team made some decision for the Lord." "I will never forget Knoxville," said Boggs. " . . . The high schools just came in mass." Eager students would arrive so early that revival services sometimes started 30 minutes before the scheduled time "because the place was already filled," Smith recalled.[67] Students from the Tennessee School for the Deaf participated as well after revival leaders visited their campus and enlisted an interpreter.[68]

After moving to the University's gymnasium for the Saturday night service, the response was so great that the revival was extended for four days at the First Baptist Church despite final exams. Commitments kept coming with 49 conversions among 250 public decisions made during the final service. Among them was Ted Daffer, a popular guard on the UT football team. Long after the 11 days and nights of powerful meetings, revival was said to have lived long "in the churches, schools and homes of Knoxville."[69]

NASHVILLE—FROM CHURCH TO THE RYMAN

Stirrings of the Youth Revival Movement were happening across Tennessee before any of the large meetings led by-first wavers were planned. In 1946, Bob Entrekin, BSU director in Knoxville prior to Udell Smith, had adapted the successful open-air meeting concept used effectively in Texas. Entrekin had also raised enough money from local churches to provide a sound system for student revival teams. His colleague, Charles Roselle, led students in Nashville to erect a tent between 16th and 17th Avenues for downtown services that same year.[70]

Union University in Jackson held a revival, sponsored by the BSU, in November with the popular theme, "I'd Rather Have Jesus."[71] By 1947 the concept had spread to other parts of the state. Four Carson-Newman college students formed a revival team for the summer of 1947[72] and a locally-led Memphis Youth Revival was held that July.[73]

Students and their leaders widely embraced the youth revival concept. In 1948 the Nashville students took on the task of raising $2,400 to acquire a car to be used in their mission efforts, including transportation to churches to lead youth revivals. The plan called for each Baptist student in the city to give at least one dollar and to seek additional funds from local church members. Student Work Department head Rogers Smith, in reporting this project to a statewide audience, noted that the "Nashville students are not allergic to receiving donations from without the Nashville area."[74]

The Youth Revival phenomenon featuring large services led by popular leaders out of Baylor was not limited to the eastern Tennessee cities of Chattanooga and Knoxville. Under the leadership of Floyd North, students planned Nashville's first major citywide revival for Feb. 12-19, 1950. Howard Butt and Frank Boggs were brought to town for a series of meetings that began at Nashville's First Baptist Church and concluded at the historic Ryman Auditorium. Bill Cody, who had just become BSU director at the University of Kentucky, provided "masterful guidance" in planning the meeting.[75]

"Nashville's first citywide youth revival had its real beginning in the hearts of a small group of students who attended Student Week at Ridgecrest in June 1949," according to North. "There they heard Frank Boggs and Howard Butt for the first time and gathered some thrilling echoes from a Knoxville youth revival in which Frank and Howard had led." Butt spoke at each of the Nashville revivals and "his Spirit-imbued appeals were irresistible," North reported. Boggs' voice, he added, was "amazing in power and interpretation of God's message."[76]

Attendance grew from 1,600 to a crowd of 5,000 at the closing session at Ryman Auditorium, according to one report. State student work director Rogers Smith declared the revival—resulting in approximately 350 decisions including 64 professions of faith—to be "one of the greatest spiritual awakenings in many, many years."[77] North said many other commitments were of great significance considering that "many, including BSU council members, had plugged along for months and years on a parent-pleasing, conscience-easing level" before discovering and using "the real power of God."[78] The *Nashville Banner* carried an editorial commending the revival for making "what may well be a lasting impression on the religious life of this community." That youth were drawn to a youth-led meeting, the editorial stated, "attests to the potentialities of such a movement as well as the readiness of youth to embrace spiritual interests."[79]

YOUTH REVIVALS ALL AROUND

So many well-attended youth revivals were held across the south in the late 1940s and early '50s that the young Texans and others sharing their zeal would sometimes use the term "citywide" as a noun. For example they would say, "We had a great citywide there last year."

While every service even remotely connected to the Youth Revival Movement was of eternal importance, determining and detailing each one would be an impossible task. For certain, there were many more—all across Texas and well beyond—than could be profiled in this volume, assuming they all could be identified.

"I don't see how I survived it," said Howard Butt of the extensive travel he did during the busiest years of the Youth Revival Movement. Butt led many more revivals than he can recall and most of his records from the revival years were destroyed in a Texas flood years ago.[80]

All across the land, however, many grateful persons can testify to the life-changing impact of an exciting youth revival held in their town.

Ward Gasque is one of many with such a story. A New Testament scholar and a founding professor of Regent College in Vancouver, British Columbia, Gasque credits a 1954 youth revival service in Florence, South Carolina, with making a tremendous impact on his life. Gasque had lived in a Florence hotel that his father had acquired and given the family name. Age 12 at the time of his father's death, Gasque spent the next couple of years as "sort of a delinquent teenager."[81] At age 14, Gasque returned home from "very wild living at Myrtle Beach" to get more money and clean clothes. With "a sense that something was going to happen," he went to hear Butt preach in a youth revival at Florence Memorial Stadium.[82]

It was a Damascus Road conversion experience for young Ward, and a redirection of his life toward ministry and biblical scholarship. "I was soundly converted," recalled Gasque, who took seriously the challenge to pray, study the Bible, and share his faith with others. For several years he led Bible studies and outreach efforts for youth and pursued his theological training.[83]

The effectiveness of youth sharing and demonstrating their faith as a means of reaching other youth was not lost on perceptive student leaders like Bob Denny. "Youth naturally crusades," Denny once wrote, while "adults ordinarily seek a comfortable level of existence."[84] Though well-educated, including a law degree, Denny warned of becoming too "intellectually respectable" in presenting the gospel message. He considered the early youth revivals to be a return to an old-fashioned time when "getting right with the Lord" was the primary concern.

Denny made a strong case for the effectiveness of personal testimonies and "plain, simple gospel preaching." He also urged a close relationship between revival planners and local congregations where post-revival "follow-through" could be done.

Young people in leadership roles will make mistakes due to their inexperience, Denny admitted. However, he insisted that "it is better to have the mistakes of activity than those of inactivity."Most importantly, "their testimony to those of their own age is more effective than that of adults," Denny added. As he well demonstrated, Denny said adults were needed in the revival movement as "spiritual coaches" to both "avoid some of the blunders" and to " use youthful talent efficiently."[85]

Endless stories about changed lives resulting from youth-focused, youth-led evangelism during the heyday of the student revivals could be told. Memorable events were held all across the South, like the tri-city youth revivals in Roanoke, Virginia, in 1951 and '52. Hundreds jammed the sanctuary and neighboring rooms of the First Baptist Church in August 1951 to hear Howard Butt preach and Frank Boggs sing.[86]

In April of that year, the twosome also held services at Tabernacle Baptist Church in Richmond. The following two

Wednesday prayer meetings were used for testimonies from those impacted by the revival.[87] Charles Wellborn, by then a popular *Baptist Hour* radio preacher, came to Richmond in the spring of 1951 as well to speak to an associational youth rally at the First Baptist Church.[88]

In August of 1952, Jack Robinson and Dick Baker led another citywide revival in Roanoke. At the final service, revival planners had the wives of the two young evangelists reached by telephone so Robinson and Baker could greet them—very publicly—on their second wedding anniversaries that they shared on August 26.[89]

When Southern Baptists gathered in San Francisco that June of 1952, the Youth Night rally drew 15,000 persons and was considered by one observer as "probably the greatest youth service in the 106-year history of Southern Baptists."[90]

Marian Smith, who played piano for a 1949 Kentucky BSU revival team, reported that 13 youth revivals were conducted across the state that summer attracting 29,480 persons and resulting in 134 conversions. An additional 20 revivals were held in Kentucky "where college students did the work," she added.[91]

Two Mississippi College students, Charles Tolbert and Frank Hart Smith, helped arrange and promote approximately 91 spring and summer revivals throughout Mississippi in 1949. They assisted churches "that had never had a youth meeting to make plans." Cumulative totals of 1,512 decisions including 484 professions of faith were recorded.[92]

While youth revivals were being held in churches and communities of all sizes across the South in the late 1940s and early '50s, larger citywide meetings with the popular young evangelists continued to expand. In Hopkinsville, Kentucky, for example, a 1952 revival at the high school stadium made a tremendous impact that was felt throughout the town for many years. "That was a fun meeting," recalled Howard Butt, who preached during the Hopkinsville revival. "The standout was the impact (the revival) made in a top social and professional group."[93]

Among the young professionals touched by the event were physician Gabe Payne and his wife, Maybelle. After hearing Howard Butt preach in front of the large banner emblazoned with simply "Try Jesus," the Paynes made commitments that led them to a lifetime of volunteer service in medical missions. "We were church members and Christians, but we had never really gotten caught up in an evangelistic situation," Maybelle Payne recalled nearly 50 years later about the revival's impact on her and her late husband. "It changed our lives and so many of our young friends who were not Christians." Payne added that William Peyton Thurman, pastor of Hopkinsville's First Baptist Church at the time, carried on the spiritual awakening started by the revival. As a result, many significant decisions were made. "I've forgotten how many young people went into the ministry, but I could probably count a dozen," Payne recalled. [94]

Keeping count is a hard thing to do when considering the overall Youth Revival Movement, conceded Ralph Langley. Like Butt, he has "never put a number" on the revivals he helped lead during those glory years when meetings were packed and public commitments were abundant. However, memories of God's power at work in places like Dothan, Alabama, and at Carson-Newman College in Jefferson City, Tennessee, will always remain fresh.

In the Dothan revival, Langley recalled spending hours before and after the nightly services visiting individually with more than a dozen local business leaders. Because of his work, the local sports editor could not meet Langley until around midnight following one service. "He received the Lord," Langley said of the late night witnessing opportunity. That decision led the sports editor, Reuben Herring, on a journey of spiritual growth to the point he became editor of the popular Southern Baptist publication, *Home Life*.[95]

During the Carson-Newman spring revival, led by Langley prior to the Knoxville citywide meeting in 1950, "the campus just shook." Langley said the meeting was "so prayed up" that the commitments came like shaking ripe fruit from a tree.[96]

New Orleans got in on the movement with a double dose of revival in 1950. Two citywide crusades were held with BSU director Mary Lee Vines at the helm.

The first, with Tulane University student James J. Crumpler as general chairman, occurred in February during the days leading up to the rowdy and rambunctious Carnival Week celebration in the French Quarter. About 1,000 young people attended each service at the First Baptist Church and 84 professions of faith were recorded.[97]

Students staged the fall revival at First Baptist Church of New Orleans as well. Howard Butt, Buckner Fanning, and Frank Boggs led the services under the theme, "Christ for Me." The theme became a reality for 149 "students and young business people who professed their faith in Jesus, dedicated their lives in special service, or rededicated themselves to greater Christian living."[98]

The broader context of a spiritual awakening did not go unnoticed by Baptist student leadership. The November 1950 edition of *The Baptist Student* magazine carried this notation:

> In recent months reports of thrilling youth revivals have continued to reach *The Baptist Student.* We have heard from big cities, small college communities, from students who participated in the simultaneous evangelistic campaign west of the Mississippi River last spring.
>
> As these reports were being received, we, too, read of Billy Graham's successful meetings in Los Angeles, in New England, in South Carolina. We received letters telling of evangelistic efforts in Latin America, out in the Orient, over in Italy. And we, too, read news dispatches from college campuses, from Japan and Korea telling of manifestations of God's power.
>
> What does it all mean? Are these reports evidence of the beginning of a world-wide spiritual awakening for which many have been praying?
>
> . . . By their own commitment at Ridgecrest, Southern Baptist students are now praying four hours a day for the simultaneous evangelistic crusade which will take place in more than 18,000 Baptist churches east of the River in the Spring.

> . . . Certainly we live in a day of deep spiritual need. Civilization is unstable. But God's promises and power remain constant. Tremendous spiritual victories are ours for the claiming. [99]

STAR POWER HELPS DRAW CROWDS

Reluctant young college students found themselves leading the Waco youth revivals of 1945 and '46. They would have gladly enlisted more experienced worship leaders had it not been for the urging and encouragement of their BSU director Bob Denny. "We had absolute confidence that we had no confidence," Jess Moody said of those early experiences.[100] Yet Denny assured them of their usefulness and quietly pushed them ahead.

Frank Boggs recalled how "all of us were in our twenties" while effectively leading the widely attended services. Through the years that followed, they were never nervous in front of large crowds, Boggs said, "because we started doing that before we knew better."[101]

"We were all the little boy with the lunch," said Moody, using a biblical example to express how the young revival leaders were used despite their inexperience and yet-to-be-developed talents. Though "green, with limited abilities," Ralph Langley said they were faithful to the task.[102] The student evangelists rose to the occasion and gained confidence as they went along leading mass revivals. Experience proved to be a good teacher.

Boggs and his Baylor roommate, Dick Baker, were always assigned to different teams as the Movement spread. Though young musicians, they faced high expectations as they were called to lead congregational singing, direct a large choir, and sing solos.[103]

Though each of the young preachers became highly respected pulpiteers, they admitted that their earliest sermons were less than homiletical masterpieces. "We had only one sermon each," recalled BO Baker, "but we thought that sermon had to be preached." The sincerity and passion of the messages worked with the convicting power of God to reach the hearts of many fellow students and youth. Young people could relate to them as peers. "We learned very early that kids can win kids," Langley observed. "It was mighty good to bring peer pressure into divine operation . . . . There is a sense in which peer pressure can be positive, and the whole Youth Revival Movement was peer pressure par excellence in a divinely positive sense to get kids involved with kids."[104]

The young revivalists did not stay "green" long, nor did they remain unknown. Moving about from city to city, their notoriety grew as their faces appeared on large promotional posters and in newspaper ads, and thousands came to hear them preach or sing. "The press thought that what we did was important," Moody recalled.[105] The revival leaders were often interviewed by local media, and their words and photographs would appear in secular newspapers.

Young people who experienced the moving services would sometimes travel to other towns to hear the popular revival leaders again. Demand for the services of the dapper young evangelists was high.

Harold Sanders, pastor of the First Baptist Church of Tallahassee, Florida, knew the appeal. In a letter to Baptist students at Florida State University, he announced that he had "a big fish on the line!" He was referring to having Howard Butt, Frank Boggs, and artist Jack Hamm lined up for a citywide "Crusade for Christ" in 1951. Sanders encouraged the Baptist students to start a "whispering campaign" about how big the revival would be. He assured the students they "can't over-sell the ability, consecration or winsomeness" of the three men.[106]

Promotional materials helped raise the celebrity status. The gifted musical leaders and preachers were described in glowing terms. Howard Butt was promoted as "a millionaire businessman" or "the 24-year-old vice president of a major grocery store chain." Charles Wellborn was noted for his intellect, debating success, and military experience.

The stylishly dressed, dynamic young men on the revival teams were gaining star power. That had been true of Jackie Robinson—whose athletic prowess needed no exaggeration—since the first revival. Robinson's basketball skills had led Baylor to the final game of the national championship and earned him a gold medal as part of the U.S. Olympic team. Southern Baptist student ministry leader Frank Leavell praised Robinson as "student, athlete, preacher, Baptist (and) Christian, but the greatest of these is Christian!"[107]

Additional "star power" could bring even greater excitement to the revival meetings. During a special youth night service led by Howard Butt at a large revival at Bayfront Park in Miami in the spring of 1954, Neva Jane Langley, Miss America 1953, played the piano and gave her Christian testimony.[108]A distant cousin to Ralph Langley, Neva Jane had been active in the Baptist Student Union at Florida Southern College. She once stated that "The BSU was the one organization on campus that kept reminding me of my duty to Christ."[109]

The Miami crusade which resulted in about 1,200 public decisions also featured baritone Fague Springman—who used the stage name Lee Fairfax and had performed for three presidents. Additionally, Karl Steel of Wheaton College presented "nightly sermons painted in fluorescent chalk."[110]

The quick trip from being unknown and inexperienced students to becoming popular leaders of mass revivals resulting in thousands of spiritual decisions could certainly puff the egos of still young evangelists. Lots of prayer and laughter, as well the steady hand of leaders like W. F. Howard, were needed to keep things in balance.

"We did it for each other," said Jackie Robinson of how the young men kept their humility despite growing attention and great success. He added that problems only surfaced "when we tried to be somebody else." Robinson, the gifted basketball player, said he sometimes tried to appear very intellectual in his presentation, but "that was Wellborn." On the other hand, he added, Butt was more effective when he did not talk about his athleticism! Prayer, more than anything else, was the key to staying humble, said Robinson. "I always wept," he recalled of the times the young evangelists prayed together, "because I felt so unworthy."[111]

"We had a pattern of giving God all the credit," said Howard Butt, who added that healthy laughter was also a part of keeping the right perspective. Married in 1949, Butt said his wife, Barbara Dan, "had a great calling to keep me humble" when praise came his way. However, Butt admitted that handling all the attention and "extravagant" praise from even fellow evangelist Billy Graham was not easy. Trying to live up to such high expectations, Butt said, played a role in his battle with depression in the late 1950s. "I was not mature enough in Christ to handle it as well as today I wish I had," Butt confessed. Despite their immaturity, said Butt, "I believe God used it for his glory. We were just carried along on the wings of he Spirit."[112]

FROM A MOVEMENT COMES A PLAN

Organizers of the Waco revivals had a passion before they developed a plan. However, the positive results of the early revivals justified following a similar course of action when planning and leading future youth revivals.What emerged was a methodology steeped in spiritual preparation, extensive publicity and an organizational structure that assured involvement from a large number of local young people. Though altered to some degree in each setting, the many citywide revivals held across the South had amazing similarities.

After taking on early responsibility for overseeing the recruitment, training, and assignment of revival teams from Texas, W. F. Howard quickly developed a system that was effective in providing guidance to local revival planners and in keeping the young evangelists squarely on track.

"(Dr. Howard) was the greatest influence in the lives of a lot of us," said Bruce McIver, noting that the popular leader among students scheduled "hundreds of revivals."[113]

"The Howards really were so important to this whole thing," acknowledged Boggs, noting, like others, the role of Mrs. Hazel Howard, who worked so closely with her husband and the revival teams. Should a problem arise, prayer would be Dr. Howard's first response, not his last resort. "He would say, 'We're going to have a time of prayer,'" Boggs recalled. "Howard would then get down on his knees and the students would follow his lead, although some of them were not used to doing that in their churches. The praying would go on for a long time."[114]

W. F. Howard also had very practical ideas about how to form and train youth revival teams. In the May 1954 issue of *The Baptist Student*, he offered his insight for others to consider. "The most potent reservoir of youth revival talent is found on the campuses which engage in a year-round ministry of youth evangelism," Howard wrote. "One successful summer or school year of activity in this field will do more to enlist top-flight talent than will any other recruiting effort." To effectively recruit good youth revival leadership, Howard suggested "making the campus youth revival program an integral part of the total BSU ministry." Howard said that the BSU can give "both a sane balance and a cutting edge to youth evangelism, which no other alignment can produce."

Other steps to effective recruiting, according to Howard, included creating a youth revival committee as part of the BSU council, agreeing upon leadership qualifications and selection process, accepting applications from and interviewing all who are interested, and using many student leaders in each engagement. "We must be on alert for team opportunities in addition to those involving preaching and music," said Howard, suggesting that "by giving relatively small assignments to inexperienced students" they might grow to be entrusted "with gradually heavier team responsibilities." He also pointed out that useful talent did not always include stage presence.

Once selections were made, Howard placed a strong emphasis on adequate training including youth revival clinics, reading resources, periodic evaluation sessions, "on-the spot observation," and requesting constructive criticism from host church leaders. The most important part of the training process, Howard assured, was constantly reminding the students of maintaining "a self-accepted spiritual discipline which promises constant Christian growth." He emphasized to students and their leaders that the BSU director "will be the key to the inner lives of the students."[115]

Early participants on Texas youth revival teams and many that came along later agreed that W. F. and Hazel Howard took the selection and training of young evangelists very seriously. Bruce McIver remembered times when they would interview a large number of students, invite about 120 to youth revival clinics, and then appoint about 60 to revival teams.[116]

"Mrs. Howard was as involved with that as he was," recalled Jim Slatten, longtime Richmond, Virginia pastor. Slatten remembered going through the detailed application and interview process as a Baylor student and then not being selected by the Howards.

How did he handle the rejection? Slatten and his friend, Perry Ellis, headed to Virginia where Ellis' father, a pastor in Portsmouth, set up six revivals for them to lead. "For three summers running," Slatten said, "Perry and I were a revival team in Virginia."[117] Such is the case with a movement.

W. F. Howard's high expectations of student revival leaders also included good personal hygiene, gracious manners, and impeccable morality. "He made us wear ties . . .and use deodorant and polish our shoes," Bruce McIver remembered 50 years later. "He had a lot of rules," McIver added, and there were "a lot of ethical things we talked about." Frank Boggs described Howard as "the machinery that enabled us — and the whole thing — to happen."

"It just all fell together," said Howard, frail and as humble as ever in 1999, while sharing with former first-wave evangelists who knew better. Then in a soft voice but with keen insight, he added: "It was a miracle in the making that the dimensions of which we could not appreciate or recognize."[118]

AN IMMEASURABLE SPIRITUAL IMPACT

Some memories of the student revivals can run together after 50 years. "It's all sort of a blur," confessed Jack Robinson when reflecting on the many incredible revival experiences during a 1999 reunion.[119] While dates and places might be hard to sort through at times for the first-wave evangelists, the impact of the revival movement and many compelling stories remain unforgettable.

To provide an exhaustive list of every youth revival would be extremely difficult if not impossible for at least two reasons. First, the movement was not started as an official denominational program in which statistics were reported annually. As Robinson once pointed out, it just "caught like wildfire."[120]

Second, it would be difficult to know exactly which services to count. Hundreds of revivals were scheduled through the office of W. F. Howard. At times they featured first-wave teams from the early Waco crusades. Then second-wave evangelists and even later students were enlisted and assigned to lead services in Texas and beyond. Other state BSU programs carried out similar programs as well.

In some cases, an early student revival leader would be enlisted for a particular engagement not directly related to the youth revival program. The names of Butt, Boggs, Langley, Robinson, Fanning, Baker, and others showed up on programs for all kinds of church, student, and denominational events for many years during and after the revival movement.

Determining precisely how, where, and when the Youth Revival Movement went would be an overwhelming task. What can be stated as fact, however, is that the repercussions from those revivals are well beyond measure.

Such is the nature of movements. Unlike a ballgame where there are specified innings or a time clock, the beginning and end of movements are indeterminable. Though some statistics are helpful, the full results of a revival can never be reduced to numbers on a scoreboard. In terms of a *spiritual* movement, statistics—even when significant—are less important than embracing the belief that God has used the efforts of youth revivals to bring about much greater good than any person could ever know.

The Youth Revival Movement of the 1940s and '50s indeed led to countless life-changing decisions. And it shaped the lives of those who were used to lead it as well.

"Those experiences have colored my entire life," said Howard Butt of the amazing revival years sparked by the honest prayer of young Baylor students in 1944.[121] His colleagues would certainly agree, as they would with their mentor, W. F. Howard, who shortly before his death simply stated, "I am still amazed at it all."[122]

NOTES

[1] O. P. Gilbert, *The Christian Index*, 7 Mar. 1946, 8.

[2] John Jeter Hurt Jr., *The Christian Index*, 29 Nov. 1945, 8.

[3] Editorial, *The Christian Index*, 21 Feb. 1946, 8.

[4] Robert S. Denny, "Youth Evangelism," *The Baptist Student*, May 1952, 28-31.

[5] Personal communication with Howard Butt, 16 Aug. 2001.

[6] Winnie Dudley, "Texas Youth Revival Catches Fire at Ridgecrest," *The Baptist Standard*, 20 June 1946.

[7] Frank Boggs, interviewed by John D. Pierce, 29 Oct. 2001.

[8] Revival Revisited: A Public Symposium at Samford University, 18-20 June1999, unedited video.

[9] Denny, *Student*, May 1952.

[10] Boggs, interview.

[11] Dudley, *Standard*, 20 June 1946.

[12] Boggs, interview.

[13] Revival Revisited, video, 1999.

[14] Ibid.

[15] Henry Greer, interviewed by John D. Pierce, 11 Oct. 2001.

[16] Revival Revisited, video, 1999.

[17] Greer, interview.

[18] Billie Lovell, *Atlanta Journal*, 19 Apr. 1952.

[19] Greer, interview.

[20] Lovell, *Atlanta Journal*, 19 April 1952.

[21] Howard Butt, letter to student leaders in Atlanta, from Greer's notebook.

[22] Greer, interview.

[23] *Alabama Baptist*, 9 and 16 June 1949.

[24] *Sports Illustrated*, 30 Aug. 1993.

[25] *Alabama Baptist*, 2 June 1949.

[26] Revival Revisited, video, 1999.

[27] *Alabama Baptist*, 7 July 1949.

[28] Revival Revisited, video, 1999.

[29] *The Builder* (Hunter Street Baptist Church, Birmingham, Ala.), 29 July 1951.

[30] *Alabama Baptist*, 26 July 1951.

[31] Ibid.

[32] Ibid., 25 Oct. 1951.

[33] *The Mobile Register*, 21 Apr. 1954.

[34] *Alabama Baptist*,20 May 1954.

[35] *Baptist and Reflector*, 10 Nov. 1949.

[36] *The Chattanooga Times*, 5 Nov. 1949, 16.

[37] *Times*, 5 Nov. 1949, 16.

[38] *News-Free Press*, 12 Nov. 1949, 6.

[39] *Baptist and Reflector*, 10 Nov. 1949.

[40] *News-Free Press*, 12 Nov. 1949, 6.

[41] "Introducing...Chattanooga Youth Revival Team," undated promotional piece.

[42] *Chattanooga News-Free Press*, 9 Aug. 1950.

[43] Hilda M. Spence, "'God's people' to lead nation," *News-Free Press*, 9 Aug. 1950.

[44] Editorial, "Inspiring Youth Revival Meetings," *Chattanooga News-Free Press*, ed. Brainard Cooper, 12 Aug. 1950.

[45] *The Informer*, newsletter of the Hamilton County Baptist Association, June 1951.

[46] *The Informer*, September 1951.

[47] *News-Free Press*, 10 Aug. 1951, 1.

[48]Ralph Langley, interviewed by John D. Pierce, 27 Nov. 2001.

[49] Buckner Fanning, letter to Bruce McIver, 26 June 2001.

[50] Langley, interview.

[51] *News-Free Press*, 4 Aug. 1951.

[52] George Burnham, "Elderly Negro Gets Spirit of Revival," *News-Free Press*, 18 Aug. 1951.

[53] Burnham, *News-Free Press*, 18 Aug. 1951.

[54] Revival Revisited, video, 1999.

[55] *Informer*, Sept. 1951.

[56] Revival Revisited, video, 1999.

[57] Udell Smith, *Baptist and Reflector*, 3 June 1948.

[58] Udell Smith, interviewed by John D. Pierce, 31 Oct. 2001.

[59] *Southwide Baptist Digest*, March 1950, 7.

[60] Dean Stone, "Knoxville," *The Baptist Student*, Nov. 1950.

[61] Smith, interview.

[62] Ibid.

[63] Revival Revisited, video, 1999.

[64] W. F. Howard, quoted in *The Baptist Student*, Nov. 1950.

[65] *The Baptist Student*, Nov. 1950.

[66] Boggs, interview.

[67] Smith, interview.

[68] *The Baptist Student*, Nov. 1950.

[69] *Student*, Nov. 1950.

[70] Charles L. Nored, *Make the Campus Different: Seventy-five Years of Baptist Student Union in Tennessee* (Murpressboro TN: 1999), 60.

[71] *Baptist and Reflector*, 9 Jan. 1947.

[72] Ibid., 29 May 1947.

[73] Ibid., 21 Aug. 1947.

[74] Ibid., 26 Feb. 1948.

[75] *Southwide Baptist Digest*, March 1950, 7.

[76] Ibid.

[77] *Baptist and Reflector*, 2 March 1950.

[78] *The Baptist Student*, Nov. 1950.

[79] *Nashville Banner*, 20 Feb. 1950. Editorial reprinted in the *Baptist and Reflector*, 2 March 1950.

[80] Howard Butt Jr., interviewed by John D. Pierce, 30 Nov. 2001.

[81] Ward Gasque, interviewed by John D. Pierce, 27 Nov. 2001.

[82] James A. Rogers, "Unpromising teenager now biblical scholar," *Florence Morning News*, 1974.

[83] Gasque, interview.

[84] *The Baptist Student*, May 1952.

[85] Ibid.

[86] *The Roanoke World-News*, 21 Aug. 1951.

[87] Letter from Tabernacle Baptist Church of Richmond, VA, to Howard Butt, 13 April 1951.

[88] *Religious Herald*, 3 May 1951.

[89] Jack Robinson, interviewed by John D. Pierce, 27 Nov. 2001.

[90] *The Baptist Student*, Dec. 1951.

[91] Marian Smith, "Kentucky Youth Revivals," *The Baptist Student*, May 1950.

[92] Frank Hart Smith, "Mississippi's Report," *The Baptist Student*, Feb. 1949.

[93] Butt, interview.

[94] Maybelle Payne, interviewed by John D. Pierce, 9 Nov. 2001.

[95] Langley, interview.

[96] Ibid.

[97] *The Baptist Student*, November 1950.

[98] Ibid., June 1951.

[99] Ibid., Nov. 1950.

[100] Revival Revisited, video, 1999.

[101] Boggs, interview.

[102] Revival Revisited, video, 1999.

[103] Boggs, interview.

[104] Revival Revisited, video, 1999.

[105] Ibid.

[106] Harold G. Sanders, letter, 31 Oct. 1951.

[107] Frank H. Leavell, "The Editor's Outlook," *The Baptist Student*, November 1948.

[108] "'Christ Crusade' coming to an end," *Miami Herald*, 27 March 1954.

[109] *The Baptist Student*, June 1953.

[110] *Miami Herald*, 27 March 1954.

[111] Robinson, interview.

[112] Butt, interview.

[113] Revival Revisited, video, 1999.

[114] Boggs, interview.

[115] *The Baptist Student*, May 1954.

[116] Revival Revisited, video, 1999.

[117] Jim Slatten, interviewed by John D. Pierce, 25 Oct. 2001.

[118] Revival Revisited, video, 1999.

[119] Ibid.

[120] Ibid.

[121] Butt, interview.

[122] Revival Revisited, video, 1999.